THE NATIONALS
PAST TIMES

*The History and New Beginning of Baseball
in Washington, D.C.*

James C. Roberts

TRIUMPH
B O O K S
CHICAGO

Library of Congress Cataloging-in-Publication Data for hardcover edition

Roberts, James C., 1946–
    Hardball on the Hill : baseball stories from our nation's capital /
James C. Roberts.
        p. cm.
    Includes index.
    ISBN 1-892049-26-0 (HC)
    1. Baseball—Washington (D.C.)—History. I. Title.
GV863.W18 R63 2001
796.357'64'09753—dc21

                                                          2001017282

This book is available in quantity at special discounts for your group or
organization. For further information, contact:

Triumph Books
601 South LaSalle Street
Suite 500
Chicago, Illinois 60605
(312) 939-3330
Fax (312) 663-3557

Printed in Canada

ISBN-13: 978-1-57243-754-8
ISBN-10: 1-57243-754-5

Interior design by Amy Flammang
Cover design by Preston Pisellini
Cover images courtesy of the Washington, D.C., Public Library and the
Ronald Reagan Presidential Library.

For the Roberts Team
Mandy, Andrew, Melissa, and Timmy
All-Stars, every one

CONTENTS

FOREWORD

Baseball and politics have been constants of American life since virtually the beginning of the Republic, and nowhere more so than in the nation's capital. In *The Nationals Past Times*, Jim Roberts takes the reader on a fascinating journey of discovery and rediscovery into the kaleidoscope of Washington, D.C., baseball.

If horse racing is the sport of kings, then baseball is the sport of presidents (at least American presidents), and the author traces the unique relationship that has existed between the presidency and baseball for more than 100 years.

We also encounter a host of legendary figures along the way, including General Abner Doubleday, Walter Johnson, Clark Griffith, "Shoeless" Joe Jackson, and my grandfather and namesake, Connie Mack—a great figure in the history of the game and also a man of tremendous character who has been a hero and an inspiration to me all my life.

Speaking of my grandfather, it was a thrill for me to see the photograph reprinted in this book (page 122) of him playing catcher for the Washington Senators in 1888. The game was played on the old "Swampoodle Grounds," located where Union Station now stands. It was the first time I had seen the photo, and I was fascinated to learn that my grandfather got his start in baseball a quarter of a mile from my old Senate office.

The Nationals Past Times also focuses extensively on baseball's connections to Capitol Hill, where I spent much of my time for 16 years, first as a congressman and then as a senator. The book traces the colorful history of the game on Capitol Hill from the construction of the city's first baseball diamond in 1859, through the century-long rivalry of the congressional baseball game, to the recent congressional efforts to restore the good name of "Shoeless" Joe Jackson.

Equally compelling, however, are the stories of some lesser-known people such as Claire Donahoe, the first woman to sign a contract with the All-American Girls Professional Baseball League; Lacy Ellerbe, an All-Star player in the Negro Leagues; and Vic Price, the 1999 National Little League Volunteer of the Year.

Mr. Price has said that "Baseball is more than a game—it's a part of our heritage." That quote summarizes what this book is all about. Baseball *is* a special part of our heritage as Americans, and in *The Nationals Past Times* a part of that heritage is wonderfully preserved for us and those to come.

—Connie Mack
Pacida, Florida

PREFACE:
Baseball Returns to Washington

Even more amazing than the fact of baseball's return to Washington is the fact that it took so long for the game to return.

"Baseball owners and would-be owners have realized for years that Washington is a great market," says Phil Wood, a well-known radio broadcaster and baseball authority in Washington.

Wood adds that the old claim that Washington was never a good baseball town is rubbish. "There is a high correlation between winning and attendance," Wood says, "and the Senators rarely won." Nonetheless, Wood notes, in 1969, 1970, and 1971, the last three years the Senators were in Washington, they were in the middle third of major league teams in attendance. Moreover, all of the cities with similar attendance records during those years still have their teams in place.

Efforts to bring a team back to Washington began almost before the Senators were out of town.

In October 1971 Earl Foreman, a businessman and owner of the Virginia Caps (formerly the Washington Caps) basketball team, announced that he was going to buy the San Diego Padres and move them to Washington. The effort came to naught, however.

In 1973 Joseph Danzansky, owner of Giant Foods Inc., formed a partnership with Robert Wittig and Robert Schatner to purchase the Padres from owner C. Arnholdt Smith and move the team to D.C. Major League Baseball unanimously approved the deal and it appeared that the Padres' move to Washington was imminent. So imminent, in fact, that Topps

Baseball Cards had "Washington National League" trading cards printed with the Padres players on them.

San Diego mayor Pete Wilson threatened to sue Major League Baseball if the team was moved. MLB insisted that Danzansky indemnify the league in the event of an unfavorable lawsuit verdict. Danzansky refused, and MLB executives redoubled their efforts to find a buyer who would keep the Padres in San Diego. That buyer appeared in the person of Ray Kroc, founder of McDonalds, and with his purchase of the Padres, Washington's hopes of obtaining a team were once again put on hold.

Just two years later, however, an Indianapolis businessman named Emil Bernard held a press conference at the D.C. Armory to announce that he was going to buy the Giants and move the team to Washington. That deal never materialized, and later San Francisco businessman Bob Lurie and Bud Herseth, an Arizona cattleman, purchased the Giants to prevent the team from moving to Toronto. Herseth decided to sell to Bernard. Lurie reminded Herseth, however, that their coownership agreement provided that, should either partner decide to sell, the other partner had the right of first refusal. Faced with a certain legal battle, Heskith backed down and the Giants remained in San Francisco.

In the mid-eighties, foreseeing an expansion of major league teams, a local ownership group headed by John "Chip" Akridge launched an effort to demonstrate Washington's enthusiasm for acquiring a team by selling season tickets. More than 15,000 people bought the tickets, with the money deposited in an escrow account. There these funds languished for several years because, despite the impressive display of support, no team was forthcoming. Instead Washingtonians had to watch resentfully as franchises were awarded to six other cities: Tampa Bay, Seattle, Phoenix, Miami, Denver, and Toronto.

Washington's fortunes were dealt a particularly severe blow in 1992 when the Baltimore Orioles moved into a spectacular publicly financed ballpark named Camden Yards. The new ballpark was the first of the retro-stadiums and inspired a wave of imitations in cities across the country. Camden Yards became immensely popular, with the Orioles selling out almost every game and many fans making the drive from Washington and its suburbs.

The combined population of the Washington and Baltimore metro areas is approximately 7½ million people, making it the fourth largest in the nation. The Baltimore Orioles are the only major league baseball franchise in the area, and Orioles owner Peter Angelos has been determined to keep it that way. Predicting disastrous attendance losses for Baltimore if Washington ever got a new team, he has proclaimed his implacable opposition to any such development, using his allies in the Democratic Party (to which he is a major donor), appeals to the loyalty of his fellow owners, his close friendship with MLB commissioner Bud Selig, and the threat of lawsuits to thwart the hopes of prospective franchise owners—of whom there have been many.

One of the most enthusiastic and persistent of these was Virginia businessman William L. Collins III, a former minor league baseball player and minor league franchise owner. In 1993 Collins and a group of investors formed the Virginia Baseball Club, an organization with the announced intention of bringing major league baseball to northern Virginia. Over the next 11 years the Collins group would spent $13 million in pursuit of their dream, coming tantalizingly close to achieving it before losing out to Washington at the end of 2004.

One near miss came in 1996, when Collins announced an agreement with Drayton McLane, owner of the Houston Astros, to buy the Astros and move the team to northern Virginia. Houston voters had declined to build a publicly financed baseball stadium (to replace the multipurpose Astrodome built in 1965), which McLane said was necessary to make the franchise financially viable. Without it, he wanted out. Collins went so far as to write a check for $100 million to McLane, but before it could be cashed, Bud Selig asked McLane to hold his fire while the League tried to muscle the Houston city government. MLB's campaign worked and, facing the impending loss of the Astros, Houston reluctantly agreed to build a stadium—the ballpark that became the ill-fated Enron Field in 2000 before being renamed Minute Maid Park.

The Astros stayed in Houston, courtesy of Major League Baseball, which, in Phil Woods' opinion, had learned to use Washington as a "hammer" to bludgeon reluctant states and municipal governments into building franchise owners lavish ballparks at public expense.

Major League Baseball intervened again in 2002 in a three-team deal involving Montreal, Boston, and Miami. The estate of Tom Yawkey, owner of the Boston Red Sox from 1933 to 1976, decided to sell the team and had potential buyers in John Henry, Tim Werner, and Larry Lucchino, owners of the Florida Marlins. Major League Baseball enabled the deal by agreeing to purchase the moribund Montreal Expos from owners Jeffrey Loria and

David Sampson for $120 million. Loria and Sampson then purchased the Marlins, allowing Henry and company to buy the Red Sox (for an astonishing $800 million, the most paid for a sports franchise at that time).

The upshot: Major League Baseball owned a franchise, but Washington still did not.

Meanwhile, in 1999 a rival group, the Washington Baseball Club, was formed by businessman Fred Malek, a part owner of the Texas Rangers (and a former business partner of President Bush). The ownership group, consisting of eight general partners and three limited partners, featured a powerful consortium of wealthy businessmen (D. Raines, CEO of Fannie Mae, and James Kinsey, founding CEO and chairman emeritus of America Online); international attorneys (Vernon Jordan and Stephen W. Porter, senior partner at Arnold and Porter); and well-known celebrities (Darrell Green, former Washington Redskin). The Washington Baseball Club, as the name suggests, was dedicated to bringing a major league team to Washington, D.C. Behind these two well-funded groups the governments of Virginia and the District of Columbia stepped up to the plate.

In January 1999 Anthony Williams took office as mayor of Washington, D.C., and almost immediately announced that he was determined to bring baseball back to the District. Williams' two predecessors, Sharon Pratt Kelley and Marion Barry, had also gone on record as favoring baseball's return, but they had never pursued the matter aggressively. In any case, the District was confronted by so many crises during their hapless administrations, including the flight of residents and corporations, that they would have lacked time and energy to pursue baseball, even if it had been a high priority—which it wasn't.

It was with Mayor Williams, however. This mayor, unlike his predecessors, proved to be very pro-business, and in this more favorable climate new residential and business construction boomed.

Among the most successful of the new projects was the MCI Center in downtown Washington. Home to both the Washington Wizards basketball team and the Washington Capitals hockey team, the center doubles as a venue for concerts and other events. The MCI Center sparked the rejuvenation of the adjacent area, which is now alive with restaurants, bars, and stores. Although it was privately financed, it provided a compelling demonstration of the possible economic benefits of a sports facility—an example that Williams would be able to use effectively in selling the idea of a baseball park.

In 1996 Virginia's Republican governor, George Allen, and pro-baseball forces in the state legislature passed legislation creating the Virginia Baseball Stadium Authority, intended to facilitate the construction of a baseball complex in northern Virginia

Under the leadership of executive director Gabe Paul, the authority staff worked with the Virginia Baseball Club headed by Collins (whose group put $6 million into the effort) to identify prospective sites. An ideal site was identified in Arlington, across the Potomac River from Washington, in a largely abandoned railway yard. Residents in the surrounding communities loudly expressed their opposition, however, and began a noisy "not in my backyard" campaign. The plans to acquire the land were dropped.

The authority then teamed up with the Diamond Lake real estate firm to propose a joint development in Loudon County near Dulles Airport. The 460-acre complex, modeled after the Texas Rangers facility in Arlington, Texas, would make the ballpark the centerpiece for a huge new residential and commercial community. Projected to cost $360 million, the plan called for a 42,000-seat ballpark to be built on land donated by Diamond Lake, which also pledged to build 10,000 surface parking spaces. The rather complicated financing plan called for one-third financing by the state (in the form of a rebate of state income, sales, and property taxes); one-third local government (10 percent tax on tickets and all concession items sold); and one-third by the team (mainly through rental fees). An architect was chosen, architectural plans were drawn up, and the Virginia baseball coalition appeared to be well positioned to attract a team.

Most knowledgeable observers actually believed that northern Virginia, not Washington, was the hands-down favorite over all of the other bidders for the Expos to land the team. And, in truth, northern Virginia did have a lot going for it, the foremost advantage being location. Loudon County, home of Dulles airport and the proposed stadium site is the fastest growing county in the entire nation. Moreover, Loudon and its neighboring counties boast a total of more than 3 million people and the Dulles corridor is a booming hi-tech area home to hundreds of businesses. Major League Baseball's relocation committee, headed by White Sox owner Jerry Reinsdorf, was well aware of this and saw it all first-hand when they visited northern Virginia in early 2004.

Another advantage of the site was its distance from Baltimore. Northern Virginia congressman Tom Davis said, "We took the committee for a helicopter ride around the beltway at rush hour, and I pointed out to them that from northern Virginia, you basically can't get to Baltimore in the evenings." Surveys showed that the Orioles draw only about 4 percent of their attendance from northern Virginia, and Peter Angelos had let it be known that he would not oppose a team being located there. The fix appeared to be in.

But a new wrinkle developed. In January 2003 Democrat Mark Warner became governor of Virginia, and although he publicly supported the idea of bringing baseball to northern Virginia, when the deal was his for the taking in September 2004 he turned his back and walked away. The legislation establishing the Virginia Baseball Stadium Authority included a provision that required the authority to come back to the legislature for final approval of a construction deal. When the authority went to Wall Street to seek funding for ballpark construction they found financiers eager to invest, but they required the state of Virginia to declare its "moral obligation" to guarantee the loan.

Gabe Paul and others saw no conceivable problem with this. "Our financing plan was absolutely sound," he says. "For the state to put up any money, it would have been necessary for the team to draw less than a million fans per season for a period of 30 years, which was unimaginable. The worst team in the league draws more than that."

Paul adds, "I talked with the governor about the baseball deal over a period of about two years and he never said boo." Presumably, it never occurred to Paul that the governor had any problems with the authorizing legislation.

Yet, Paul says that at 10:00 on the evening of September 23, the night before he was supposed to meet with MLB to negotiate the deal, he received a call from the chair of the Authority, Keith Frederick, advising him that Warner had withdrawn his support for the financing plan. After years of work, with success within his reach, a crestfallen Gabe Paul had to tell Major League Baseball that the northern Virginia deal was off.

Major League Baseball, however, had a ready—though less attractive—fallback position: Washington, D.C. While the relocation committee members were negotiating with Virginia, they were doing the same with Washington, D.C.—as indeed they were with Norfolk, Portland, and Las Vegas.

In April 2004, following numerous meetings with the relocation committee, Washington mayor Anthony Williams accepted MLB's demand that any ballpark in D.C. be financed by majority public funds. A site on the Anacostia waterfront had also been agreed to.

Thus, when the Virginia deal fell through, Commissioner Bud Selig had only two important calls to make. The first one was the unpleasant one—to his friend Peter Angelos. Sources in the Orioles organization say that on September 28 Angelos was meeting in his office with a business-man making a proposal. The phone rang and Angelos reportedly excused himself and took the call in an adjoining room. When he returned several minutes later he appeared upset and distracted and told his visitor they would discuss the proposal some other time. The call he had taken was from Bud Selig.

On September 29, at Washington's historic City Museum, a nervous but excited Mayor Williams, surrounded by baseball supporters, waited for a call he had been told to expect. The call came and it was from the commissioner.

"Congratulations," Selig said. "It's been a long time coming."

The room erupted in cheers led by the mayor, wearing an old Senators cap. Among those joining him in singing "Take Me Out to the Ball Game" was council president Linda Cropp, a name that would became famous nationwide by year's end.

It is unclear how familiar Cropp was with the details of the deal Williams had made with MLB, but it is certain that she understood that it required public financing and that she approved the deal or at least did not oppose it.

Under the D.C./MLB agreement, construction of the new 41,000-seat, $460-million ballpark would be paid for through the sale of city bonds. The bonds would be repaid over a 30-year period from three sources: 1) team rent payments ($5.5 million per year); 2) in-stadium taxes on tick-ets, concessions, and merchandise (an estimated $12.2 million per year); and 3) a tax on businesses in the district with revenues over $3 million (an estimated $21 million per year). In subsequent weeks, however, signifi-cant opposition arose to the agreement, which was portrayed by the oppo-nents as a sweetheart deal for wealthy baseball team owners, building them a ballpark for rich suburban fans by using funds that should have benefited D.C.'s poor by building libraries and improving schools.

In the municipal elections five weeks later, three council members who favored the baseball deal were defeated and replaced by three oppo-nents, including the flamboyant and controversial former mayor Marion

Barry, who passionately proclaimed his intention to kill the deal. Unless the council approved the construction legislation by December 31, the new council convening in January would vote it down. Mayor Williams, however, remained confident that he had a solid majority on the council for the stadium vote, which was scheduled for later that month.

After the decision was made to relocate the Expos to Washington, District officials and MLB executives had to scramble, with only six months available to field a team at RFK stadium. Under team president Tony Tavares, season tickets went on sale in November and fans had made approximately 17,000 deposits of $300 each. At RFK stadium sports construction pro Allen Y. Lew was brought in from New York to head up the crash effort to renovate the facility for baseball. Lew quickly upped the projected budget from $13 million to $18.5 million.

Then what to call the team? Commissioner Selig favored the name "Senators," the official name that Washington's American and National League teams had had from 1957 to 1971. Mayor Williams favored "the Greys" in honor of the Negro Leagues team that had played in Washington in the 1930s and 1940s. In the end both sides compromised on "the Nationals." The "Nats" had been the official team name from 1905 to 1957, but in truth the Nationals and the Senators were virtually interchangeable. The Nationals had the added virtue of being the name of one of Washington's first two baseball clubs in 1859.

On November 23 Mayor Williams joined Tavares at a ceremony at Union Station at which they removed a blue curtain to unveil the new team name and logo. "Baseball is about our way of life," Williams said, adding, "It's about community. It's about opportunity. And now, with the Nationals, it's about our nation's capital, Washington, D.C."

The fun was temporarily interrupted for the several hundred attending when District resident Adam Eidinger jumped onto the rostrum yelling, "This is a bad deal, people." Eidinger continued to yell until several supporters, led by 73-year-old Charlie Brotman, a former in-stadium announcer for the old Senators, wrestled him to the floor. Eidinger's outburst proved to be a minor nuisance for those present. A much more dangerous threat would soon emerge.

Sensing the growing opposition to the baseball deal, council president Cropp, a savvy politician with mayoral ambitions, began expressing doubts about it. In late November she stated that she would introduce a bill to amend the agreement by requiring that the ballpark be built on city-owned land adjacent to RFK stadium. The mayor complained loudly that such a move would fundamentally alter the agreement made with MLB and would therefore be a deal-breaker. He remained publically confident, however, that he had a solid majority to defeat the Cropp plan.

When further study revealed that the RFK site would require millions of dollars of environmental cleanup, plus other unforeseen costs, Cropp dropped her proposal. She did, however, send a letter to Major League Baseball asking for concessions on cost overrun payment, late completion penalties, and other items.

In the face of growing opposition other council members also started going wobbly, protesting the diversion of revenues from schools, libraries, and other pressing needs of the district. Williams, his concerns growing, promised to add revenues in order to placate wavering council members. Cropp, meanwhile, postponed the vote on the stadium vote from late November to December 15 in order to give Major League Baseball time to respond to her letter.

In early December Selig traveled to Washington and, at a luncheon for a thousand people, passionately and sentimentally announced baseball's return to Washington, D.C. He sat next to Cropp at the luncheon, but the two appeared to have little to say to each other.

On December 15 MLB's response to Cropp arrived and, while it offered some minor concessions, Cropp said that she found the letter condescending and arrogant in tone and unresponsive to her requests.

On December 15 the D.C. City Council convened to discuss and vote on the mayor's baseball stadium plan with the mayor as part of an SRO crowd of supporters and opponents in attendance. Thirteen hours of often contentious debate followed. At the last minute (actually midnight) Cropp left the rostrum and began drafting a statement. When she returned the council president stunned those present, and soon millions around the nation, by introducing an amendment to the mayor's bill requiring at least 50 percent of the financing to come from private sources. The amendment carried by a vote of 10–3, and then the amended bill passed by a 7–6 vote with Cropp providing the deciding vote. Outside the council chambers an angry and shaken Mayor Williams denounced the vote, saying that the dream of baseball in Washington was close to dying.

These events were the lead story in Washington newspapers the next morning and the hot topic of the sports talk shows. The next day the leading question was what the reaction of Major League Baseball would be;

unconfirmed reports had Bud Selig foaming with rage. Baseball's answer was not long in coming. MLB president Robert DuPuy released a terse statement calling the D.C. council bill a violation of the carefully negotiated agreement between MLB and the District and "wholly unacceptable." Fans who had purchased season tickets were advised that they could get refunds and all Nationals employees were ordered to cease business and marketing operations. The statement went on to say that because the agreement with the District government remained in force until midnight December 31, no offers to purchase the Nationals would be entertained until January 1, 2005.

All over the Washington metro area baseball fans reacted first with shock and then with anger at what they considered Cropp's betrayal—among them Mayor Williams, who was reportedly so furious that he refused to talk with Cropp for two days. For her part, Cropp admitted that she had indeed blindsided the mayor but significantly added that if Major League Baseball showed flexibility, she was prepared to reopen the stadium issue for more discussion and a new vote at the council's last scheduled meeting on December 21.

For their part, having talked tough in public, MLB officials privately indicated their willingness to negotiate and a flurry of calls ensued between MLB, the mayor, and his staff, who were also in close contact with Cropp and her staff. MLB agreed to share insurance payments with the District in the event of cost overruns. Instead of requiring completion damage up to $19 million per year in the event of construction delays, the two sides agreed that the penalty would be the forfeiture of rent payments to the District for the period of the delay.

For her part Cropp agreed to drop her demand for 50 percent private financing in return for a pledge from the mayor that he would vigorously seek such funding. With the assurance now that the District government would insure that the ballpark would be built, the deal was back on. On December 21, at the last council meeting of the year, Cropp introduced a bill incorporating the agreed upon changes and it passed by one vote: 7–6.

At year's end the one large problem not resolved was a compensation package for Orioles owner Peter Angelos that would keep him from dragging Major League Baseball and its owners into a protracted and expensive lawsuit. One reported provision of such a proposed agreement would guarantee Angelos (and any family members who might inherit the Orioles) a guaranteed minimum resale price of $360 million for the team—much more than Angelos originally paid. That figure would grow, contingent on growth in local revenue (about $129 million for 2003). Another plum being offered the irascible Angelos was a 60 percent share for some period of time in a new regional TV-sports network to be operated by the Nationals and the Orioles. A 60 percent stake, or even an equal share in the network, would be a huge plus for Angelos because the majority of the viewers would come from the Washington metro area, not Baltimore.

On December 29, two days before the deadline, a jubilant Williams signed the stadium legislation surrounded by children wearing red, white, and blue caps and T-shirts—the colors of the Washington Nationals. In the wake of the announced agreement, the management team for the Expos went into high gear to field an improved team for the new Nationals.

With a projected $50 million payroll figure to work with, general manager Jim Bowden and manager Frank Robinson recruited Colorado Rockies outfielder Vinny Castilla, White Sox pitcher Esteban Loaiza, and Expos pitcher Tony Armas, among new acquisitions.

It had taken 33 long and frustrating years, with several near-misses, and in the end it came only after three months of bitter wrangling and in a narrow one-week window of opportunity, by a one-vote margin, just 10 days before the swearing in of a new council opposed to the agreement. But in the end justice was done for legions of long-suffering baseball fans in the Washington metro area. The national pastime was back in the nation's capital.

ACKNOWLEDGMENTS

This book, like baseball itself, was a team effort. In this case the general manager of the *The Nationals Past Times* team was Mitch Rogatz, president of Triumph Books, who saw the possibilities in the collection of baseball stories I dropped on his desk, and who also saw the need for a tighter focus. This book of Washington baseball stories is the result of his advice, and it is a better book for it.

Blythe Hurley is the managing editor of Triumph Books and her great talent, patience, and good humor were all sorely tested during production of this book. She handled missed deadlines, unreasonable requests from the author, and impossible publication-date pressures with aplomb. Having surmounted all obstacles and produced a completed book on time, Blythe was still able to chuckle when I quoted the famous line of legendary Pittsburgh Pirates announcer Bob Prince: "We had 'em all the way."

Triumph's Ken Samelson did a great job of fact checking the manuscript and Tom Bast, also of Triumph, gave many helpful suggestions. Four of the chapters in this book were published in somewhat different versions in the *Washington Post*, and I am indebted to *Post* editors Rose Jacobius, Mae Israel, and Gene Weingarten for their advice and editing magic.

Several employees of Radio America were also extraordinarily helpful. Foremost among them was Chris Graham, who performed yeoman service (literally) in typing much of the manuscript and in helping with the research. My thanks also to my secretary, Nicole McKan, and to Lezlee Brown and Peter Trahan, who helped in a variety of ways; to Kyle Key, who processed the photographs; and to Nicole Sitler and David Koch, who transcribed many of the interviews.

I would also like to thank Dale and Cleta Mitchell for their invaluable support and advice, and American Conservative Union Chairman David Keene for his excellent story suggestions. I also owe a debt of gratitude to Edward L. Sanderson, whose book manuscript, *Jimmie Trimble: An Informal Biography*, provided invaluable information used in the writing of the Epilogue.

I am also indebted to Bob Wolff, longtime Washington Senators broadcaster (and Hall of Fame member), for his help and for granting permission to quote from his delightful memoir, *It's Not Who Won or Lost the Game—It's How You Sold the Beer*.

Again, like baseball, this book begins and ends at home, because without my family it is unlikely that I would have undertaken the project. Coaching my children in baseball has intensified my love of the game and provided a host of experiences that are reflected in several chapters of this book.

A final word of thanks is owed to my wife Patti for her understanding and support. She also patiently tolerated my dereliction of household duties and endured visits to obscure baseball fields, endless Harry Caray impersonations, and many other indignities during the writing of this book. If MVP honors were given for this effort, the award would go to Patti.

Author's Notes

"Baseball in Blue and Gray" was originally published in *The Washington Times* on April 3, 1999.

"The Gipper's (Other) Game" was published in the 2000 edition of *The National Pastime*, published by SABR, the Society of American Baseball Researchers.

A shorter version of "In a League of Her Own" was published in the *Washington Post* on June 11, 1998.

An abbreviated version of "When It Was a Game" was published in the *Washington Post* on November 1, 1997.

"Quest for the Cup" was published in abbreviated form in the *Washington Post* on September 8, 1996.

An abbreviated version of "For the Love of the Game" was published in the *Washington Post* on September 30, 1999.

INTRODUCTION

Le baseball *est revenue á* Washington. Pardon my French, but in Montreal that's how they would say, "Baseball has returned to Washington." They are words I have waited 33 years to hear.

Many embittered fans said it would never happen, but on September 29, 2004, it did. After an absence of 33 years, Washington, D.C., mayor Anthony Williams announced that major league baseball was coming back to the nation's capital.

There would be some anxious moments ahead, to be sure, as political wrangling on the D.C. City Council almost killed the deal with Major League Baseball, but the train got back on the tracks and on December 30, 2004, Mayor Williams signed the legislation providing funding for a half-billion-dollar baseball complex on the Anacostia River, 15 blocks from the U.S. Capitol, to be completed in 2008. In the interim, the Washington Nationals prepared to play at RFK Stadium, which was to be reconfigured for baseball at a cost of $18 million.

Washington area baseball fans responded by buying 17,000 fall season tickets in the first month after they went on sale, and Nationals memorabilia went flying off the shelves. "I think we're going to have a very successful franchise in Washington," said David Cope, the Nationals' senior vice president for marketing.

That's been the assertion that tens of thousands of Washington base-ball fans have made for years. Having endured more than three decades of mind-numbing frustration, their joy at finally getting a team is tempered only by a lingering bitterness over the fact that it didn't happen years ago.

Sitting in the press box at Fort Lauderdale Stadium one March day a few years ago, I got really galled (Gauled?) reading the PR releases for the Montreal Expos, who were playing the Baltimore Orioles that day at the end of spring training. Pitchers were *lanceurs*, catchers were *receveurs*, out-fielders were *voltigeurs*, the coaches were *instructeurs*, etc. What a disgrace, I thought. The capital of French Canada has a professional baseball team and the capital city of the United States of America—where baseball is the national pastime—doesn't.

Every time I thought about this outrage, I got steamed. Montreal didn't even seem to want a baseball team. The Expos generated only a little over $40 million in total revenues, the smallest amount in either league, and average attendance could have been accommodated in the average college auditorium.

My rage growing, I yelled, "The team should be in Washington, for *Dieu's* sake!"

The first edition of this book was written in 2001, partly in the belief that that would be the year major league baseball would finally return to Washington. The planets all seemed to be in alignment. The D.C. metro-politan area then had close to 5 million people and one of the wealthiest populations in the nation to boot. Two investment groups with plenty of cash were waiting. The Expos and several other small-market teams were ripe for sale.

And yet nothing happened. Since 1971, seven cities had been given franchises by Major League Baseball, but Washington continued to be frozen out by a sports monopoly that seemed to be totally impervious to logic, fairness, and even financial self-interest.

Yet the case for bringing baseball to D.C. was so overwhelmingly pow-erful that not even Major League Baseball could ignore it forever.

The first crack in the ice came in 1999, when Major League Baseball's commissioner, Bud Selig, told the *Washington Times* that he was no longer opposed to teams moving and that Washington was a prime candidate for the first franchise that became available.

It would take five more agonizing years, but at the end of 2004 it finally happened, and in the Preface I explain how.

Even without major league baseball, however, Washington is very much a baseball town. Washington supplies one-fourth to one-third of the attendance at Orioles games in nearby Baltimore. The Washington area supports three minor league teams and two of the eleven wooden-bat, college All-Star leagues recognized by Major League Baseball. Baseball can be seen at the college level on at least 10 local campuses and the game is played at dozens of public and private high schools. At the grassroots level—at least in the suburbs—the game is doing well too, despite all the competition from other sports, such as soccer and lacrosse.

Moreover, Washington, D.C., has contributed to the game of baseball throughout its history. The man featured in baseball's creation myth—General Abner Doubleday—is buried at Arlington National Cemetery. Ten of the first thirty-eight inductees into the Baseball Hall of Fame had a Washington connection. The Washington Nationals club, founded in 1859, continued in various guises, most famously as the Washington Senators, until 1971, making the Nats one of the longest-lived baseball organizations in the nation.

A unique relationship between the presidency and the game of baseball was forged during the Civil War and continues to this day with the 91-year-old custom of the president throwing out the first ball of the season. No other city can boast such a relationship (nor for that matter can any other sport). Baseball's congressional connections also go deep in Washington. "Hardball on the Hill" (meaning Capitol Hill) was a reality as early as 1859. And three of the Nationals' first fields were located on Capitol Hill. The annual congressional baseball game between the Republicans and the Democrats has been played for most of the past 100 years, with many of the players demonstrating a surprisingly high level of skill. Across the street the Supreme Court has helped immensely to solidify baseball as the national pastime by declaring it a sport, not a business subject to interstate commerce regulation—the only such waiver granted to any sport.

Washington has been important to baseball in many other ways. *Baseball Weekly*, the nation's largest circulation publication devoted to the sport, is published here by the Gannett company. SABR, the Society of American Baseball Researchers, was founded here by Robert Davids. SABR members have made an important contribution to preserving the history of the game, making use in many cases of the archives of the Library of Congress and the National Archives, repositories of baseball documents and artifacts surpassed only by the Hall of Fame in Cooperstown.

Although all the chapters in this book have a Washington connection, I think most of the stories will have a wide appeal. Washington is the nation's capital, after all, and much of what happens here is relevant to Americans across the country. Also it was my intention to appeal to the general reader. This is not an "inside baseball" book of the kind written by George Will in *Men at Work* or *Pure Baseball* by Keith Hernandez. Those books are superb examples of the genre but they assume a high level of baseball sophistication on the part of the reader. The stories told in this book were selected because of their human-interest value and hopefully will strike a chord with a more general audience.

This was also my intention with the coaching stories in the "On the Field" section. Although the games described were played in the unique environs of the capital city, they should resonate with anyone who has coached, played, or watched baseball at the T-Ball and Little League levels.

My day job is serving as president of the American Studies Center, a nonprofit foundation that I founded some 20 years ago. The ASC supports two subsidiaries: Radio America, a national news/talk network, and the World War II Veterans Committee. Founding and directing an organization such as this offers a host of rewards but also presents its own set of challenges, fund-raising foremost among them. My major diversion from the more tedious aspects of my work is baseball—watching it, coaching it, and writing about it. Over the past 15 years or so I have written articles on various aspects of the game for numerous publications, from large circulation dailies such as the *Washington Post* to small niche journals such as *The National Pastime*, published by the SABR. Some of those pieces are included in this volume.

A few years ago I got the idea of putting these occasional articles together in book form. When I showed the manuscript to Mitch Rogatz, the president of Triumph Books, he read it and said, "There's a lot of good material here, but you need a sharper focus. Why don't you give it a Washington spin?"

I reluctantly agreed to do this, but I'm glad now that I did. Although baseball in Washington, D.C., turned out to be an enormous—make that overwhelming—subject, exploring the many facets of the topic has been a fantastic adventure.

From the exciting discoveries recently made about the game's early days to the ongoing debate about its future; from major league baseball to the T-Ball fields of Great Falls, Virginia; from the Hall of Fame in Cooperstown, New York, to college baseball in the Shenandoah Valley; from the Negro Leagues to the All American Girls Professional Baseball League; from Shoeless Joe Jackson to Pete Rose; from Ronald Reagan to George W. Bush—all have Washington connections and all have proved to be fascinating pieces in the mosaic of American baseball.

Many critics say that baseball is no longer the national pastime. And it is true that the game is dogged by a number of problems and is challenged by many newly popular sports. But that being said, baseball is showing a new vitality at many levels that suggests that its problems can be overcome if the leaders of the game show the courage and common sense to make the needed changes.

This book takes note of baseball's problems and discusses some ideas for reform. Mainly though, it's a celebration of the game—still the world's greatest game—in the capital of the world's greatest nation.

I

IN THE PAST

1

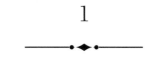

A Capital Game

Author Hank Thomas and antiques dealer Blair Jett were in their third day of rummaging through their friend Miller Young's attic, and they were growing discouraged. They had offered to help clean out the attic, partly in the hope of finding hidden treasure, after Young sold his house in the Washington suburb of Damascus.

Treasure for Thomas—a grandson of the great pitcher Walter Johnson—meant baseball materials, and Young's attic seemed like a fertile field since his great-grandfather, Nicholas Young, had been one of the founders of the National League in 1876 and had served as its president from 1885 to 1902.

Miller Young, however, had frankly expressed skepticism because he was convinced that he had all the family's baseball materials locked in a safe.

The two nevertheless doggedly continued their search of the hundreds of boxes and a dozen bureaus crammed with all manner of junk.

Then Thomas heard Jett cry out, "Oh boy! Oh boy!"

"I knew from the tone in his voice that he had found something fantastic," Thomas said.

Indeed he had. Jett had discovered a cache of baseball documents related to the Washington Nationals—a team founded in the District of Columbia in 1859—just 13 years after the rules of the game had been codified by Alexander Cartwright in New York City.

The constitution and bylaws of the Washington Nationals ballclub, dated November 27, 1859. Photo courtesy of the Washington Historical Society.

The Nationals played at a field located at the intersection of 6th and 7th Streets and Maryland Avenue N.E., about eight blocks from the U.S. Capitol. In literal terms, the "Nats," as they came to be called, were the first people to play baseball on Capitol Hill.

Among the items was a scrapbook containing the club's charter, articles on the Nationals' games clipped from the *New York Mercury*, and a collection of game tickets and invitations to social events sponsored by the team.

The collection had been compiled by Edmund F. French, a clerk in the Treasury Department, who gave it to Nicholas Young, a clerk in the War Department and the great-grandfather of Miller Young.

Among the documents in the plastic bag were a number of letters addressed to the National League of Professional Baseball Clubs. Nicholas Young was one of the founders of the league in 1876. He served as its first secretary until 1885, when he became league president, an office he held until 1902. The National League still goes by the same name, of course, and this year marks the 125th anniversary of its founding.

Rather than sell the documents to a private collector, Miller Young decided to donate them to the Washington Historical Society so that they could be accessible to researchers and historians.

Thumbing through the fragile yellowed pages, the reader is struck by the genteel tone of the newspaper accounts of the time—as well as the lives of the players.

Describing a visit by the Nationals to play the Pastimes in Baltimore, for instance, the *Mercury* reported, under the headline "Healthful Game of Baseball":

> *It is gratifying to report that this admirable field sport continues in Baltimore and one of the most interesting match games has been played by the Pastimes of this city and the Nationals of this metropolis. The National Club arrived on the early train and were met by a committee of the Pastimes who, taking possession of their ball, did the honors up to 1:00 where they were escorted to Mr. Charles Hoffke's Saloon and partook of a refreshing lunch. At 2:00 they took them in a special car furnished by the city passenger railway and proceeded to the grounds on Madison Avenue.*
>
> *The trial of skill and physical ability over, the participants somewhat wearied by their assiduous efforts, enjoyed for a brief season the cool refreshing breezes of the country and then returned to Mr. Hoffke's saloon. The bill of fare embraced many delicacies of the season.*

The first game recorded by the Nationals was played against the Potomacs on May 5, 1860, with the Potomacs winning 35–15.

A *Mercury* article dated March 31, 1861, reports "commenced play on ground between 6th and 7th Streets east near Maryland Avenue, Capitol Hill."

Less than three months later, however, a report notes, "changed our ground to square south of President's house."

Teams played on this ground—now known as the Ellipse—throughout the Civil War, and Abraham Lincoln is reported to have watched some of them.

An article published on August 28, 1865, reports on a game between the Nationals and the Atlantics and a meeting with Lincoln's successor, Andrew Johnson:

> *The reception committee of the National Baseball Club accompanied the Atlantics to the White House on Wednesday morning and obtained an interview*

Invitations and ticket stubs from the Washington Nationals and other 19th-century baseball teams in Washington, D.C. Photo courtesy of the Washington Historical Society.

for them with the President, although a host of people were already awaiting an audience. The members were serially introduced to the President and expressed their regrets that he was not present to give the game a national importance.

The President replied that nothing but urgent business prevented his witnessing the match and promised to visit the playground in September when the Excelsiors visited the capital.

Thanking the Atlantics for the compliments of their call, he bowed his acknowledgements and retired.

The meeting with President Johnson was among the first in what has developed into a unique relationship between the presidency and baseball. Over the past century and a half, both institutions have sought to ally each with the other, to the advantage of both.

In their book *Baseball: The President's Game*, William S. Mead and Paul Dickson note that every president except Rutherford B. Hayes has had some documented association with baseball.

A Revolutionary War soldier named George Ewing wrote of playing a game of "base" at Valley Forge on April 7, 1778, and of General Washington it is reported by another soldier that "he sometimes throws and catches a ball for hours with his aide-de-camp." The game played by the general and his troops at Valley Forge was almost certainly "rounders"—a British antecedent of baseball.

Andrew Johnson was the first president to call baseball "the national game." Johnson was a great fan, hosting teams at the White House and giving federal workers the day off for a special round-robin tournament featuring the Washington Nationals, the Philadelphia Athletics, and the Brooklyn Atlantics.

His successor, Ulysses S. Grant, was also a fan, and he and his staff are said to have watched games played south of the White House from the rooftops of a neighboring government office building. Grant also watched the New York Gothams play their first game at the New York Polo Grounds in 1876.

Chester Arthur, another baseball fan, was host to the Cleveland Forest Citys at the White House on April 13, 1883, stating on that occasion that "good ballplayers make good citizens." Arthur's successor, Grover Cleveland, received the Chicago White Stockings at the White House in 1888 and reminisced about baseball with the team's owner, Cap Anson. In an interesting historical twist, Cleveland was the namesake for Grover Cleveland Alexander, the great pitcher portrayed more than a half century later by President Ronald Reagan in the film *The Winning Team*.

In his second term, Cleveland invited government clerk John Heydler to recite a popular new poem, "Casey at the Bat," while Heydler was delivering a package to the White House. Years later Heydler went on to become president of the National League.

Benjamin Harrison, who defeated Cleveland, was an enthusiastic baseball fan and also the first president to attend a major league game. On June 6, 1892, Harrison saw Washington lose to Cincinnati 7–4 at Washington's Swampoodle Grounds.

William McKinley threw out the first ball for the Columbus, Ohio, team to open the season of 1892 and he told a reporter for *Sporting Life* that he hoped to do the same during his first year as president. However, on Opening Day, to the disappointment of 7,000 Senators fans in National Park, he failed to show up.

Teddy Roosevelt was one of the only presidents to dislike baseball, privately dismissing it as a "mollycoddle game." T.R.'s three sons were avid players and fans of the game, however, and the president took pride in their success. He was also too politically savvy to publicly express his disdain for the sport, and when called upon to comment on it went through some Clintonesque verbal contortions to say something that sounded positive without connoting his support.

Roosevelt also received two teams at the White House, including the New York Highlanders, then managed by one Clark Griffith. In 1912, Griffith became manager of the Washington Senators; William Howard Taft was the first of nine presidents that the wily Griffith would court for baseball's benefit, as well as his own.

Taft was a huge baseball fan (at 330 pounds he was huge in every respect), and he attended games as often as he could fit them into his schedule. On April 14, 1910, Taft threw out the first ball to open the Washington Senators' baseball season. The great Senators pitcher Walter Johnson caught the ball, and the ceremonial pitch established a venerable tradition that still endures today.

It was in 1899, during the McKinley administration, that Washington's professional baseball team officially became known as the Washington Senators. The team had gone by various names, beginning with the Nationals, during its 40 years as an amateur and then later a professional baseball team. The moniker of "Senators" had been used informally and with increasing frequency in the last decade of the 19th century, and the 1900 *Roger's Baseball Guide* reflected the new name for the first time.

Woodrow Wilson was an enthusiastic baseball player as a boy and remained an avid fan until he died. In his last years Wilson was largely incapacitated by a stroke; watching baseball games was one of his few sources of enjoyment. He would have his chauffeur drive him to Griffith Stadium and park in the bullpen area, where he could watch the game in relative privacy.

Warren Harding liked baseball as much as Wilson did and became a fan and friend of a number of players, including Ty Cobb and Walter Johnson. In 1922, during Harding's administration, the Supreme Court also showed its partiality to the national pastime, ignoring a mountain of empirical data and setting aside common sense to rule that baseball was a sport and not a

Congressional pages choose sides for a baseball game on the Mall in 1922. Photo courtesy of the Baseball Hall of Fame.

business, and hence was not subject to regulation under the Interstate Commerce Clause of the Constitution. This exception, provided to no other sport, has been both helpful and harmful to baseball in the years since.

Silent Cal Coolidge maintained the link between the presidency and baseball, although his wife, Grace, was a more enthusiastic fan.

Herbert Hoover loved the game, as did Franklin D. Roosevelt. Clark Griffith, owner of the Senators, courted FDR assiduously, and the president patronized Griffith Stadium frequently in the years before World War II broke out.

Mrs. Henry Wallace, wife of the vice president, throws out the first ball in a Senators game circa 1934. Lowell Thomas, the famous broadcaster, clowns around to Mrs. Wallace's right. Photo courtesy of the Washington, D.C., Public Library.

Following the attack on Pearl Harbor, baseball commissioner Kenesaw Mountain Landis wrote to Roosevelt asking him whether professional baseball should continue while the country was at war. FDR responded in a letter to "My dear Judge" that, speaking personally, he hoped that the game would go on.

And go on it did. The draft or enlistment of over 500 major league players, however, meant that the sport's depleted team rosters had to be filled by the young, the old, the lame, the halt, and the nearly blind. Teenagers and retired players suited up again to keep the Washington Senators and other teams on the field, supplemented in some cases by truly amazing players with "special needs."

Among these was Bert Shepard, a pitcher for the Senators who was shot down over Germany while flying a mission as an Army Air Corps pilot. Shepard was taken prisoner by the Germans and had a badly injured leg amputated. Liberated in late 1944, Shepard returned to the States, had a new artificial leg made, and returned to the Senators, first as a coach and then as an active pitcher, playing in a number of games in 1945.

That year saw the end of World War II and the return of the president to the ballpark in the person of Harry S. Truman, who threw out the first ball at a Senators game on September 8, 1945, six days after Japan surrendered.

Truman and almost all of his successors were avid baseball fans. Dwight Eisenhower played professional baseball in the Kansas State League for the summer before entering West Point and during another summer while a cadet there. Ike played for money to help pay for his education using the pseudonym Wilson. Playing for pay was forbidden by NCAA rules and Ike had signed a pledge that he had not done so. Had his cover-up been discovered, he would have certainly been expelled from West Point, with who knows what impact on the course of history.

As president, Eisenhower was a frequent and enthusiastic attendee at Griffith Stadium, often scoring the game on his scorecard. It was during his administration that Congress held hearings on proposed legislation that would strengthen professional baseball's antitrust exemption.

In 1958 the Senate Commerce Committee held hearings taking testimony from a number of players, managers, and, in a legendary exchange with Senator Estes Kefauver, from Casey Stengel, the crusty manager of the New York Yankees. Casey testified in his best Stengelese:

> I would say that I wouldn't know, but I would say the reason why they would want it passed is to keep baseball going as the highest baseball sport that has gone into the baseball sport and from the baseball angle. I'm not going to speak of any other sport. I'm not in here to argue about other sports. I'm in the baseball business. It's been run cleaner than has ever put out in the hundred years at the present time.

Undaunted by this sea of scrambled syntax, the chairman moved on to ask Mickey Mantle: "Do you have any observations with reference to the applicability of the antitrust laws to baseball?" In one of the classic ad-libs of all time, in a deadpan voice, Mickey stated, "Well, my views are pretty much the same as Casey's."

Presidents throwing out the first ball, a tradition that lasted from 1910 to 1971 in Washington, D.C. From left to right, first row: William Howard Taft, Woodrow Wilson, Warren Harding. Second row: Calvin Coolidge, Herbert Hoover, Franklin D. Roosevelt. Third row: Harry S. Truman, Dwight D. Eisenhower, John F. Kennedy. Fourth row: Lyndon B. Johnson and Richard Nixon.

President John F. Kennedy is linked most closely with football, but he was also an enthusiastic baseball fan. Kennedy was the last president to visit Griffith Stadium and the first to visit the new D.C. Stadium (later named RFK Stadium after his brother, Bobby). JFK threw out the first ball to open the 1961 season on April 10, 1961, and in so doing ushered in a new style of ballpark.

RFK was the first multiuse stadium designed to accommodate baseball, football, and other sports; its nondescript doughnut design was soon copied in cities around the country. These sterile, forbidding stadiums, many with artificial turf, offended baseball fans and contributed to major league baseball's decline from the 1960s through the 1980s.

The trend was reversed by the spectacular success of Camden Yards, which opened in 1992 in nearby Baltimore. Camden Yards, with its old-fashioned look and downtown location, sparked a construction boom of similar ballparks that continues in cities from coast to coast. These ballparks have paid tremendous dividends for the owners and the game, drawing fans in droves and helping to revive baseball from the low reached in the aftermath of the 1994 strike.

Richard Nixon was perhaps the most knowledgeable baseball fan ever to occupy the White House. He frequented games throughout most of his life and was a keen student of the sport. Nixon and his son-in-law, David Eisenhower, compiled a number of all-time best all-star teams for various eras in the history of the game.

Gerald Ford played baseball in college, as did George Bush; both played for the Republican team in the annual congressional baseball game. Bush took Queen Elizabeth II to a game at Camden Yards and flew Ted Williams and Joe DiMaggio to Toronto, where he and Canadian Prime Minister Brian Mulroney threw out dual first balls.

Jimmy Carter is remembered for playing softball with reporters and campaign workers during the 1976 campaign. As president, he declined to do the Opening Day honors and attended only one major league game, the last game of the 1979 World Series in Baltimore. The Pittsburgh Pirates won 4–1. Throughout the 1990s, however, Jimmy and Rosalyn became frequent game attendees, joining Atlanta Braves owner Ted Turner and his wife Jane Fonda to cheer on the Braves in many playoff and World Series games. Carter even defied the forces of political correctness to defend use of the "tomahawk chop" by Atlanta fans.

Former President Bill Clinton waves to the crowd at Camden Yards before throwing out the Opening Day pitch on April 5, 1993.

Ronald Reagan, like John Kennedy, is usually associated with football; but it can be argued that it was baseball—specifically his experience as a Chicago Cubs announcer on Des Moines WHO radio—that propelled him into the limelight as first an actor and then a politician.

George Bush kept his baseball glove in his desk drawer and a copy of the *Baseball Encyclopedia* close at hand in the Oval Office. He loved talking baseball and reminiscing with retired players about their careers in the majors.

Bush's successor, Bill Clinton, grew up playing the saxophone rather than baseball, but he was a loyal fan of the St. Louis Cardinals, as were most young people in the South and lower Midwest in those days. St. Louis' powerful KMOX radio had an enormous reach, and a string of Cardinals radio affiliates boomed the sound of Cardinals announcers Harry Caray and Jack Buck throughout the area.

Meanwhile Clinton's future wife, Hillary Rodham, was growing up a Cubs fan in the northern suburbs of Chicago. It came as a surprise to many baseball fans (especially to partisan Republicans and hardened Washington cynics), that Hillary managed to switch the president's longtime loyalty to the Cardinals to that of their bitter rivals, the Cubs.

Clinton visited the ballpark a number of times as president and was present on September 6, 1995, when Cal Ripken made history playing in his 2,131st consecutive game.

Clinton and then–Vice President Al Gore tried to use their influence to end the bitter baseball strike of 1994. They failed, and Clinton correctly predicted dire consequences for baseball in the wake of the strike.

In late 1999 First Lady Hillary Clinton surprised a lot of people again when she disclosed a "lifelong passion" for the New York Yankees. Skeptics noted that Hillary's previously unknown support for the Yankees was disclosed only after she decided to run for the U.S. Senate, representing New York.

The 2000 presidential election put George W. Bush in the White House and, like most of his predecessors, Bush is a fan of the national pastime. Indeed, before winning his current office, Bush was once the co–managing partner of the Texas Rangers organization. It can be argued that the new president has a closer association with baseball than any of his predecessors. There is reason to hope that the first decade of the new millennium will be a golden era for the nation's pastime in the nation's capital.

2

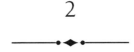

LAST IN THE AMERICAN LEAGUE

"First in war, first in peace, last in the American League." It's the jibe that dogged Washington Senators fans for much of the twentieth century. In truth, however, things were worse in the nineteenth century, when the team was also last in several other leagues.

The Senators' mostly dismal history is chronicled in a book titled simply *The Washington Senators*, by Morris A. Beale. Beale called the Senators, "The world's oldest baseball club," a dubious claim when the book was written in 1947 and one obviously not true since 1971, when the team left Washington and became the Texas Rangers. There is no doubt, however, about the fact that the Senators—known also at times as the Nationals and the Statesmen—had a very old pedigree.

The Nationals were chartered in 1859 by a group of government clerks. The team played other local clubs and military units during the Civil War, opening its 1865 season with a game against the 133rd New York Volunteer Regiment, which was passing through Washington from Appomattox on its way home to be mustered out.

In 1867 the Nationals went on a western tour, playing teams in Columbus, Cincinnati, Louisville, St. Louis, Chicago, and Rockford, Illinois. The team chalked up a phenomenal record, demolishing every team but Rockford by overwhelming scores (for instance, the Nats downed St. Louis, 113–26) and proved to be a huge draw everywhere they went. *Spalding's*

Baseball Guide called the tour "the first extended tour of a professional baseball organization" and gives the team credit for spreading the appeal of baseball throughout the Midwest.

On St. Patrick's Day, 1871, Washington resident Nicholas Young called a meeting of all the professional baseball teams in the country, and the National Association of Professional Baseball Clubs was organized. The association lasted until 1875, when it disbanded because of contract disputes, gambling controversies, and general internecine warfare. In 1876, Young drew upon lessons learned in that ill-fated association to draw up a constitution for a new league, the National League of Professional Baseball Clubs—the National League that still exists today.

The Nationals were not part of this league, however, and were rated by *Spalding's Baseball Guide* as a "non-league club" for the next 10 years. During that time they played in the International League, the local Departmental League, and the Union Association.

The Nationals' home field was the Capital Grounds, located near the present-day Senate office buildings. It was built in 1875 on Capitol Hill, using land later occupied by Union Station and the old post office building. The field became known popularly as the "Swampoodle Grounds," sharing the nickname of that marshy area of the city.

In 1886 Young became president of the National League and the Nationals—having changed their name to the Statesmen—were invited to join. During their first year the Statesmen finished seventh, or next to last.

That year a tall, skinny lad by the name of Cornelius McGillicuddy joined the team as its catcher. His cumbersome name was soon shortened to "Connie Mack" by the press, and it was by that name that he was known in 1889 when he left Washington and marched into baseball immortality.

In 1887 a new star arose on the team in the person of William E. Hoy. Despite being deaf and mute, Hoy was superb in both centerfield and on the basepaths. During his rookie year, Hoy set a then-record for stolen bases with 82.

Despite such heroics, the Statesmen finished in seventh place that year and last the next year. Faced with declining attendance and financial woes, the National League took over the franchise and moved it to Cincinnati. The next year team owner Walter Hewitt started a new team, this time in the Atlantic Association. The new organization—now called the Senators—moved to a new field at 16th and Euclid Streets N.W. However, by August, this team too had collapsed.

In 1891, baseball promoter Harrison Bennett formed yet another franchise, this one in the American Association. This team moved to another new field at 7th and Boundary Streets N.W.—the site on which Griffith Stadium would later be built. In December the wheel of fortune turned yet again as the National League bought out the American Association League, bringing Washington once more into the national game.

The team rattled around the cellar for the next 10 years, joining the new American League in 1901. There they continued their desultory ways for the next decade, the fans' frustrations eased only by a few exceptional talents.

Unquestionably foremost among these was Walter Johnson, "The Big Train." Probably the greatest pitcher in the history of the game, Johnson signed on with the Senators in 1907. For the next 21 years Johnson

Walter Johnson, the Washington Senators' "Big Train," probably the greatest pitcher who ever lived

dominated the opposing batters of every team, posting some astonishing numbers. Despite the fact that during his 21 years with the team the Senators finished in last place twice, next to last four times, and third from last three times, Johnson won 417 games while losing 279. Twice he won 30 games or more and 12 times he won 20 or more. He led the league in strikeouts 12 times, striking out an amazing 313 batters in 1910, and finished his career with a 2.17 ERA. His ERA was under 2.0 during 11 of his 21 years. In 1908 Johnson pitched three shutouts in four days; he holds the all-time shutout record of 110 games. And as if all that weren't enough, in 1925 he batted .433—an astonishing achievement for any player (no one has hit over .400 since Ted Williams did it 60 years ago). For a pitcher to do it is unbelievable.

Johnson was born in Kansas, hence his second nickname "the Kansas Cyclone," but he was discovered pitching in Idaho. There a Senators scout reported back that Johnson "threw so fast you can't see 'em." He added, "He knows where he's throwing, because if he didn't there would be dead bodies strewn all over Idaho."

It was this blazing fastball that became the Big Train's hallmark. An opposing third baseman, Jimmy Austin, said, "On a cloudy day you couldn't see the ball half the time, it came in so fast."

On one overcast day, Cleveland shortstop Roy Chapman was at the plate facing Johnson. Chapman took two called strikes on fastballs that he heard but didn't see. Dejected, Chapman walked to the dugout.

"But Ray," the plate umpire yelled, "you've got one strike left."

"Never mind, Billy," Chapman replied, "I don't want it."

So overpowering was Johnson's fastball that he never bothered to develop another pitch—no curve ball, no slider, no change-up. "Walter's idea of a change-up," Ty Cobb once remarked, "was to just throw harder."

In 1912 and 1913 the Johnson-led Senators were strong contenders for the pennant. In 1924 and 1925 they won back-to-back pennants (two of only three won by the team) and in 1924 they won their one and only World Series. For the most part, however, the underfunded Senators languished; Walter Johnson was about all they had going for them.

Clark Griffith, the Senators' manager from 1912 to 1920 and chief owner from 1920 to 1955, is thought of as synonymous with the Washington Senators. It was his knowledge of the game, showman's flair, and uncanny ability to get the most out of the team's financial resources that kept baseball in the nation's capital for the first half of the twentieth century.

Opening Day, 1911, at the park that was to become Griffith Stadium.

The son of a fur trapper, Griffith was born in a log cabin in Clear Creek, Missouri, in 1869. The family soon moved to Bloomington, Illinois, and Griffith made his professional pitching debut in 1888 with the Central-Interstate League's Bloomington team. Three years later he was signed by St. Louis's major league team, going on to pitch for Boston's American Association team in 1892 and for Oakland in the Pacific Coast League in 1893, where he compiled a 30–18 record. From 1894 to 1899 Griffith pitched for Cap Anson's Chicago Colts, winning 21 or more games each year. He became known as the "Old Fox" because of his wily ways on the mound, utilizing an arsenal of six or more pitches, including the screwball and scuffball, which he claimed to have invented.

In 1901, when Ban Johnson started the American League, Griffith became player/manager for Charles Comiskey's Chicago White Sox, winning 24 games and leading the new league in shutouts. That year the Sox took the first pennant in the new league's history. Then from 1903 to 1908 Griffith was skipper of the New York Highlanders, predecessors of the Yankees. In 1909 he became player/manager of the National League's Cincinnati Reds, a position he held until 1912, when he took the helm of the Washington Senators.

The Senators' fortunes improved immediately under Griffith's direction, and the team placed second in 1912 and 1913. And, although the Nats won only three pennants during Griffith's 45 years in command, they were in last place only six times—the popular impression to the contrary notwithstanding. In 1920 Griffith retired as manager and became general manager and principal owner of the team.

A succession of managers followed. Bucky Harris was called the "boy wonder" during his first stint at the helm, from 1924 to 1928. During his first year as manager, the Senators won their first American League pennant and their only World Series; they repeated as A.L. champs in 1925. Harris was an old boy wonder by the end of the last of his three terms (1950–1954). In between were managers "Big Train" Walter Johnson (1929–1932), Joe Cronin (1933–1934), Ossie Bluge (1943–1947), and Joe Kuhel (1948–1949). The Senators' third and last appearance in the

Senators player/manager Bucky Harris greets Connie Mack, owner/manager of the Philadelphia Athletics. Photo courtesy of the Washington, D.C., Public Library.

World Series came in 1933, under manager Joe Cronin. They lost to the New York Giants, 4 games to 1.

Lacking a major market advertising budget or attendance base, Griffith used every P.R. trick in the book to hype the team. He always made a point of courting the support of the residents of the White House, and achieved a particularly good rapport with FDR.

When the United States entered World War II, baseball commissioner Kenesaw Mountain Landis employed Griffith as an emissary to Roosevelt. Griffith strongly lobbied for the continuation of baseball during the war— a position the president himself endorsed in a letter to Landis. During the war the Senators lost three players, who were killed in action—the most of any major league team.

For the first two decades following the war, Senators fans had little to cheer about except some great performances by a few individual players, including Hall of Fame pitcher Early Wynn in the 1940s and slugger and fellow Hall of Famer Harmon Killebrew in the 1950s. While the New York Yankees racked up pennant after pennant during this period, the Senators had to be content with merely making the first division half the time. In fact, the envy caused by the great Nats-Yankees disparity of that era became the basis for the hit Broadway musical *Damn Yankees* in 1955.

For many Washington fans of that time, part of the attraction of going to see the Senators play was to see the great players on the visiting teams— Joe DiMaggio, Ted Williams, Lou Gehrig, Bob Feller, Mickey Mantle, and all the rest. Some 37,000 fans showed up in 1946 to see an exhibition staged by Griffith in which Indians pitcher Feller had his fastball gauged by a radar gun (velocity recorded by "Rapid Robert": 107 mph).

Opposing hitters loved Griffith Stadium, especially after the fence was pulled in on the left-field side in 1950 to accommodate a beer garden. No one loved it more than Mickey Mantle, who made history on April 17, 1953, when he blasted a home run over the bleachers and onto a neighboring street. This famous tape measure home run clocked in at 565 feet.

The biggest asset the Senators had going for them in the post-war period was not a player but an announcer. From 1947 to 1961, Bob Wolff entertained, regaled, informed, educated, lobbied, and interviewed radio listeners and television viewers in the Washington area as the announcer for the Senators. So lousy were the teams during most of that period that Wolff rarely gave the score on his broadcasts! Despite the limitations imposed on him by the Senators, Wolff went on to become one of the most

Senators owner Clark Griffith (left) and Bob Wolff. Photo courtesy of Bob Wolff.

successful broadcasters in the business, winning the Baseball Hall of Fame's Ford Frick Award in 1995.

Following his discharge from the navy in 1946 (during which time he wrote a manual totally revising the navy's supply system—a manual that the navy adopted), Wolff got a job as sports director for Washington's radio station WINX, owned by the *Washington Post*. The following year, WTTG, Washington's first television station, went on the air. Wolff signed on as the first TV broadcaster in Washington history, telecasting Senators games as well as those of the Washington Capitols basketball team and University of Maryland basketball and football games. During the baseball season Wolff broadcast the Senators games on television and radio, as well as hosting pregame and postgame shows, which he had recorded earlier for radio. He did all this *daily*.

Famous for his work ethic and thorough preparation, Wolff also became renowned for his interviews—not just with athletes but also with

Bob Wolff with "Mr. Quotable," Yogi Berra. Photo courtesy of Bob Wolff.

the "man in the stands." On Memorial Day in 1957, Wolff spied Vice President Richard Nixon and his daughter Tricia in the stands at Griffith Stadium and persuaded the vice president to do a "man in the stands" radio interview while withholding his identity until the end. Nixon happily played along for over seven minutes. Some of the dialogue:

"How long have you been here in the nation's capital? For some time?"

"Well, off and on, I've been here about 10 years."

"Oh, well, you're practically a native right here now."

"Practically a Washingtonian by this time."

"I see. What sort of work do you do, sir?"

"I work for the government."

"For the government?"

"Yes, yes, for the government."

"Oh?"

"My boss is President Eisenhower."

"Your boss is President Eisenhower? What sort of work do you do, sir?"

"Well, I'm the vice president."

"Ladies and gentlemen, our guest has been the vice president of the United States, Vice President Richard Nixon . . . "

When the Senators left Washington for Minneapolis in 1961, Wolff went along too. He later went on to New York, where he became the voice of Madison Square Garden. He is still a television personality in the New York area, making him the longest-running announcer on television today. Wolff says that he loves living and working in New York, but looks back fondly on his years in Washington.

In 1955 Clark Griffith died and his adopted son, Calvin, inherited the team. The son lacked his father's loyalty to Washington and had long been aghast at the team's poor bottom line. Rumors about an impending move began swirling around town.

According to author Bill Gilbert, *Washington Post* owner Phillip Graham became concerned about the prospect of losing the Senators in

Bob Wolff interviews Vice President Richard Nixon for one of his "man in the stands" features. Between them is Nixon's daughter, Tricia. Photo courtesy of Bob Wolff.

1957 and asked the paper's star sportswriter, Shirley Povich, for advice about how to prevent the move.

Povich advised Graham to plant a question about the possible move at one of President Eisenhower's press conferences. Povich explained that Del Webb, the chairman of the American League Expansion Committee, owned a construction company with extensive federal government contracts, and that incurring the president's displeasure was not a risk he would want to take. Graham talked with Eddie Folliard, the *Post's* White House correspondent, who in turn spoke with James Haggerty, Eisenhower's press secretary. Haggerty told Ike about the idea and the president agreed to go along with it.

Thus, at the next White House press conference, Folliard, following the script, said something like, "Mr. President, there are reports circulating to the effect that the Senators might leave Washington. What are your thoughts on this?" Eisenhower, acting shocked, stated that he would be extremely disappointed if the nation's capital were left without a professional

Senators third baseman Harmon Killebrew and outfielder Bob Allison sign autographs for Washington Star *paperboys, June 15, 1959.* Photo courtesy of the Washington, D.C., Public Library.

baseball team and that he hoped it didn't happen. This gambit, according to Gilbert, bought the Senators three years of extra time in Washington.

Nonetheless, in 1961 the American League did approve the Senators' move to Minnesota. But perhaps sensitive about leaving the capital without baseball, the National League also approved Washington as the site of an expansion club. Thus it was that the new team—also called the Senators—was in place for their second season when President John F. Kennedy inaugurated the 1962 baseball season by throwing out the first ball at the just-built D.C. Stadium.

Bill Gilbert was hired as the new team's publicity director by the general manager, retired Air Force Brigadier General Elwood Quesada. In Gilbert's view the advent of Quesada was the beginning of the end for baseball in Washington. "Quesada was not suited temperamentally or intellectually for the job," said Gilbert, adding, "He had all kinds of grandiose plans but had no idea how to accomplish them."

Things got off to a bad start in March when Quesada became furious that construction at D.C. Stadium was behind schedule. "The place was a

An aerial view of Griffith Stadium

virtual quagmire," Gilbert recalled, "and he ordered me to organize a press conference there in the mud at which he denounced the construction company."

Once the season started, Quesada got further bogged down in trying to micromanage the team. "He asked me to call Willard Scott and other DJs in the area," Gilbert recalled, "and request that if the weather forecast for home game days called for rain, they not report it." When Gilbert refused to do this, Quesada arranged a luncheon for the same local media at which he made the same request. The radio and TV hosts and reporters were understandably incensed by this scheme, and relations with Quesada went downhill from there.

In May, Quesada fired Gilbert, which caused additional P.R. problems. In the fall the owners of the team fired Quesada.

Things never really turned around for the Senators. Fans, who loved the friendly, quirky feel of Griffith Stadium, never warmed to D.C. Stadium (later renamed RFK Stadium)—a concrete donut really designed for football. The result was that 10 years later, in 1971, the new Senators left town again—this time for Dallas, where they became the Texas Rangers.

Thirty years later, the former president of the Texas Rangers has come to Washington as president of the United States. Does he feel at all guilty that, because of the Senators' move to Texas, the nation's capital has not had professional baseball for 30 years? The situation begs for an enterprising reporter to say, "Mr. President, I have a question. . . . "

3

BASEBALL IN BLUE AND GRAY

Visitors to Arlington National Cemetery will find the impressive tombstone of Civil War General Abner Doubleday. General Doubleday participated in a number of battles in the war including Gettysburg, where he distinguished himself in combat. He is also cited for having command of Fort Sumpter in Charleston in 1861, when he ordered the first Union shot of the war to be fired on the Confederate forces who had begun bombarding the fort.

The Fort Sumpter action gave General Doubleday a footnote in the history books but, as any baseball fan knows, his greater claim to fame is that he is supposedly the father of baseball. Specifically, in 1839 in the remote New York village of Cooperstown, Doubleday is supposed to have created the rules that made baseball the game we know today.

There is only one thing wrong with this story: it is a complete fabrication. This utterly bogus and preposterous claim, apparently invented out of whole cloth, is one of the most amazing hoaxes ever perpetuated on the American public.

The essential facts are as follows: At the turn of the century, America was beginning to flex its muscles as an emerging world power and the burgeoning sport of baseball had already become known as America's "national pastime." A long running debate was underway about baseball's beginnings, with people such as journalist Henry Chadwick arguing

General Abner Doubleday. He didn't start baseball, but he helped start the Civil War at Fort Sumpter.

(correctly as it happened) that baseball was the direct descendent of a number of British ball and stick games, especially one called "rounders."

By this time, however, Albert Spalding, a wealthy businessman and baseball promoter, had become fixated on the notion that America's national pastime had to be a sport invented in America and untainted by any foreign connections. In 1907 Spalding persuaded Abraham Mills, president of the National League, to set up a commission to settle the dispute. The committee was heavily stacked in favor of the Spalding position.

During the course of their investigation the commission received a letter from an elderly man, Abner Graves, who claimed he had played baseball with Doubleday as a boy and that in 1839, in Cooperstown, he had witnessed Doubleday create the new rules for the local ballgame. On the slim evidence of a 68-year-old recollection the commission declared Doubleday to be the father of baseball and Cooperstown to be the place of its birth. Graves's reliability can perhaps be put in context by noting that the old man shot his wife a few years later and was committed to a mental institution. Nonetheless, on this gossamer myth, baseball's most sacred temple was built.

In 1939, the Baseball Hall of Fame was opened in Cooperstown to enshrine the game's holiest relics (including Babe Ruth's bat and Ty Cobb's glove) and to immortalize its greatest players. To Cooperstown each year come the three or four players, managers, and announcers elected for induction. Through its quaint streets and green and leafy greenswards wander thousands of baseball fans, drinking in the quiet beauty of base- ball's pastoral birthplace. Most of them probably don't know the real story.

If the title "the father of baseball" belongs to anyone, it is Alexander J. Cartwright, a New York businessman and sporting club member who, in 1846, reworked the various rules of existing ballgames to produce a game that was closely akin to the version of baseball played today. The first game played according to those rules was held on Elysian Fields park in Hoboken, New Jersey, in 1846.

There is no evidence that General Doubleday played baseball or even witnessed a game, much less invented it. In his meticulously kept diary the game is never mentioned and it is a documented fact that he was a cadet at West Point during the time in which he was supposedly at Cooperstown organizing the first game. It is quite certain that the old gen- tleman went to his grave in 1893 completely oblivious to any association with the sport that would one day make him famous.

But, although the general didn't start baseball, a plausible case *can* be made that he started the Civil War.

As it turns out, there are connections aplenty between baseball and the war—the two things filmmaker Ken Burns describes as the "two Rosetta Stones" for deciphering the American character. The stories of both are indeed intertwined, and even after the myths have been stripped away, it's still a compelling tale.

In the 15 years between the playing of Cartwright's first game and the eve of the Civil War, baseball had spread throughout New England and the Midwest. Cartwright traveled to the West Coast, introducing the game along the way, and even sailed to Hawaii, where he immediately gained enthusiastic new converts. Baseball was also played in parts of the South at the time, particularly in Virginia and the Carolinas and in and around the ports of New Orleans and Galveston, although its spread was slower in the more rural and remote parts of the South.

The Great Emancipator, Abraham Lincoln, was himself a baseball player and fan—although here fact and fiction are densely intertwined.

There is a well-known story, for instance, that Lincoln was playing baseball on the Springfield, Illinois, common when he was informed of the arrival of a delegation dispatched from the Republican party's convention in Chicago to advise him that he had received the Republican presidential nomination. According to the account published in Albert Spalding's book *America's National Game*, Lincoln supposedly said, "Tell the gentlemen that I am glad to know of their coming; but they'll have to wait a few minutes till I make another base hit." A painting depicting this event hung for many years in Lincoln's home in Springfield.

Although the story is considered by most experts to be apocryphal, it is true that Lincoln did play the game and that he was an enthusiastic spectator. During the Civil War the Nationals—Washington's semipro team—played baseball on the grounds of the White House, and Lincoln is reliably reported to have been a frequent spectator.

There is also a story, apparently true, that he once stopped the White House guards from expelling a group of boys who were playing baseball on the lawn.

One giant whopper told about Lincoln was popularized in the 1940s by radio announcer Bill Stern. According to Stern, when Lincoln lay dying after being shot by John Wilkes Booth, he summoned General Abner Doubleday to his side and with his last breath said, "Abner, don't let baseball die."

By the late 1850s, baseball was rapidly eclipsing cricket as the most widely played ballgame in America. In 1857, the publication *Porter's Spirit* editorialized that it was time "to set up a game that could be termed a 'native American sport,'" and concluded that "baseball must be regarded as a national pastime." *The New York Clipper* called baseball "the national game amongst Americans; and right well does it deserve that appellation."

To these publications, "baseball" meant Cartwright's New York version of the game, but other variations still competed. For instance, the first intercollegiate game—played between Williams and Amherst Colleges in 1859—was played according to New England town-ball rules, which made for longer and slower games. There was a Philadelphia version of the game as well, but the New York game was gaining ascendancy.

In 1860 Henry Chadwick, an English-born reporter for the *Brooklyn Eagle*, published the first book on baseball, *Beadle's Dime Baseball Player*. It was essentially a collection of his articles about the game that had been published in his newspaper over the previous three years. Although Chadwick traced baseball's origins to rounders, he wrote that baseball had changed so much "as almost to deprive it [rounders] of its original features beyond the mere groundwork of the game." He also lauded the game's positive impact on health and character and published the rules of the National Association of Baseball Players.

When hostilities broke out and armies were raised in both the North and the South, their ranks contained thousands of men who played baseball—especially in the North. According to the Baseball Hall of Fame Library, which compiled the statistics, 11 members of the National Baseball Association served in the military during the Civil War.

Many of baseball's fledgling organizations were hurt by the war. In New York City, for instance, two-fifths of the baseball clubs folded because

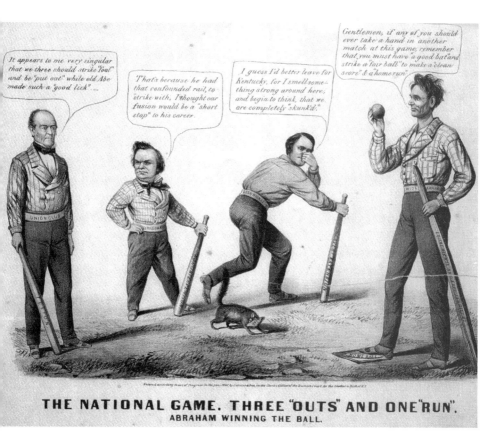

"The National Game," a Currier and Ives cartoon depicting Abraham Lincoln and some of his opponents, circa 1860.

players had enlisted. This attrition affected mainly those who entered the military as enlisted men. Less affected were the baseball clubs of the affluent, since it was possible to pay a man to take your place in the military. Many wealthy baseball club members did this and were therefore able to carry on the clubs' intraleague rivalries throughout the war. Nonetheless, there was a serious decline in the clubs everywhere during the four years of hostilities. Overall the number of nationally recognized clubs fell from 62 to 28.

Still, the game remained popular on the home front. For instance, at Elysian Fields in Hoboken, New Jersey, an all-star game was played on October 21, 1861, between teams from Brooklyn and New York. The game drew an audience of 15,000 spectators. In September of 1862, an estimated 15,000 fans watched a game in New York City between the Atlantics and the Brooklyn Eckfords on the same day that word arrived about the Battle of Antietam.

Nor was the game limited to the North and South. "The Rocky Mountain Boys" are reported to have played baseball in Denver in 1862. Baseball was also played in prison camps in both the North and South.

One of the most famous paintings of the Civil War is of Union soldiers playing baseball in 1862 in the Confederate prison camp at Salisbury, North Carolina. The painting, by Otto Boetticher, a major in the Union army and a prisoner in Salisbury, shows a large crowd watching the game in the prison yard.

Charles C. Alexander, a baseball historian, questions the accuracy of this incident in his book *Our Game*, writing that "The depiction of well-clad and ostensibly well-fed Yankees playing baseball in a neat prison camp . . . could have little relation to reality given the thirty-four percent death rate among the more than 10,000 men held there."

However, this argument was effectively rebutted in an article in an issue of *Baseball America*. The author, Jim Summer, a curator at the North Carolina Museum of History in Raleigh, noted that during the first two years of the war, conditions in the prison were not bad by war-time standards. He also quotes accounts written by three prisoners that refer to baseball having been played there. Among these was a diary entry for May 21, 1861, by William Crossley, a Union soldier from Rhode Island:

And today the great game of baseball came off between the Orleans's and the Tuscaloosans [prisoners transferred from New Orleans and Tuscaloosa] with

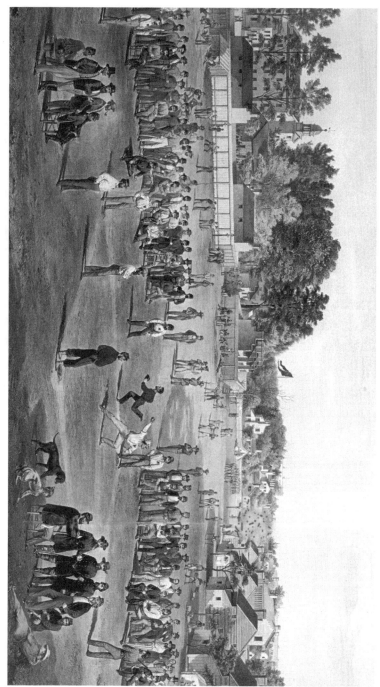

Union prisoners playing baseball in a Confederate prison in Salisbury, North Carolina, circa 1862, in a painting by Union Major Otto Boetticher

apparently as much enjoyment to the Rebs as the Yanks, for they came in the
hundreds to see this sport.

It is also true that Confederate soldiers learned the game in Northern
prison camps. There are accounts of rebel prisoners learning to play baseball in the camp on Johnson's Island in Lake Erie, for instance. And a New
Orleans newspaper account from after the war noted that the city's traveling baseball team, the Southern Club, was made up of men who had
organized as prisoners on Johnson's Island.

Even winter baseball thrived, with an adaptation called "ice baseball,"
played on Sylvan Pond in Hoboken, New Jersey, and Capitaline Skating
Pond in Brooklyn in the winter of 1864. In the winter of 1865, the
Atlantics and the Gotham team played a three-game series at Hoboken
with the Atlantics winning the final game 50–30. In 1865 the Philadelphia
Athletics played a doubleheader against teams from Burlington and Mount
Holly; the Mount Holly game had to be called because of a severe snow-
storm.

In many other cities, including Washington, D.C., baseball continued
to be a popular diversion during the war. The game was also popular
among the armies and navies of both the North and South. In the North,
the U.S. Sanitary Commission recommended that "when practical, amuse-
ments, sports, and gymnastic exercise should be favored among the men,"
with baseball listed as one of the approved sports.

In *America's National Game*, Albert Spalding wrote that thousands of
Union soldiers took the game with them to war and that in the South,
"The same leaven was working in the Confederate ranks. The New
Orleans boys also carried baseballs in their knapsacks."

In one famous story some 40,000 Union soldiers watched a game
played at Hilton Head Island on Christmas Day 1862 between soldiers
from the 105th New York Infantry and an all-star team. One of the all-
stars supposedly was A. G. Mills, who was destined to serve as future president of the National League.

Baseball in the ranks of North and South is well documented by
author Bell Irvin Wiley, probably the best-known writer on the lives of
the common soldier of the time. In his book *The Life of Billy Yank: The
Common Soldier of the Union*, Wiley writes, "Baseball appears to have been
the most popular of all competitive sports in the Union Army." In his
companion volume, *The Life of Johnny Reb: The Common Soldier of the*

Confederacy, Wiley writes, "Next to music Johnny Reb probably found more frequent and satisfactory diversion in sports than in anything else. When leisure and weather permitted, soldiers turned out in large numbers for baseball."

So what was the net effect of the Civil War on baseball? Author Thomas Dyja says that "In the short term, the war probably retarded the spread of the sport, but in the long term it probably helped to spread the growth of baseball by introducing it to thousands of men who had not seen or played the game." Dyja notes that in 1860 there were 62 baseball clubs in existence. The number fell to 32 in 1863 and 30 in 1865. However, by 1867, two years after the end of the war, the number of clubs had exploded to 202.

The intertwining of baseball and the Civil War has even produced an excellent historical novel, *Play for a Kingdom*, also by Thomas Dyja. Reached at his office in New York City, Dyja said, "I've been a baseball fan—Cubs—and Civil War buff since I was eight years old, and I've done a lot of reading about both." Dyja said that several years ago while reading Albert Spalding's *Baseball: America's National Game*, he came across a passage that electrified him. Spalding wrote:

> It is said that in Virginia in the long campaign before Richmond, during periods when active hostilities were in abeyance, a series of games was played between picked lines from Federal and Confederate forces. I have heard rumors of this series repeatedly, but have not been able to trace this to any authoritative source.

"If the story wasn't true," Dyja said, "it deserved to be." He set out to do the research for a novel based on it.

"One day after a long frustrating day of research at the Brooklyn Historical Society, I was about ready to pack it in," Dyja said, "when I happened to notice a file marked 'Civil War' on a countertop." Tearing into the file, Dyja found the mother lode he had been looking for—a daily record of the activities of the 14th Brooklyn Regiment, including the scores of its baseball games with other units of the Union Army of the Potomac.

Now the task was to find a Southern counterpart for the 14th Regiment. "I was reviewing maps and regimental histories at the New York Public Library," Dyja recounts, "when I came across the 12th Alabama, whose first duty in the war was to bury the dead of the 14th Brooklyn at Manassas. I had exactly what I needed."

After three years of research and writing, *Play for a Kingdom* was published in 1997 and received almost uniformly favorable reviews. Producer Ron Howard has secured the movie rights.

The book tells the story of Company L, a battered unit of the 14th Brooklyn, in the Battle of Spotsylvania in the spring of 1864. Company L has been assigned to guard the army's flank and its men are deployed in the deep woods around their periphery. Tired and disgruntled, some of the soldiers decide to seek diversion playing a game of baseball. As they are warming up in a clearing, a voice with a Southern drawl rings out, "Do you call that a speedball?"

Emerging from the woods, a company of the 12th Alabama Regiment approaches the Union soldiers. The Rebels suggest a nine-inning truce for an interarmy game of baseball. The Northerners agree and both teams begin to play—a dangerous diversion indeed, given the likelihood of court martial or death if this gross violation of military rules were to be discovered. Woven in and around the baseball competition are gripping battle scenes, an intricate espionage plot, and the individual portraits of a number of soldiers—all vividly drawn.

Dyja notes that baseball and the Civil War have much in common and much that make them forever interesting. In an article in *Civil War Times*, Dyja wrote, "Both are feats of minutia and laden with detail. There is always some obscure fact to be discussed, some personal story to be told." Dyja adds that "baseball and the Civil War are not just keys to understanding America. They *are* America, and anyone who studies them closely will find the encounter an experience of personal identity."

Does Dyja invest too much hope in baseball? Perhaps. But if he does, he is in plenty of distinguished company and has plenty of predecessors. At the end of the Civil War, for instance, many looked to baseball as a sport that could reunite the country.

For example, a New Orleans newspaper editorialized shortly after the end of the war, "Would it not be pleasant to see the hatchet buried in the great national game, despite the efforts of politicians to keep up ill feeling between the sections?"

In 1869, commenting on the visit of the New York Mutuals Club to New Orleans, the publication *Wilkes' Spirit* said, "This National game seems destined to close the National wounds opened by the late war. It is no idle pastime, which draws young men separated by two thousand miles together to contest in Friendship, upon fields but lately crimsoned with their brothers' blood in mortal combat."

National reconciliation was, of course, a burden that baseball alone could not carry. But this game, which by the war's end had truly become the national pastime, probably did a great deal to "bind up the nation's wounds." Then as now, hopes and dreams were invested in the game. And for 150 years, far longer than most institutions, baseball has stood the test.

THE GIPPER'S (OTHER) GAME

Ronald Reagan and the National Pastime

From 1932 to 1937, "Dutch" Reagan was a sportscaster for radio station WHO in Des Moines, Iowa, broadcasting Cubs games. As Reagan explained it in his autobiography *An American Life*:

I was doing the games by telegraphic report. Well, just picture that the fellow sat on the other side of a window with a little slit underneath, the headphones on, getting the Morse code from the ballpark, and he typed out the play. And the paper would come through to me saying something like, "S1C." That means strike one on the corner. But you're not going to sell Wheaties yelling "S1C!" So I would say, "So-and-so comes out of the windup, here comes the pitch . . . and it's a called strike breaking over the outside corner to a batter that likes the ball a little higher.

An event during this period provided Reagan with the grist for a story that he has told more often than any other, and that eventually found its way into *Ripley's Believe It or Not*. As Reagan described it (again in his autobiography):

One day I saw Curly—the Teletype operator—start to type, so I started another ball toward the plate. Then I saw him shaking his head, and I thought it was a miraculous play. But when the slip came through it said, "The wire's gone dead." Well, with those other five or six fellows out there doing the same game, I knew that if I said, "We will pause for a brief interlude of transcribed music until they get the wire fixed," everybody would switch to other stations.

Then I remembered the one thing that doesn't get in the score book—foul balls—and I knew I was on my own. I looked at Curly on the other side of the window, and he was helpless. It was the Cardinals and the Cubs, and Dizzy Dean was pitching. I made Dean use the resin bag and shake off a couple signs to take up time. Then he threw another one, and another. Bill Jurges was at bat, and when he hit a foul, I described kids in a fight over it. Then he fouled one to the left that just missed being a home run.

About six minutes and 45 seconds later, I'd set a world record for someone standing at the plate—except that no one keeps such records. I was beginning to sweat, when Curly sat up straight and started typing. When he handed me the slip, I started to giggle, and I could hardly get it out. It said, "Jurges popped out on the first ball pitched."

For Reagan the Teletype story was just one of many baseball-related jokes and anecdotes that he told throughout his career on the "rubber chicken circuit."

It also reflects a lifelong enthusiasm and affection for the national pastime. "How could I not love baseball?" Reagan said on many occasions. "It made me what I am today."

This will no doubt surprise many who associate Reagan with football. It is true that Reagan played football rather than baseball in high school and college and his best-known movie role was that of Notre Dame football player George Gip in *Knute Rockne: All American*, a role that gave him the well-known nickname "the Gipper."

The choice was dictated in part by his nearsightedness. As Reagan recalled, "I never cared for baseball . . . because I was ball-shy at batting. When I stood at the plate, the ball appeared out of nowhere about two feet in front of me. I was always the last chosen for a side in any game. Then I discovered football: no little invisible ball—just another guy to grab or knock down."

But indeed, as Reagan said, it was baseball that was to make him famous. In 1932 young "Dutch" Reagan, fresh out of Eureka College in Illinois, decided that the new and burgeoning medium of radio offered him the best opportunity for success in the Depression-era economy. He was a quick study and had a certain stage presence thanks to his acting experience in college plays, but he had no radio experience.

After being repeatedly rebuffed by Chicago radio stations, Reagan took the advice of a program director who suggested that he try a station in a smaller market. He traveled to Davenport, Iowa, and knocked on the door of the station there.

Told by the program manager, Peter MacArthur, that he couldn't be hired because of his lack of experience, Reagan angrily asked how he could gain experience if no one would hire him. As he headed for the door, Reagan, to his surprise, heard MacArthur ask him to come back.

"Could you announce a football game?" MacArthur asked. Reagan said he would give it a try and, stepping up to a microphone for the first time in his life, he retold a half of a football game he had once played in as if he were watching it. Impressed by the young man's raw talent, MacArthur offered him a job on the spot.

Reagan had found his first big break. Quickly proving himself an adept announcer, he was transferred in early 1937 to a sister station, WHO in Des Moines. Although Des Moines was a small city, WHO had a powerful 50,000-watt signal that enabled the station to be heard for hundreds of miles. Reagan thus quickly became a regional celebrity.

Colonel Barney Oldfield, later to become Reagan's publicist, was also a radio personality, working at the time for a station in Lincoln, Nebraska. He remembered that "Reagan had a reputation as being one of the best broadcasters in the Midwest."

In 1936, *The Sporting News* conducted a write-in poll of its readers asking them, "Who is your favorite baseball broadcaster?" Of those announcers not in cities with major league teams, Reagan finished fourth. Assessing his talents, the publication called him an "Iowa air ace" with "a thorough knowledge of the game, a gift for narrative, and a pleasant voice."

One of Reagan's fans during this time was Jim Zabel, a man who would eventually succeed him at WHO. Zabel, then living in Davenport, listened to Reagan regularly on the radio and recalled that Reagan "had a natural glibness about him and a great voice and a great quickness of mind." As an announcer, "he was very colorful, very good at describing the purple shadows coming across the field, that kind of thing."

A powerful testimony to Reagan's prowess as an announcer, Zabel said, is the fact that many people preferred listening to his re-creations of Cubs games to the live broadcasts coming from Wrigley Field.

Ronald Reagan as an announcer for WHO in Des Moines, Iowa, in the 1930s.
Photo courtesy of WHO.

Pictures of Reagan during this time convey the image of a young star—albeit a local one—beloved by his listeners and sponsors. One of the more famous photos shows a dapper young Dutch smoking a pipe with an accompanying inscription, "yours for Kentucky winners and Kentucky Club—Dutch Reagan."

In later years, Zabel interviewed Reagan 18 times and noted that the conversations always seemed to drift back to his happy days in Des Moines and to baseball. "He could remember going to Wrigley Field and how much he liked that and what a colorful place it was," Zabel recalled. "He hated the fact that they were getting rid of all the old baseball parks at the time. He liked baseball the way it was, with all its mystical lore."

In one of the later interviews, Zabel asked Reagan what would have happened to him if he hadn't gone to Hollywood. Reagan's answer: he was very happy when he was working in Des Moines and guessed that he would have stayed there for several years and then, when the opportunity arose, he would have gone to Chicago and auditioned to be the Cubs' announcer.

That, of course, was not to be. Reagan did go to Hollywood and the rest, as they say, is history.

Yet Zabel is convinced that many of the skills that made Reagan a leading actor and later a popular president—the ability to set a scene, to tell a story convincingly, to project the full scale of emotions—were honed during his days re-creating baseball games at WHO.

In the spring of 1937, Reagan got his second big break. He had persuaded the WHO management to let him accompany the Cubs to spring training on Catalina Island, 26 miles offshore of Los Angeles.

In Los Angeles he ran into Joy Hodges, a film agent for Warner Brothers whom he had known in Des Moines. Hodges arranged for a screen test at Warner Brothers and soon after his return to Des Moines, Reagan received a telegram advising him that he had passed the screen test and that a $200-a-week contract was on the way. Reagan soon became a leading film star, going on to appear in more than 50 movies.

In 1952, near the end of his movie career, Reagan was tapped to play the role of pitcher Grover Cleveland Alexander in *The Winning Team*.

Calling the experience "the happiest chore I've had since *Knute Rockne: All American*," Reagan immersed himself in learning the craft of pitching by working with the great Cleveland Indians pitcher Bob Lemon, who was hired as his advisor and an extra on the film.

Reagan's daughter Maureen recalls that her father, working overtime at home, developed the irritating practice of throwing pebbles at her feet by the swimming pool as he developed his pitching form.

Reagan was then dating his future wife, Nancy Davis. One day, Reagan recalled, "She came out on the set . . . and I said 'How would you like to have a baseball autographed by all these great ballplayers?' Oh, she thought that would be great. I started out, looked back, and there were tears in her eyes, and she was standing there. And I said, 'What?' And she said "Can't *I* go get them?'"

In addition to Lemon, a number of major league players, including Gene Mauch, Hank Sauer, and Peanuts Lowery, worked as advisors on the film. Nancy frequently accompanied Reagan to the set.

Bob Lemon recalled, "He [Reagan] was very graceful and easy to teach. I had this little quirk in my own motions where I did a little leap after I released the ball, so I would be in position to field a ball back to me. By the time they started shooting the movie, Reagan was doing exactly the same thing."

Promotional poster for The Winning Team. *Reagan played Grover Cleveland Alexander in the movie.* Photo courtesy of Robert Shapiro.

Reagan developed a real respect, affection, and sympathy for Alexander, or "Alex," as he called him, expressing regret that Alexander had developed a reputation as a drunk and noting that one reason the pitcher drank was that he was an epileptic and, being ashamed of his affliction, preferred to explain his seizures as drunkenness rather than give the real reason for them.

The dramatic high point of the movie recounts Game 7 of the 1926 World Series when Alexander, who had pitched a full game the day before, was called in as a reliever in the seventh inning. Alexander struck out famed Yankees hitter Tony Lazzeri with the bases loaded to win the game for the Cardinals.

In another dramatic moment, Alexander was knocked out by a ball hitting him between the eyes as he tried to steal second base. This make-believe injury was prefigured for Reagan by a serious injury he himself did suffer three years earlier, in June of 1949, when he was on a celebrity soft-ball team playing the Minor League Hollywood Stars in an exhibition game.

Johnny Grant, then a DJ for L.A. station KMPC, was the announcer for the game. As Grant, now honorary mayor of Hollywood, recalled, "The game was a benefit for the City of Hope hospital and was played on the old Wrigley Field in downtown Los Angeles. Bob Hope was pitcher, Donald O'Connor played second base, and Janet Leigh was one of the cheerleaders. Either Henry or George Tobias was playing first base."

Bill Demarest was the umpire; he had called two balls and a strike on Reagan, Grant said, adding, "Then Reagan bunted and tried to beat out the bunt by sliding into first base." Instead, he slid hard into the first baseman and, as Reagan recalled, "My leg broke like a wet cigar."

"You could hear the pop of the leg all the way to the stands," Grant recalled, "and the game was stopped while Reagan was carried off the field and taken to the hospital."

When Reagan's son Michael visited his father in the hospital, his comment was, "Well, I hope that at least you were safe." His father replied, "You know, I don't know if I was or not."

Reagan remained in the hospital for two months while the leg—which had been broken in four places—healed.

Cleveland Indians pitching ace Bob Feller recalled receiving a letter from Reagan during that time. As Feller told the story in his autobiography, *Now Pitching: Bob Feller*, Reagan made the acquaintance of a 10-year-old boy in the hospital whose father, a World War II hero, had become mentally unstable and shot himself and the boy's mother.

The boy was in the hospital for a lengthy period of psychological treatment, wrote Feller, and Reagan had taken an interest in him. "They became even closer when they discovered that they both loved baseball."

Reagan, who had interviewed Feller at WHO, wrote that the boy was "an ardent fan and it seemed to be his one real interest. Of course, I became head man when I tossed your [Feller's] name around as someone I knew personally." The boy had a birthday coming up, Reagan explained, and he asked Feller if he could send him a baseball autographed by the Indians players.

Reagan closed the letter saying, "You'd contribute a lot toward pulling this little guy out of a dark world he's making for himself. I know this is an imposition, Bob, and I would hesitate to bother you if I didn't believe it could do a lot to really help a nice little kid who can very easily end up going haywire."

"By that time," Feller wrote, "the old sports announcer from Station WHO in Des Moines, who interviewed me on his radio show while I was still a high school pitcher, had become a successful movie star. I was impressed with the sincerity of his request—how he said he hoped I would remember him, even though he was famous now, and how genuine he was in his interest in the boy's recovery. I sent Reagan a ball autographed by the whole team."

Years later, in 1981, Feller was chatting with Reagan at the White House and mentioned the letter to him. "We talked about baseball and Iowa—and about that autographed baseball for the little boy more than 30 years before. I told him I remembered it well and that I even kept the letter over the years.

"He couldn't believe it. There wasn't anything in 1949 to believe it was a letter from a future president, but that wasn't why I kept it anyhow. I kept it because of what Ronald Reagan did, taking the time to write out a two-page letter in longhand to help a kid he hardly knew. That seemed to me to be a special act of human kindness, and the memories of deeds like that are worth preserving. That's why I kept the letter.

"The president asked me to send him a copy, which I was pleased to do as soon as I got back to Cleveland. After only a few days I got another letter from Reagan, only this one was on White House stationery instead of a hospital's. He told me:

*Thank you again for sending the baseball more than 30 years ago. I'll confess
I'm more than a little overwhelmed that you kept the letter*

*I'll sign this one the same way. I remember in '49 I did it in case you
didn't remember me. Now I'll do it for "Auld Lang Syne."*

Again, thanks and best regards.

Ronald Reagan

"Dutch"

As governor from 1967 to 1975, Reagan continued to follow the
sport. And following his two terms as governor, Reagan hit the "rubber
chicken circuit" as a highly paid lecturer; baseball stories and jokes were
staples of his repertoire. In a speech to the Conservative Political Action
Conference in Washington, D.C., in February of 1977, Reagan told of a
young married couple with a new baby:

*The wife asked her husband to change the baby's diaper, but he begged off,
saying he didn't know how. Well, the man was an avid baseball player and
so she said to him, "Look, pretend that the diaper is a baseball diamond. Fold
second base until it touches home plate and lay the baby's bottom where the
pitcher's mound would be. Now bring first base, third base, and home plate
together and fasten with a safety pin." Then she said, "Oh, one more thing; if
it starts to rain, the game isn't called. You just start all over again."*

In February of 1980, shortly after his inauguration as president,
Reagan spoke to another CPAC gathering and told this apocryphal story
about a player:

*You know, one day the great baseball player/manager Frankie Frisch sent a
rookie out to play center field. The rookie promptly dropped the first fly ball that
was hit to him. On the next play he let a grounder go between his feet and then
threw the ball to the wrong base. Frankie stormed out of the dugout, took his glove
away from him, and said, "I'll show you how to play this position." And the next
batter slammed a line drive right over second base. Frankie came on it, missed
it completely, fell down when he tried to chase it, threw down his glove, and
yelled at the rookie, "You've got center field so screwed up nobody can play it."*

A month later, on March 27th, the new president had a special treat
when he spoke to a White House luncheon for members of the Baseball

Hall of Fame. The president was seated between Duke Snider and Willie Mays, and he chatted with the likes of Joe DiMaggio, Warren Spahn, and Harmon Killebrew.

At the podium, the president told the old-timers, "Nostalgia bubbles within me and I might have to be dragged away." Speaking off the cuff, he reminisced and told stories including "one that has been confirmed for me by Waite Hoyt. Those of you who played when the Dodgers were in Brooklyn know that people from Brooklyn have a tendency to refer to someone by the name of Earl as 'Oil.' But if they want a quart of oil in the car, they say, 'Give me a quart of 'earl.'" So one time, Waite was sliding into second. And he twisted his ankle. And instead of getting up, he was lying there, and there was a deep hush over the whole ballpark. And then a Brooklyn voice was heard above all that silence and said, 'Gee, Hurt is hoit!'"

Days later, Reagan was almost killed by a bullet fired by would-be assassin John Hinckley. Maureen Reagan wrote in her book, *First Father, First Daughter*, that as he lay in the hospital severely weakened, "One of the ongoing dialogues that day was between Dad and his ever-present doctors concerning the president's scheduled commitment to throw out the first baseball of the major league season in Cincinnati the following Wednesday. Dad's always been a big baseball fan, and he said he had waited all his life to be invited to throw out the first ball on Opening Day; this was his first Opening Day as president, and he didn't want to miss it."

Reagan didn't throw out the first pitch that year, but he did so in Baltimore to open the 1982 and 1996 seasons. Mike Deaver, then deputy chief of staff, recalls one trip to Baltimore with a chuckle. "When we arrived," he said, "they escorted Reagan to the pitcher's mound where he began to chat with players and Orioles officials. As they talked, I noticed that they kept moving slowly towards home plate. When they were about halfway there," Deaver remembered, "someone said to Reagan, 'I think this is about right, Mr. President,'"

Reagan politely declined, Deaver recalled, and he explained, "I think I can do it from the mound." The president then "walked back to the pitcher's mound and fired a ball right across the plate. The crowd went wild. This was just one example of people always, always, underestimating Reagan."

Late in 1981, Reagan's longtime association with the Cubs surfaced in a *New York Times* item that chagrined the new president. A *Times* reporter

Throwing out the first ball at Baltimore's Camden Yards. Photo courtesy of the Ronald Reagan Presidential Library.

noted with incredulity that Reagan had declined to join the Emil Verban Society, the Washington, D.C.–area Cubs fan club.

Shortly thereafter, society president Bruce Ladd received an urgent call from Mike Deaver, who made it plain that the invitation had disappeared in the White House correspondence bureaucracy and that *of course* the president would join the society. Not long after that call, an astonished Ladd received a call from the president himself, who apologized profusely for the snafu and began immediately reminiscing about his days with the Cubs.

"He named every player on the Cubs 1935 pennant-winning team, including their positions," said a still-amazed Ladd, adding, "It's clear to me that his Cubs experience is permanently imprinted on his mind."

In 1987 Reagan was awarded the Ernie Banks Positivism Award by the Emil Verban Society and, although he couldn't attend the luncheon, he sent a special videotape with remarks recorded for the group.

Secret Service agent John Barletta became close to Reagan during the White House years. Because Barletta is an excellent horseman, he was picked to accompany Reagan on his rides around the ranch. Barletta is a longtime fan of the Los Angeles Dodgers and it was a dream come true for him to find out that the Reagans were good friends with Tommy Lasorda, legendary manager of the Dodgers.

Lasorda gave Dodgers warm-up jackets to President Reagan, Nancy, and Barletta, which they all used on horseback rides at the ranch or at Camp David. The three were also given use of Lasorda's box at Dodger Stadium, which they used five or six times after Reagan left the White House.

Although Nancy did not follow baseball closely, she enjoyed watching the games too, according to Barletta. In particular, she became a fan of catcher Mike Scioscia and enjoyed talking with him.

During his stays at the ranch Reagan would frequently call up to the Secret Service command post and ask what the agents were doing. "On a number of occasions we would tell the president we were watching a baseball game," Barletta said, "and he would come up and watch with us."

Reagan also attended a World Series game in Baltimore in 1983, and on September 30, 1988, he threw out the ceremonial first pitch at Wrigley Field and did one and a half innings of play-by-play with Cubs announcer Harry Caray. "You know, in a few months I'm going to be out of work and I thought I might as well audition," he told Harry.

Two former Cubs announcers, President Ronald Reagan and Harry Caray, in the booth at Wrigley Field. Photo courtesy of the Ronald Reagan Presidential Library.

Caray later commented, "You could tell he was an old radio guy. He never looked at the monitor once." The president, who had begun his career as a Cubs announcer, had come full circle.

Reagan returned on another occasion to join Harry Caray in the announcer's booth following his departure from the White House; he also joined Vin Scully for some play-by-play during the All-Star Game of July 12, 1989.

Perhaps the reason for Reagan's success is, as David Broder has suggested, his long-suffering experience as a Cubs fan. Wrote Broder in 1981:

For four years, Ronald Reagan broadcast games of the Cubs and in the process became that rarest of nature's noblemen, a Cub fan. Nothing before or since those four years has prepared him more fully to face with fortitude the travails of the Oval Office. As a Cub fan, he learned that virtue will not necessarily prevail over chicanery, that swift failure follows closely on the heels of even the most modest success, that the world mocks those who are pure in heart, but slow of foot, but—(and here's the famous Reagan optimism)—that the bitterest disappointment will soon yield to the hope and promise of a new season.

5

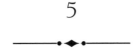

IN A LEAGUE OF HER OWN

On May 31, 1998, almost 55 years to the day after she took the field in the first women's professional baseball game, Claire Donahoe took the mound at Baltimore's Camden Yards to throw out the first ball.

Donahoe was honored as the first woman drafted for the All-American Girls Professional Baseball League—the "league of their own" made famous by the 1992 Penny Marshall film starring Geena Davis, Madonna, and Tom Hanks. Donahoe played in the AAGPBL from 1943 to 1946 as a center fielder for the Racine, Wisconsin, Belles.

The incident was just one in a lifetime of amazing experiences that have taken Donahoe to ballparks from Chicago's Wrigley Field to bomb-damaged, post-war Germany; from imperial Iran to the dusty villages of Ethiopia; from the Bolivian Andes to Baltimore's Camden Yards—not to mention a ceremony at the Baseball Hall of Fame and a chat with Hillary Clinton.

It is a story that truly puts Claire Donahoe in a "league of her own," far surpassing what her cameo role in the film suggested.

Claire Schillace was born in 1921 to Sicilian immigrant parents in the Chicago suburb of Melrose Park. Her mother died when she was 12 and she and her five siblings were raised by their father, Vincent, a steel worker and a very traditional man who felt that "a woman's place was in the home cooking and washing dishes." For the rest of his life he would be alternately frustrated, proud, and perplexed by his independent daughter, who early on displayed an exceptional talent for baseball in games with her brothers.

Claire was a star softball player on the girls softball team at Proviso High School, a Catholic school in Melrose Park, Illinois, and a "die-hard" Cubs fan who recalls that the entire school played hooky on Opening Day to go see a game at Wrigley Field. In 1942 Donahoe enrolled in Northern Illinois State College and began playing for a women's softball team in one of Chicago's many industrial softball leagues.

With America mobilizing for war in the fall of 1942, Philip K. Wrigley, owner of the Chicago Cubs, called the club's assistant general manager, Ken Fells, to his office.

"Wrigley believed that the War Manpower Act was going to result in the shutdown of major league baseball," recalled Fells, now in his nineties and retired in Scottsdale, Arizona. "He asked me to think about something to replace it with, and what we came up with was a women's baseball league." Wrigley agreed to provide start-up funding and Fells quickly deployed the Cubs scouting force throughout the United States and Canada to recruit players. "We had less than nine months to put the thing together," Fells pointed out.

The women's softball leagues, popular throughout the country, were the obvious places to focus on; it was in scouting one of the Chicago teams that a Cubs scout saw Claire Schillace playing.

Finalist candidates from throughout the States and Canada were summoned to Chicago and other cities in May of 1943 for tryouts; Schillace was told to report to Wrigley Field. So impressed were the scouts that she was accepted without a tryout; she was one of the first four woman to be selected. Two of the other three had been schoolmates at Proviso High School. After she was summoned to Fells's office, Donahoe recalled, "He showed me four uniforms and said 'Which team do you want to be on?'"

"I said, 'Well, I like the yellow one.' That was the uniform of the Racine Belles and I played on that team for my four-year career."

The young recruit was "thrilled" by her good fortune. "I couldn't believe that I was offered $75 a week to do something I loved doing," said Donahoe. "That was big money in those days. Frank Sinatra was making $70 a week at the time in Baltimore." She eagerly signed the agreement presented to her and in so doing became the first woman in American history to sign a professional baseball contract.

The four teams initially established were expanded to eight by the end of the year—all in small Midwestern cities of at least 65,000—the idea being that if major league baseball shut down, the teams would be moved into major-league ballparks.

"We just started a new kind of baseball," said Fells. The new hybrid kept some softball practices, such as the underhand pitch, but the extra fielder was eliminated, the bases were placed farther apart, and sliding was permitted.

Wrigley's vision was that the players "look like ladies, but play like men"—a tough standard that required the players to attend charm school classes and wear makeup, short skirts, and tights instead of uniforms with pants. At the same time, they were expected to play aggressive ball. The result was that "Many of us got terrible strawberries on our legs sliding into base," Donahoe said. "Treating bruises was one of the jobs of the chaperones that were assigned to the teams."

The former Claire Schillace, left, poses with fellow players selected for the All-American Girls Professional Baseball League, which played during World War II.

The chaperones were essential, Donahoe pointed out, since so many of the girls were teenagers that had never been away from home and since the teams were on the road so much. "We played every day—126 games a season, including doubleheaders on Sunday," Donahoe recalled. "It got so bad, we'd pray for rain. The all-night train rides could get really tiring, and we always had to be dressed up in skirts when we traveled."

Despite the arduous travel schedule, Donahoe remembers her baseball years fondly. "The people of Racine were wonderful to us. We were wined and dined," she said. "And the Elks, Kiwanas, and Moose Clubs were always organizing events for us. Families would invite us to corn roasts or hamburger fries or whatever."

It was the same on the road, where local groups would often invite the Belles to events organized for their home teams and the girls were given free access to golf, swimming, and tennis at local country clubs.

Donahoe and her teammates chafed somewhat under the chaperoning and 10:00 P.M. curfews but "found ways to slip out." Romances developed along the way, as did a close camaraderie reinforced by endless jokes and pranks. Particularly memorable, Donahoe said, was the time she and some teammates encountered a hooker on the street and paid her to knock on the hotel-room door of their manager and aggressively impersonate the new player expected to join the team the following day,

Not surprisingly, conflicts sometimes arose with the umpires, who were all men. Donahoe recalled with a chuckle the game in which a Bostonian teammate yelled "bahstad" at an umpire who, not understanding her pronunciation, did nothing. He did understand the next player who called him "blind," however, and threw her out of the game.

Exasperated by an ump who consistently called low pitches strikes, Donahoe once hiked up her socks and said, "Would you please look at my knees."

"I am," the umpire replied, "believe me, I am."

As the number of teams grew and the players became more experienced, the quality of play improved as well. By 1946, pitchers had gone to a sidearm pitch and the size of the ball had shrunk from 12 to 11 inches. By 1954, the year the league folded, the size of the ball was 9 inches, the same as a regulation baseball. The distance between the bases had expanded to 85 feet, versus 90 in major league baseball, and the pitcher's mound was 60 feet from home plate—only six inches shorter than in men's baseball. In effect, the girls of the AAGPBL were playing professional men's–caliber baseball.

Bill Allington, then manager of the Rockford Peaches, filmed parts of some of his team's games. Only a few copies survive. Watching the grainy images, the viewer sees a totally unique form of baseball, one with a grace and beauty that is breathtaking to watch. The Wrigley-mandated skirts, however impractical on the field, lend an almost ballet-like appearance to the game as the women pivot to turn double plays, stretch to scoop up grounders, and race to field fly balls. This unique combination of feminine beauty with superb athletic ability demonstrates powerfully why thousands of loyal fans turned out 50 years ago to watch the "girls of summer."

One late summer day at Racine's Horlick Field, the Belles were waiting out a rain delay in the dugout. A steady downpour had formed huge puddles on the field, making play impossible and a rescheduling of the game increasingly likely. Nonetheless, in the stands a lone fan insistently bellowed "play ball," leading the players to wonder aloud about "that jerk" and what his problem was.

When the game was finally called off, Schillace walked up into the stands to investigate. The noisy fan was George Donahoe, a man newly returned to civilian status from service with the American army in Europe. The two hit it off immediately and before long they were engaged.

By 1946, the luster was beginning to wear off the game for Claire Schillace. The war was winding down and it was clear that the major league ballplayers serving in uniform would be back on the field soon. "I'd had my fling with baseball," Donahoe said. "I was due to get married and I decided it was time to get out."

George Donahoe had taken a job establishing schools for the military families that were moving to Germany. "He sent me a picture of a bombed out building," Claire recalled. "A bathtub was hanging down the side by a pipe and on the picture he wrote, 'I hope you enjoy our new apartment.'" The two were married in Frankfurt on September 20, 1947, and had a brief respite from the devastation visible everywhere by spending a weekend honeymoon in a hotel nearby.

The couple spent eight years in Germany, where George served as principal at the new American high school. Claire worked as a science teacher at the school. One of her students was a lad named Norman Schwartzkopf, whom she remembers as "an ordinary boy, good and well behaved."

The good behavior didn't always prevail outside the classroom, however. "Norman lived in the boys dormitory," Donahoe recalled, and "one day he and some other boys were brewing beer in the dorm and the word got back to the M.P.s. Well, his father was head of the M.P.s and when he heard they were on the way, he panicked." Leading his first evacuation maneuver, the boy jumped out of the second-story window and broke his leg. Years later, Donahoe read the now-famous general's autobiography and noted wryly that "he didn't tell that story in the book."

Two sons, James and Michael, were born to the Donahoes during their eight years in Germany, and Claire wasted no time teaching them to play baseball. During summers she volunteered as a college counselor with the American Youth Organization teaching baseball to both American and German youths.

In 1955 George Donahoe took a job with USAID and the family moved to Iran. In Tehran, Donahoe signed the boys up for Little League at the local military base and when the colonel coaching the team quit midway through the season, she filled in as his replacement. A woman coaching a boys baseball team was unusual enough in American circles. It was shocking indeed to the two aristocratic Iranian boys on the team. But Donahoe took the challenge in stride, leading the Tehran Orioles from last place at midseason to second place at season's end.

Conditions were primitive in 1950s Iran and of all the American luxuries they missed, Donahoe recalled that the greatest deprivation was the lack of Coca-Cola. "One time a friend of mine went on vacation to Aden and brought back two bottles of Coke for me," she remembered. Clutching the bottles of the precious beverage away from her grasping, Coca-Cola–deprived children, Donahoe fled into the bathroom, locked the door, and downed both bottles while the kids howled in anger and pounded on the door.

After three years, the family (now with the addition of a third child, Joan) was assigned to Ethiopia; Coca-Cola figured prominently in Donahoe's greatest adventure there as well.

On a flight from Rome to Addis Ababa, Donahoe stoically endured the challenges of flying Ethiopia Airlines. "They had a second deck above the passengers for their livestock and every time we hit an air pocket, they would squeal and squawk," she recalled.

Suddenly the 20-seat plane developed engine trouble somewhere over the Sudan. When the pilot announced that the passengers should prepare for an emergency landing, "The copilot asked what he could do to help."

Told to "prepare to meet your maker," the copilot fainted, Donahoe laughingly recalled.

Following a crash-landing on the dirt runway of a remote desert airstrip, the passengers emerged, shaken, from the damaged aircraft. The dazed survivors were startled to see a camel caravan passing by. "It was like a mirage." Donahoe said, "and the first camel was carrying two cases of Coke."

Not knowing how long they would be stranded in the desert, the passengers stampeded toward the caravan and bought all the Coke from the camel driver. "I don't know how much we paid him," Donahoe said, "but I'll bet he could have retired right then and there."

Fortunately, help arrived in a few hours and Donahoe was soon back home, home being Debrehan, an impoverished town 65 miles from Addis Ababa. Life was tedious in the remote area and Donahoe had to develop her own sources of entertainment. One of her favorite diversions was to race her Volkswagen across the desert roads against the local Galla tribesmen, who rode horseback. "They were excellent riders," she remarked, "and they could keep up with me at 35 miles an hour." Another diversion was showing movies in the local American school where she taught. On those occasions the townspeople would gaze in wonderment not at the screen, but at the projector that was making the magic images.

Special challenges included occasional visits from lions to the schoolyard and the harassment of a baboon family that lived in a nearby gully. Not wanting her children to forget baseball, Donahoe encouraged her boys to teach the game to the local children. The boys unfortunately took this encouragement a bit far, teaching their pitching skills to the baboons in the gully. The animals used these newly acquired skills to throw rocks at the school windows, shattering the panes, which had to be replaced at great expense and effort from England.

Donahoe remembers getting up at 3:00 in the morning to listen to baseball scores on the Voice of America, waiting expectantly for news about her beloved Chicago Cubs (a team then a decade-plus from their last pennant and 40 years and counting from their next).

After 13 years abroad, she also longed to go home—but a reassignment to the States was not to happen before one more duty post. Two and a half years later the Donahoe family—now six strong with the addition of a third son, John—found themselves 11,000 feet up in the Bolivian Andes in a town named Calecoto.

The family adapted to the high altitude, warm days, and cold nights and Donahoe took her accustomed job as a teacher in the local school. She once again coached Little League as well, and her team found Calecoto a hitter's paradise, with balls seeming to travel forever in the thin mountain air.

In 1965 George got the long-awaited transfer to AID headquarters in Washington, D.C., and the family returned home after 18 years abroad, settling in Chevy Chase, Maryland. Many years of happy, normal, suburban life followed. Claire taught science at Kensington Junior High School, coaching the girls softball team as one of her collateral duties.

With all the time spent abroad, Donahoe had long since lost contact with her teammates in the All-American Girls Professional Baseball League. Her children were aware, of course, that she had played for the AAGPBL, but the league itself had long ago fallen into obscurity following its demise in 1954, and for Donahoe her playing days were a distant memory.

Then in 1990, Donahoe received a call from Dottie Willse Collins, a former player for the Peoria Peaches. Ascertaining that Donahoe was the former Claire Schillace, Collins asked her if she remembered Dottie Wilse. "Oh yes, I remember you." Donahoe replied. "I hit a home run off you and you were the most feared pitcher in the league."

"Well, you're in the Hall of Fame and they're making a movie about us and they want you to help," Collins said. Almost too astonished to talk, Donahoe agreed and a call from Columbia Pictures soon followed, offering her a job as an advisor to producer Penny Marshall, who was soon to begin filming A League of Their Own.

The next four weeks were a crash refresher course for Donahoe, who hadn't played professional ball in more than 40 years. She made a quick trip to Herman's Sports Store, telling the kindly but perplexed clerk that no, the bat, balls, and glove "are not for my grandchildren, they're for me."

Invited to play catch with her in the front yard, a chagrined adult son said, "How about the back yard?" There the two spent hours playing catch, "a lot of it spent on our hands and knees looking for stray balls, lost in the pachysandra." The neighbors were amused by the daily training and a friend approaching her door one morning was startled to see Donahoe swinging a bat in the kitchen.

Spring training over, Donahoe reported for duty at the film set in Skokie, Illinois, where she and a dozen other league veterans spent two weeks coaching Marshall and stars Geena Davis, Rosie O'Donnell, Madonna, and Elizabeth Anne Ramsey (of Mad About You fame) in the fundamentals of the game—which were totally new to most of them. The inexperience was painfully apparent with Ramsey (who portrayed Donahoe in the film) when she failed to catch a ball and ended up with a broken nose.

Anxious to avoid this kind of catastrophe with star Geena Davis, who played a catcher in the movie, the producer tried wrapping a tennis ball in leather only to see it bounce repeatedly out of the mitt. The solution eventually proved to be a softer "T-ball" of the sort used by six- and seven-year-old beginners.

"I was amazed at the tricks they use making movies" Donahoe said, recounting a scene in the film where Geena Davis hits a home run over the fence. "She couldn't begin to do that, and none of the extras or anyone else could do it either." The solution in this case was a catapult that hurled the ball through the air. Matched by trick photography to a clip of Davis swinging the bat, it gave the uncoordinated star a home run of Babe Ruthian proportions.

Also a surprise to Donahoe was the drudgery and long hours involved in making a movie. Particularly brutal was the scene at Cooperstown that portrays the induction of the (actual) players into the Hall of Fame. "We were on the set from 7:00 in the morning to 4:00 the next morning," she recalled, "and this included the little kids involved in the scene."

Overall, however, Donahoe and her teammates found the experience a thrill, reveling in the opportunity to rub shoulders with Geena Davis, Tom Hanks, and the other stars and to observe the spectacle of Madonna.

"Madonna? Oh yes, I met her," said Donahoe. "She had quite a reputation and we were very concerned when we heard that she was going to be involved."

Madonna played the part of Faye Dancer, a center fielder for the Rockford Peaches. "She came out on the field," Donahoe recalled, "dressed in leather boots laced up the knees, wearing bib overalls with one strap loose, revealing a red metallic bra. Her hair looked like it was spiked with black shoe polish. It was an amazing sight."

The movie was a major box office hit and focused a great deal of attention on the league, bringing notoriety to its veterans. In April of 1994, Donahoe was invited to be a guest of the Washington, D.C., Cubs fan club luncheon and was summoned to the head table for a chat with Hillary Clinton. The first lady told her that *A League of Their Own* is her mother's favorite movie. "She [Clinton] said that she [Clinton's mother] is sick that she didn't try out for the league," Donahoe said of Mrs. Rodham, who was a dedicated softball player in Chicago in the years when the league was in operation.

Donahoe was tapped to throw out the first ball at Baltimore's Camden Yards on August 24, 1992 and again on May 31, 1998, and also helped Baltimore's Babe Ruth Museum with its exhibit on the AAGPBL. She is also an active member of the league's alumni organization and looks forward to attending the semiannual reunions.

Claire Donahoe throws out the first ball at Baltimore's Camden Yards, May 31, 1998.

The meetings are tinged with sadness, however. "We're older and slower now," Donahoe said, "and quite a few of the girls have passed away." Among those are Ann Harnett and Shirley Jameson, two of the three other women who, with Donahoe, formed the nucleus of the All Girls League. Noting the death of many of the league's 550 players, and the unknown whereabouts of others, the Baseball Hall of Fame has launched a major effort to complete a file on each of the leagues' players.

A few years ago, Donahoe suffered a particularly sad loss in the death of her husband. But she remains active, sustained by her proudest accomplishment, her four children and three grandchildren, all of whom are close to "Oma." She relates with pleasure a recent visit with her daughter's family, who live in Houston. They are all fanatic followers of the Houston Astros.

During the visit her grandson Joey, age seven, announced that he wanted to be a famous baseball player. "You mean like one of the Astros?" his father asked, expecting him to mention Craig Biggio or another of the Astros' big names.

"No," said Joey. "I mean like Oma."

Author's note: Claire Donahoe passed away in 1999.

6

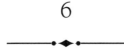

WHEN IT WAS A GAME

Lacy Ellerbe Remembers His Life in the Negro Leagues

Kansas City in the 1940s offered few amenities for black baseball players. As Lacy Ellerbe recalled, "We couldn't eat in the best restaurants, we had to sit in the balconies at the movies, and we couldn't stay in the hotels downtown."

Ellerbe, a Washington resident, played for four teams in the Negro Leagues from 1937 to 1954, when segregation prevailed in Kansas City and across much of the nation. Times have changed.

The roughly two dozen veterans of the Negro Leagues who gathered in Kansas City found the red carpet rolled out for them as the city's elite and a celebrity-studded guest list turned out for the grand opening of the National Negro Leagues Baseball Museum.

Approximately 2,000 people filled the H. Row Bartle Hall at the city's convention center for a reception, a banquet supervised by New York's Tavern on the Green chef Patrick Clark, and after-dinner dancing and partying far into the night.

Former sportscaster Bob Costas was the MC and special guests included actor Danny Glover, basketball great Kareem Abdul-Jabbar, talkmeister Larry King, film producer Ken Burns, and Rachel and Sharon Robinson, the widow and daughter, respectively, of Jackie Robinson, the man who broke major league baseball's color barrier 50 years ago.

The museum itself is a 10,000-square-foot space in a $20-million-dollar complex built in the city's 18th and Vine Street area—traditionally the African American section of Kansas City and now designated a national historic landmark.

According to curator Ray Roswell, the museum, funded at a cost of $2 million, includes a 75-seat theater featuring a film on the leagues narrated by James Earl Jones; hundreds of bats, balls, uniforms, pennants, and other memorabilia of the leagues; thousands of photographs and documents; and 15 computer stations for research.

Chairman of the museum's board is John "Buck" O'Neil, a former first baseman for the Kansas City Monarchs and a member of a fast-dwindling group of veterans of the Negro Leagues.

Larry Doby, another great star of the Negro Leagues (and the man who integrated the American League) was supposed to be a special guest, but was unfortunately in the hospital at the time.

Washington resident Mamie Johnson Goodman has the distinction of being one of three women permitted to play in the Negro Leagues in the 1950s. She is the only surviving member of the trio.

Lacy Ellerbe, who played for four teams in the Negro Leagues from 1937 to 1954

Some of the veterans attending were brought by their children, said museum spokesperson Lorraine Fraser, "because they are too old and feeble to travel on their own." The hardships of travel and the handicaps of age were in all likelihood soon forgotten by the veterans, however, as they savored a tribute 50 years late in coming, but all the sweeter for the wait.

Given the many representatives of the national media in attendance, it was also an unparalleled opportunity to tell the story of the many African American contributions to the game of baseball, such as night baseball.

"We always carried lights and two gas generators around with us in the forties," said Lacy Ellerbe. "Wilk [J. L. Wilkenson, owner of the Kansas City Monarchs] invented night baseball, but they still don't give him the credit."

According to John B. Holway, author of *Blackball Stars*, other innovations by the Negro Leagues included shin guards, batting helmets, and the hit-and-run bunt.

The leagues also gave American baseball a huge roster of now-legendary figures including Jackie Robinson, Larry Doby, Roy Campanella,

The author with the legendary Ernie Banks

Hank Aaron, Willie Mays, and Ernie Banks, who became stars in the integrated major leagues. Others such as Cool Papa Bell, Josh Gibson, Satchel Paige, and Mule Suttles were considered to be among the best in the game, black or white, but were limited to playing in the Negro Leagues before integration.

Thousands of men played for the 75 teams in the six Negro Leagues during the first half of the century, and they played a superior brand of baseball that emphasized speed, base stealing, bunting, and the hit-and-run—as opposed to reliance on the long ball, popularized in the major leagues by home-run king Babe Ruth.

The segregation of baseball has fueled endless speculation on the relative merits of black and white players. How would Babe Ruth have fared, for instance, against the pitching of Satchel Paige, Bullet Joe Rogan, and other black stars of the era?

We do know that all-stars from the Negro Leagues and the majors played each other hundreds of times in the off-season. Author John Holway has researched the period from 1900 to 1950 and identified 436 interracial games. "The whites won 168. The blacks won 268," he wrote.

Although Ellerbe generally has good memories of the interracial rivalries, things sometimes got ugly when Negro Leagues teams played white teams. "Some people would spit on us and call us apes and so forth or they would let black chickens and dogs and pigs loose on the field, but we never let it get to us," he said. "We would make sure they saw us smiling and then we would hit that ball as far as we could."

The interracial games provided some humor as well. "I remember one game the Washington Black Sox played against a white team somewhere down in Virginia," he said. "Our first batter hit a home run. Our second batter hit a home run. Our third batter hit a home run and our fourth batter hit a triple."

At that point the owner of the team, a portly white man with a deep Southern drawl, stepped up to the microphone and stopped the game. "He must have been an important man," Ellerbe said, "because everybody got quiet."

Taking the microphone, the man said to the crowd, "Folks, you might as well go home, cause our lil ole boys ain't gonna beat this team." Then he paused and said, "You know why these Black Sox boys are hittin' those balls so hahhd?"

Then the punch line: "Cause it's whaat [white]!"

Despite the limits, injustices, and indignities of segregation, most of the living Negro Leagues veterans do not look back on their playing days with bitterness or regret. Just the opposite. Lacy Ellerbe, for one, reflects on those days with pride and affection.

Ellerbe was born in the hamlet of Rockingham, North Carolina, in 1919, and he recalls his boyhood days fondly. Though Jim Crow laws were in force, black and white children played together. "We played baseball and swam and fished and rolled watermelons down the hill into the pond," he recalled.

The only things the black and white children didn't do was go to school and church together, Ellerbe said, noting, "When we asked our parents why that was so, they just said, 'That's the way it is.'"

Baseball was the main pastime of kids in Rockingham early in the century and Ellerbe thinks he began learning the game as early as age three under the patient tutelage of his father. "In those days when a baby boy was born, the first thing his father bought for him was a little bat and glove," he said. "I've seen a lot of pictures of fathers or uncles or grandfathers holding a baby and the baby has what looks like a little stick in his hand. But it was a little baseball bat."

Young Ellerbe showed great talent for baseball and, when the family moved to Washington when he was 15, the boy soon came to the attention of the Washington Indians, a black minor league team.

Over the next 20 years from 1936 to 1956 he played in the Negro Leagues for the New York Black Yankees, the Baltimore Elite Giants, the Homestead Greys, and the Washington Black Sox. He was selected as an All-Star during several of those years.

Ellerbe fondly recalls staying in hotels in the black sections of cities when they were cohesive neighborhoods with thriving businesses and a real sense of community. A week before a scheduled ballgame on a Sunday, he said, "The preacher would say to his congregation, 'You be in church early next Sunday, cause there's a game then.' And on that Sunday everybody would turn out, the men in suits and the ladies in dresses and hats. And they'd all go to the game. It was a big occasion for them."

During his baseball years, Ellerbe was married briefly and he has an adopted son, Donald, by that marriage. In 1955, he hit a home run when he proposed to his current wife, Helen. The two have been happily married for the past 45 years and have two grown sons. Ellerbe dotes on his three sons: Donald, now a teacher at UCLA, Lacy, a businessman, and Jeffrey, who played briefly for the Washington Redskins and now teaches high school.

Following his retirement from baseball in 1956, Lacy went to work for the Zoological Service of the U.S. Park Police, where he remained for the next 21 years. For the next two years he worked as a security agent at the National Press Building and then he tried retirement for 12 years. "We traveled a lot and did some enjoyable things," he said, "but after a while I just couldn't stand it. The neighbors just sat around on the porch and told lies. Then they would go in the house and get something to eat and come back outside and tell more lies."

Feeling antsy at age 72, Ellerbe went back to work, this time as a security agent at the Washington, D.C., Superior Court building. His shift was 6:30 A.M. to 3:00 P.M., a routine that seems to agree with him.

In August of 1999, Ellerbe celebrated his 80th birthday, and he shows no signs of slowing down. He is active in the community, working to revive baseball in inner city Washington, and still follows baseball at the major-league level.

A particular favorite is Baltimore Orioles shortstop Mike Bordick. "He's a real ballplayer," Ellerbe said, noting Bordick's intelligence, hard work, and total focus on the game. In general, though, he is critical of most of today's players, owners, and managers, who seem to him to be in the game just for the money.

"Baseball is business now," he said. "I'm glad I played baseball when it was baseball. We had fun."

Author's note: Lacy Ellerbe passed away in August 2000.

7

WE NEEDED HEROES

Baseball and World War II

Asked why he volunteered to join the navy when the United States entered World War II, former Cleveland Indians ace pitcher Bob Feller said, "It's simple. We were losing the war. We needed heroes—fast."

Feller was already a hero in the baseball world of 1941. A teenager from Van Meter, Iowa, he became an overnight sensation in 1936 when he began his career with the Cleveland Indians. By the fall of 1941 he had achieved a 107–54 won-lost record and appeared on the cover of *Time* magazine.

On December 7, 1941, Feller drove from Van Meter to Chicago to sign a new contract with the Indians. He was crossing the bridge over the Mississippi at Davenport when he heard on the radio that the Japanese had attacked Pearl Harbor. Said Feller, "I decided right there to enlist."

In Chicago, Feller contacted his friend Gene Tunney, a former heavyweight boxing champion who headed up a national physical fitness program for the federal government. Tunney arranged for him to be sworn in at a public ceremony that made news all over the country.

By entering the naval service, Feller lost four years of baseball at the peak of his career. He did so, moreover, when he could have gotten a deferment as the sole supporter of his family, since his father was dying of cancer. He also could have avoided combat and spent the entire war giving physical fitness training. Instead, Feller demanded combat duty, went to gunnery school, and ended up commanding a 24-man gunnery squad on the battleship *Alabama*.

Summing up his career with typical bluntness, Feller said:

We took supplies to Russia for a year, escorted the convoys to Murmansk and Archangel, through the U-boats up around the Baltic. Then we went to the Pacific and took MacArthur back to the Philippines. But not everybody liked the chief petty officers, and my answer to any of them was, "Look, this is not

Indians pitching ace Bob Feller gave up four years of baseball at the height of his career when he volunteered to serve in the navy during World War II.

a career for me. I came here to fight and win a war. I don't care what the hell you think."

Following a year of duty in the North Atlantic and the North and Baltic seas, Feller and the *Alabama* were sent to the Pacific, where he participated in eight invasions, including Iwo Jima. In that battle Feller's gun crew dueled frequently with attacking kamikaze pilots in addition to Japanese warships.

Chief Petty Officer Bob Feller (second from right) in August of 1945, the day he was discharged from the navy after almost four years of service. AP/Wide World Photo.

Feller shared these and other memories of his time in the military at the "Salute to Baseball Heroes of World War II" conference, held in Washington, D.C., in November 2000. Also in attendance were Warren Spahn (a Hall of Fame southpaw pitcher with Boston and Milwaukee), Tommy Henrich (the longtime center fielder for the Yankees), Washington Senators pitcher Bert Shepard, and Buck O'Neil (first baseman for the Kansas City Monarchs, a Negro Leagues team). Along with baseball author and historian Bill Gilbert, these great old warhorses made for a baseball fan's fantasy weekend.

According to Gilbert, author of *They Also Served: Baseball on the Home Front 1941–1945*, baseball was very important to America during the war years:

> *Both baseball and baseball players made significant contributions to our success in WWII. The sport itself continued at the urging of President Roosevelt, who considered it a morale booster for the home front and for the men and women in uniform. And so he gave the green light to allow baseball to continue during the war. But beyond that, the men who had made the sport great before the war also made unique contributions of their own. More than 500 major league baseball players served in the military during WWII, along with 4,000 minor leaguers and members of the Negro Leagues.*

Warren Spahn served in Europe as a member of a combat engineer unit. According to Spahn, the boys in the combat engineer battalion meant big trouble for Adolph Hitler:

> *When I first came into the service, they asked me what I did in civilian life, and I said I was a ballplayer. The army didn't know what to do with me. So they put me into the 14th armored division, and I spent my basic training with them. And then the Pentagon streamlined the armored force, and made the headquarters A, B, and C Company, and I was in D Company. E Company was a bridge company. So they took all the personnel from D Company and made combat engineer battalions out of them. And that's what I went overseas with, combat engineers, and let me tell you, that was a tough bunch of guys. We had people that were let out of prison to go into the service. We had the dropouts of the airforce and every other branch of the service. So those were the people I went overseas with, and they were tough and rough and I had to fit that mold too.*

Just out of basic training, Spahn and his felled rookie soldiers were shipped off to Europe. They arrived just in time for the immense German offensive that became known as the Battle of the Bulge.

In typical understatement, Spahn said, "We were surrounded in the Hertsen Forrest and had to fight our way out of there." The "fight" lasted four weeks and resulted in many American casualties. Unprepared for the German offensive, the poorly clothed, poorly supplied American troops had to survive not only the German onslaught but also the coldest winter in decades. "Our feet were frozen when we went to sleep and they were frozen when we woke up," Spahn said. "We didn't have a bath or a change of clothes for weeks."

In close proximity to the Germans, Spahn said, the American troops found baseball to be an ally:

> We had a password among the Americans: Who played the Keystone sack for the Bums? And if anybody in the United States Army wasn't a baseball fan, they were dead. Because the Germans had our dog tags, our uniforms, our equipment. I felt sorry for any of these Americans who didn't know baseball; but that was a correlation that I was very proud of, that I played baseball. And we worked our way out of there, and we went through Malmedy and Bastogne.

After surviving the Battle of the Bulge, Spahn and his unit were moved on to another engagement that became famous—the Remagen Bridge:

> Then we were ordered to go to the Rhine River, and it just so happened that the bridge at Remagen was set up for demolition, and the demolitions didn't go off. So we had an opportunity to capture the 15 or so Germans on that bridge, and captured the bridge, and then we had a bridgehead that even high command didn't know about. And, you know, what do we do then? . . .
>
> I remember the Luftwaffe coming over the mountain strafing us. They were trying to retake the bridge that we had taken, so we were under hell for a while, and then we got some artillery, and then we got some people there, and we established a line of fire with the fifty-caliber machine gun. Every fifth bullet I think was a tracer, and it looked like the Fourth of July. . . . I saw German planes go over . . . trying to bomb us, and you could see sparks when the shells hit the planes but didn't take them down. And I remember a P-38 we knocked down, and this plane was buried in the ground, and this pilot was nothing but ashes.

In what was later called "a stroke of good luck for the Boston Braves," Spahn survived a very near miss. "We as engineers were trying to reinforce that bridge; there were a lot of holes in it. But we added so much weight to that bridge that it fell. . . . And I could have been on there when it went down."

Buck O'Neil also has some powerful stories about his experiences in WWII. He battled the Japanese in the South Pacific as well as racial bigotry as a member of the Navy Seabees. "I could have stayed out of the service," O'Neil said, "but I said I got to go, I got to go."

Sent to the South Pacific, O'Neil's all-black battalion served under the leadership of white officers. On one occasion, O'Neil said, "Our unit was transferring ammunition from an LST to a destroyer and they started to play taps and a little ensign from Alabama yelled out, 'Niggers, attention on deck!'

"I climbed up the ladder and I told him, 'Don't you talk to me like that. I'm a navy man. I'm black but I'm fighting for the same things you are.'"

The captain overheard the exchange, O'Neil said, and reprimanded the ensign. "When the ensign began to think about it he started to cry, and I said to him, 'Don't cry about it, just don't do it any more.'"

O'Neil said the thing that stunned him the most about the people in the Pacific islands "was how poor they were. They didn't have enough to eat and some of the servicemen would take advantage of the women and give them food so they could have relations with them." He added, "I could never have anything to do with that."

The main lesson he took away from the war, O'Neil said, "Is that war is hell, not only for the people fighting but for the civilians too." He was quick to add, though, that he didn't suffer any lasting damage. "I came back in '46," he said, "and led the league in hitting."

Bert Shepard has one of the most amazing wartime stories to tell. A P-28 pilot in the Army Air Corps, he flew 35 missions over Germany. On the last one, he said:

> I was headed back to England. I saw a column of smoke ahead and they told me there were German planes on the ground. Well, I thought I might as well make a pass over there. I guess I flew right over a gun emplacement, because the next thing I knew my right foot was shot off. Well, I was going to call the colonel and tell him I had a leg shot off and I would get back to him as soon as I could. There was no pain or anything. The leg was just sort of numb.

Shepard never got to make the call, however. "Well, the next thing I knew, I got shot in the chin and knocked unconscious." ("Some people think I'm still unconscious," said Shepard, who has a wicked sense of humor. "But the doctors have examined me and they tell me that, no, technically I'm OK.") Moments after he lost consciousness, Shepard's plane crashed.

He survived the crash, but he would not have lived were it not for the compassion of a Luftwaffe doctor from Vienna. "When I came to, this doctor had pulled me out of the cockpit and was working on my leg," Shepard recalled. "But there were some German farmers with pitchforks gathered around and they were going to do me in because some of the American pilots had strafed German civilians and they hated us because of that." The doctor, however, "had a pistol and he waved it at them and they went away." The doctor wanted to operate but the German military on the scene objected. "So the doctor called the high command in Berlin and they gave him permission to operate and so he did and amputated my leg."

After his surgery Shepard was sent to a POW camp where he spent eight months until being liberated by the Allies. "One thing that I'll always remember about the camp," he said, is "how important baseball was to the prisoners. Whenever a new prisoner would come—say if he was from New York—everybody would ask 'How are the Yankees doing?' Even in the camp, everybody wanted to know how their favorite team was doing."

Baseball was still very much a fact of life for Bob Feller during the war as well. "I played ball in Norfolk during basic training," he said. "And I played when I was with the war college in Newport, Rhode Island, and I helped them set up a program there and got them some equipment and uniforms."

Feller kept up the pace overseas too. "I played softball in Iceland," he said, "and we played baseball at Scapa Flow in the Orkney Islands." In the Pacific, "We played ball in New Hebrides and Fiji Kawalien and all across the Pacific Pelilu, Tarraawar in the Marianas. We'd take these islands and Buck O'Neil and the Seabees would bring in bulldozers and clear the jungle and make ballfields. The best one we had was on Ulithi, south of Guam."

Feller even played aboard ship. "We'd play catch on the *Alabama* every day, conditions permitting," he recalled. "A lot of days, though, around about dusk, the Japanese torpedo planes would come in trying to get to the carriers and we would have to man the guns and do our job."

Tommy Henrich entered the U.S. Coast Guard in August of 1942 and spent the war years stateside. Perhaps because of this, Henrich said modestly, "I didn't do anything to affect anybody."

The story of his last prewar game says a lot about how the country felt about the ballplayers who were entering the service. The game was against the Tigers at Yankee Stadium on August 30, 1942, and when the announcer informed the crowd that this would be Tommy Henrich's last game before entering the military, Henrich received a thunderous wave of applause that went on and on.

"Dizzy Trout was pitching for the Tigers," Henrich recalled, "and I mentioned to him to start pitching, but he refused. He said, 'Tommy, enjoy this; this happens once in your life.'" Trout refused to pitch for another minute or two, letting Henrich enjoy the crowd's continuing ovation.

Trout knew, as did every other American league pitcher, that Henrich was a fastball hitter, and so he proceeded to throw him nothing but fastballs. Henrich swung at one and missed, took two balls and a called strike, and, with the count at 3 and 2, began to panic. "There were all these people rooting for me and I kept thinking to myself, I got to hit this to the moon," he said.

Waiting for the sixth pitch, he thought, "'For crap's sake, hit the ball someplace.' Well, the next ball comes in, another fastball, and I punch a good line drive to center field. And the crowd goes wild." To this day, Henrich said, "I think Dizzy Trout is a good guy for giving me six fastballs."

At the end of the war, many of the players resumed their baseball careers. For some, such as Washington Senators all-star right fielder Buddy Lewis, things were never the same. Lewis had logged over 2,000 hours flying more than 300 missions in the China-Burma area during the war, including dozens of flights over the "hump."

"The war really hurt Buddy," Buck O'Neil said. "He had frozen feet and frozen hands and he was never the same. He was an all-star player before the war, but he was never the same after he got back." O'Neil is a member of the Veterans Committee of the Hall of Fame and is leading an effort to get Lewis inducted, taking note of the damage done to him by serving his country in the war.

Warren Spahn had mixed results his first year back from the war. "I reported to Pittsburgh and they put a nail in the wall and said, 'Here's your locker.'"

Spahn won his first five games, after which "The team gave me permission to get married," he said. He then went on to lose eight straight games. "My wife was embarrassed to come to the ballpark," he says, "out of fear that she might get criticized for ruining my game."

The situation improved the next year, however, and Spahn went on to become the most successful left-handed pitcher in the history of the game, winning 20 or more games in 13 seasons. He was inducted into the Hall of Fame in 1973.

Bert Shepard had perhaps the most amazing postwar career among these heroic men. He played in the minor leagues before the war, but everyone assumed that, having lost half of his right leg, his baseball career was over.

Everyone, that is, except Bert Shepard. When asked what he planned to do in civilian life, he always answered, "I plan to play baseball in the major leagues."

And he did. Fitted with a new artificial leg, he returned to the Senators and amazed everyone with his pitching and fielding abilities.

War hero and pitcher Bert Shepard of the Washington Senators laces on his artificial right leg. Manager Ossie Bluege watches. AP/Wide World Photo.

Shepard was brought in as a relief pitcher for the Senators in a game against the Boston Red Sox. The Red Sox had the bases loaded with two outs when Shepard came in. He struck out George Metkovich to end the inning and, during the next five innings, gave up only one run and three hits. Shepard made history with that game—becoming the only man before or since to pitch in the majors with an artificial leg.

That was his only game in the majors, however, as five operations side-tracked his career for a considerable time. But it wasn't the end of his story. He did make it back to the minors, and played three more years as a pitcher, first baseman, and manager. In one game, knowing that he had an artificial leg, the opposing team laid down nine bunts against him, and he threw out all nine hitters. And in one season, believe it or not, he stole five bases.

For Bob Feller, the transition back to civilian life was an easy one. Setting foot on the mound in August of 1945 after a four-year absence, it was as though he had never left. Pitching at a Cleveland stadium packed with cheering fans, he struck out the first batter he faced to the sounds of a tumultuous ovation. Feller went on to pitch a complete game, which the Indians won. His career lasted eight more years, and he compiled spectacular career statistics of 266 wins and 162 losses. He was inducted into the Hall of Fame in 1962.

What might these players have accomplished if they hadn't lost those years to the war? A book titled *What If?* by Ralph Winney, a retired engineer with the Boeing Corporation, used computer models to extrapolate what the records of Feller and other World War II–era baseball players would have been if the war had not intervened.

The projections show that Bob Feller would have won 373 games instead of 266 and chalked up 1,100 more strikeouts and five no-hitters, instead of two. His 373 wins would have put him 48 ahead of Nolan Ryan. Warren Spahn would have won 20 or more games 15 times, instead of 13. Tommy Henrich would have hit 63 more home runs.

Bob Feller finds this exercise interesting but doesn't have a single regret about his war service. "I always mention it when I'm asked about my career," he said. "I am very proud of my military service. We all are. It was an honor to be able to serve our country."

8

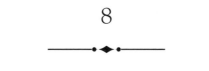

OCTOBER 8, 1956

Baseball historians will recognize October 8, 1956, as the date on which Yankee Don Larsen pitched a perfect game against the Brooklyn Dodgers in the fifth game of the World Series—the only perfect game in World Series history.

Almost 65,000 people were at Yankee Stadium that day, including two Washingtonians: Bob Wolff, the announcer for the Washington Senators, and Shirley Povich, a sportswriter with the *Washington Post*. These names would forever more be linked with Larsen's perfect game.

Wolff was in the radio booth announcing the last four and a half innings of the game. An excellent broadcaster, he had toiled in relative obscurity for the previous eight years because of the miserable perform-ance of the Senators during that time. Wolff had longed to make the big time—to announce a World Series—but that seemed out of reach.

In those days the Series was broadcast by four announcers. The radio network (in 1956 it was the Mutual Network) chose one of the four. The two competing teams also each chose one, and the sponsor selected the final announcer.

The four announcers divided their duties between the TV and the radio broadcasts; two announced the first four and a half innings on tele-vision and the last four and a half on radio. Radio was still by far the dom-inant media at that time due to the relatively small number of television

Washington Senators announcer Bob Wolff (left) did the play-by-play for the last half of the historic 1956 World Series no-hitter. Washington Post *sportswriter Shirley Povich wrote the most famous account of the game.*

sets owned by the public. The radio broadcast also included the Armed Forces Radio Network, which carried the Series worldwide.

Since the Senators never got near a World Series, that eliminated two slots that Wolff might have taken. Wolff didn't work for Mutual, so that nixed a third slot. That left the sponsor as the only option.

Fortunately, Wolff had established a rapport with the sponsor—the Gillette razor company. In his wonderful memoir *It's Not Who Won or Lost the Game—It's How You Sold the Beer*, Wolff described how he pleaded with Gillette for a shot at broadcasting the Series, only to be told, "Well, Bob, you're close. All you need is just a little bigger name." To which Wolff replied, "If I ever get on, I'll have a bigger name in 24 hours."

This catch-22 predicament might have lasted forever if not for the All-Star Game of 1956, which gave Wolff his big break. The game was played in Washington that summer, and the Gillette company decided that they needed a local broadcaster who knew the Washington scene. Wolff was the obvious choice. His broadcast won rave reviews and, when the World Series came around, he finally got that dream call from Gillette.

It was the Yankees and the Dodgers that year, which meant that Wolff would be teaming up with Mel Allen and Vin Scully—two of the greatest broadcasters in the business. The network's announcer was Bob Neal.

Game 5 arrived and the teams were tied, 2–2. Wolff had prepared with his characteristic intensity and the broadcasts had gone well. Game 5 featured Sal Maglie starting for the Dodgers and Don Larsen for the Yankees. Maglie, 39 years old, had pitched a no-hitter during the season; Wolff found himself fantasizing that the old man would do so again in the Series.

Both pitchers had done just that through three and a half innings, until Mickey Mantle hit a solo home run in the bottom of the fourth to give the Yankees the lead, 1–0. In the top of the fifth, Mantle was again the man of the hour, racing to left center to make an awesome back-handed catch on a line drive hit by Gil Hodges. However, Larsen's game was still perfect when Wolff took the microphone in the middle of the fifth inning.

Wolff had carefully rehearsed how he would call the game in case of a no-hitter. He resolved to keep the listeners informed about the exact status of the game without using the words "no-hitter"—in deference to the many superstitious fans who would have blamed Wolff for jinxing Larsen if he'd used the term and the Dodgers then got a hit.

He began: "Hi everybody. It's not only a great game—but what pitching performances. Larsen has retired all 15 men he's faced; Maglie has given up the game's only hit and only run, the homer by Mantle. We move now into the bottom of the fifth."

In the bottom of the sixth, the Yankees scored a second run off a base hit to right by Hank Bauer, driving in Andy Carey.

"No runs for the Dodgers in the top of the seventh. Larsen has retired 21 straight men. The Yankees have four hits. That's all there are in the game."

By this time, the crowd was very much a part of the drama. The tension was palpable when Larsen came to the mound in the top of the eighth inning.

Jackie Robinson, the leadoff batter, hit a grounder to Larsen, who threw him out at first.

"Hodges swings . . . a line drive . . . right to Carey. Two out. [Sandy] Amoros up. Larsen looks in, gets the sign, delivers, Amoros swings, there's a fly ball to center field, Mantle is there, under it, he has it. The Dodgers are out in the eighth inning with nothing across and their totals remain blank in the ballgame. Larsen has retired 24 straight Dodgers as we await the final chapter."

The Yankees were retired in order in the bottom of the eighth to bring on the climactic moment. In the top of the ninth, Carl Furillo flied out to shallow right field to bring on Roy Campanella—past his prime, but still a dangerous hitter. Campanella hit a grounder to Billy Martin at second base, who threw him out at first.

One out to go. Sal Maglie had now been replaced by a pinch hitter, Dale Mitchell. Mitchell was at the end of an 11-year career in the majors,

Dale Mitchell (right) with Cleveland Indians teammates Bobby Avilla (left) and Steve Gromek, celebrating a three-game sweep of the Washington Senators. Photo courtesy of Dale Mitchell Jr.

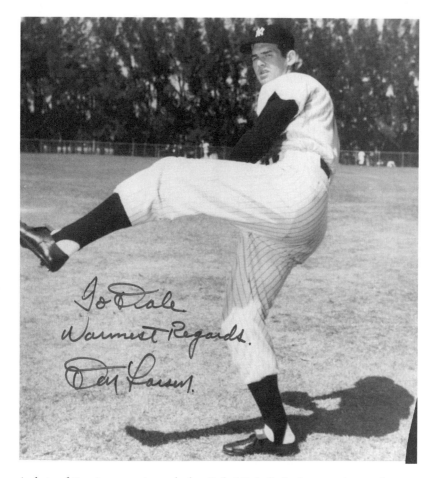

A photo of Don Larsen autographed to Dale Mitchell, the last man he struck out in his perfect game. Photo courtesy of Dale Mitchell Jr.

the first nine of which he had played for the Cleveland Indians. Acquired by the Dodgers the year before, he was now used mainly as a pinch hitter. A leadoff hitter for most of his career, he had a lifetime batting average of .312.

Larsen's first pitch was a fastball just off the plate for ball one. Then Mitchell took a called strike. The count was 1–1.

"The crowd noise was deafening," Wolff wrote. "All eyes were on Larsen . . . then suddenly the silence, the almost unbearable moment of suspense as the pitch was on its way." Mitchell fouled the third pitch off to bring the count to 1–2.

Larsen bent low to get the sign from catcher Yogi Berra. Now the pitch. Mitchell took it. The ball was in Berra's glove. But for what seemed like an eternity to Wolff, there was no call.

Then the word rang out: "Strike three called . . . a NO-HITTER . . . he's done it. A PERFECT GAME for Don Larsen and he's swarmed by his teammates. . . . Listen to the crowd roar. Don Larsen has retired all 27 Dodger batters in a row. He has pitched a perfect no-hit, no-run game, and the Yankees win the fifth game of the series, 2–0!"

In Yankee Stadium, almost 65,000 fans screamed and cheered deliriously.

Up in the press box, however, *Washington Post* reporter Shirley Povich sat stunned. Minutes later, he was still unable to think or write. He realized that he was an eyewitness to an historic event: the first, and quite possibly last, World Series no-hitter. The magnitude of the accomplishment called for great prose, but Povich had writer's block.

"He told me that he stared at the white sheet of paper until he thought he would get snow blindness," said Povich's friend, author Bill Gilbert.

But finally the words came, words that would become famous. "The million-to-one shot came in. Hell froze over. A month of Sundays hit the calendar." Larsen's feat, he continued, was one of "solo grandeur."

For Dale Mitchell, however, it was a game that would haunt him for the rest of his life. "My dad prided himself on his hitting," recalled Mitchell's son and namesake, Washington executive Dale Mitchell.

"He was a leadoff hitter for most of his career and prided himself on his hitting," Mitchell said. "He had a lifetime batting average of .312 and only struck out 119 times out of 3,984 times at bat in 11 seasons." Mitchell noted the contrast with today's players: "Batters—even leadoff hitters like Ricky Henderson—strike out 119 times *a year*."

Mitchell remembers his dad as a tough, old-fashioned ballplayer, "who was just not interested in striking out. Anytime. Period. The fact that he gained a degree of recognition for taking a called third strike pissed him off his whole life. He never softened about it. He was as hard about it the day he died as the day it happened. It was just something you did not talk about in his presence." It was Mitchell's next-to-last at-bat before retirement, ending an excellent 11-year career on a sour note that remained with him until he died.

Adding insult to injury, most observers agree that the called strike that took Mitchell out was actually high and outside. "He was well aware of that," the younger Mitchell said. "Mantle wrote that in his book and Yogi Berra said it in his book, too. But that wasn't what bothered him. He had had his share of good calls and bad calls during his career. He was just mad about striking out."

The younger Mitchell played baseball himself at the University of Oklahoma, followed by a year in the Dodgers farm system. The elder Mitchell, he noted, is regarded as the best baseball player ever produced by the university. In 1947 he had an incredible .507 batting average—still a school record.

A young Dale Mitchell Jr. gets some batting tips from his old man. Photo courtesy of Dale Mitchell Jr.

Pennsylvania Senator Arlen Specter, who attended the University of Oklahoma during Mitchell Senior's years there, shared this anecdote with the younger Mitchell: "The senator said that one day he was walking by the university baseball field," Mitchell said, "when a ball flew over the right-field fence and hit him in the chest."

"It knocked me flat on my ass," Specter told Mitchell. "I asked who had hit it and they said Dale Mitchell."

In 1986, CBS called the elder Mitchell, who was living in Tulsa. "They asked him if they could fly him to New York to do a special feature on Larsen's game with Yogi Berra and some of the others involved. My dad said there was no way he was going to fly halfway across the country to talk to the American public about striking out," Mitchell recalled. "He told CBS, 'If you want to talk to me, you can come to Tulsa.'"

The network agreed. "They sent out a crew and did a nice interview, and I'm glad he did it because it's the last interview we have of him," Mitchell said. "Four months later he died."

II

ON THE HILL

9

HARDBALL ON THE HILL

It was 7:00 A.M., June 17, 1998, and an early morning mist hung over the baseball field at Alexandria's Four Mile Run Park.

Out on the field, about 20 members of the Republican baseball team were warming up. Over on the sidelines, other players were hanging around a table where veteran lobbyist Wayne Vallis had provided a continental breakfast of coffee, pastries, juice, and—a real hit—mimosas. They were there for their final practice in preparation for the congressional baseball game, which was to be played five days later at the Baysox minor league baseball park in Bowie, Maryland, 20 miles outside Washington.

Team captain Dan Schaefer, veteran congressman from Colorado, ran the players through batting practice and fielding drills and then divided the team up for a scrimmage.

Pitching for one side was the team's ace, Steve Largent, a 43-year-old Pro Football Hall of Fame inductee and a superb all-around athlete. After serving as the winning pitcher for the last two years, was he going to make this year number three?

"I'm worried," he said. "We're playing the game a month early this year. I need a full 12-month rotation."

The opposing pitcher was "Vinegar Bend" Mizell, a former congressman from North Carolina and a major league pitcher for the Pittsburgh Pirates and St. Louis Cardinals for 12 years. During the years he was in

Congress, Mizell was so dominant on the mound that a resolution was forced through by the Democrats preventing him from pitching in the annual games.

Retired from Congress for 24 years, Mizell was still an integral part of the GOP squad during their spring training, serving up a mean variety of pitches with a remarkable speed and accuracy that made one wonder how good he must have been in his glory days.

On the sidelines, Congresswoman Ileana Ros-Lehtinen sidled up to the refreshment table. Mrs. Ros-Lehtinen has a place in the congressional game's history book as the first woman to break the game's glass ceiling—

GOP ace Steve Largent on the mound. Photo courtesy of Congressman Largent.

meaning the first woman to reach base. She had a good day at the plate, connecting nicely on a number of pitches—a success she modestly credited to the mimosas she'd been imbibing.

The congresswoman had a pleasant surprise planned for Vinegar Bend. Ros-Lehtinen is a Cuban-American; in the 1950s, Vinegar Bend Mizell was a real star in Cuba because of the time he spent playing winter ball there. Ros-Lehtinen's father was a huge fan of Mizell and had compiled a thick scrapbook of clippings from old Cuban newspapers. She had arranged for she and her father to present this scrapbook to Vinegar Bend in a ceremony during the upcoming game. (Ros-Lehtinen is especially grateful that she was able to make this long-planned presentation, since Mizell passed away six months later due to a heart attack.)

The Republican team had another female player: Jo Ann Emerson of Missouri. This made two more women than the Democrats had—a distinction that team captain Schaefer never tired of boasting about.

Emerson is a self-confessed "baseball nut." A single mother, she has long served as coach, driver, and cheerleader for her boys' baseball games and carries a ball and glove in her car at all times, ever ready for the chance opportunity of a pick-up game.

"This is an important game for us," she said. "It's Dan's last game before he retires and we'd like to see him go out with a win."

At 8:30 A.M. Schaefer assembled his troops for some last-minute instructions and a short pep talk; then the congressmen (and women) headed for their offices.

Six miles away, at a school near the Capitol, the Democrats, under the leadership of Congressman Marty Sabo of Minnesota, were ending their last practice as well. They hungered for a victory perhaps even more than the Republicans did, given their two-game losing streak against the GOP.

Democrats and Republicans alike take this game very seriously—a fact that Congressman Joe Barton of Texas makes very clear. Joe, who played for his alma mater, Texas A&M, was elected in 1984 and served as a star pitcher for the Republican team for 10 years before retiring because of his age at 47.

"We do take this game seriously," Joe said. Asked if substituting softball for baseball wouldn't increase participation, Barton noted, "We play hardball on the floor of the house and we're sure not going to start playing softball here."

But wouldn't softball attract more female players?

"We're not running a dating service for members of Congress," he snapped contemptuously.

Barton and Congressman Mike Oxley of Ohio were the leading candidates to replace retiring Congressman Schaefer as GOP manager; Barton was playing hardball in that competition, too.

Referring to the gruesome accident in which Oxley broke his arm, Joe said, "I don't play for the sympathy vote. I'm surprised he didn't get an Academy Award nomination for best dramatic performance."

Mike Erlandson and Patrick O'Keefe, the congressional staffers who actually run the game, had been persuaded to have a member of the house impersonate the recently deceased Harry Caray (longtime announcer for the Chicago Cubs), who would lead the crowd in singing "Take Me Out to the Ball Game" during the "fifth-inning stretch."

First invited was Republican Congressman Henry Hyde of Illinois, but he declined. Hyde would have been perfect for the role. He is a longtime Cubs fan, outgoing and personable, and even looks something like Harry Caray. But, given the possibility at the time that he might have to chair House Judiciary Committee impeachment hearings on President Clinton, the congressman was staying out of the limelight.

Next on the list was Congressman Leonard Boswell. He's from Iowa (so he must be a Cubs fan), and he also looks like Harry! Boswell did indeed turn out to be a Cubs fan and was delighted to do the gig. He received a pair of black, over-sized glasses and a copy of a cassette with Harry doing his schtick so he could practice.

The four-hour game special was carried in Washington on WWRC radio, and by the Armed Forces Radio Network and about 75 other stations around the nation. Co-anchors were Al From, founder and chairman of the Democratic Leadership Council and an avid Cubs fan, and Frank Donatelli, former political director to President Reagan, cohost of Radio America's *Talking Politics* program, and an equally avid Pirates fan.

An outstanding roster of guests had been lined up to be interviewed during the game, including *Baseball Weekly* editor Paul White, authors Bill Gilbert and William Mead, lobbyist "Chinch" Wollerton, and—holy cow!—broadcasting superstar and expert on the history of the game Bob Costas, who was interviewed by phone.

Since congressional baseball is not exactly major league baseball, regular commercial breaks were scheduled and missed action on the field was recapped afterwards. Interviews were also conducted throughout, with the game as background, except in the case of big plays and end-of-the-inning wrap-ups.

Finally it was game time, live at Bowie Baysox Stadium, Wednesday afternoon, June 23, 1998.

The players were on the field, people were streaming into the stands, and the broadcast booth was a web of wires and a crush of humanity as hosts, producers, and guests milled about.

A Republican barbershop quartet called "The Four Freshmen" was rehearsing the national anthem, which they sang prior to the first pitch. Someone asked for "Take Me Out to the Ball Game." They agreed and, after a brief rehearsal, sang it flawlessly, in four-part harmony. Meanwhile former Democratic Congressman Tom Downey warmed up the crowd with pregame banter on the P.A. system.

Donatelli and From (now back in the booth) set the scene and reviewed the opening lineups; the Republicans took the field.

The first inning proved to be uneventful. The two pitchers exhibited disparate styles: Largent is a power pitcher while Mel Watt, a hurler, has more finesse, relying on off-speed pitches.

That year's game was the 37th sponsored by *Roll Call* newspaper, which awards the coveted *Roll Call* trophy (it's always referred to in *Roll Call* as "the coveted *Roll Call* trophy") to the team that wins three out of five games. The GOP team desperately coveted a win that year because it would mean winning the trophy for manager Dan Schaefer, who was retiring at the end of the year.

According to *Roll Call's* Jim Curran, who has become unofficial historian of the game, the rivalry dates back to 1909, when Republican Congressman John Tener, a former major league pitcher and later commissioner of the National League, organized the first game, which was played at American Park in northwest Washington.

Given Tener's experience in the majors, the Democrats prevailed on him to play infield rather than pitch; they went on to shellac the GOP 26–16. (Some cynical observers of the GOP's congressional performance since then might contend that this pattern still persists.)

For the next half-century, games were played sporadically; the series was suspended entirely from 1958 to 1961 by Speaker of the House Sam Rayburn, who feared injuries and heart attacks among the players.

In 1962, *Roll Call* founder Sid Yudain re-ignited the series and it has been played ever since. Stars of the game over the years have included

The Roll Call *program for the 1999 congressional baseball game. On the left
is Representative Mike Oxley, the new Republican team manager. On the right is
Representative Martin Sabo, manager for the Democrats.*

former Presidents George Bush and Gerald Ford and Republicans Jim
Bunning, who was inducted earlier that year into the Baseball Hall of
Fame, and Bob Mathias, a former Olympic athlete who belted a 412-foot
home run that is still talked about.

Home runs, needless to say, are rare in this game, and years go by
without one being hit. In last year's games, Republican John Shimkus
joined the elite ranks by hitting the first homer in 10 years.

Up in the booth, William Mead, coauthor of *The President's Game*,
provided the political context for baseball in America, noting that almost
every president has had some contact with the game or one of its ances-

tors. George Washington played catch for hours in camp during the Revolution; Abraham Lincoln was both a fan and a player. William Howard Taft threw out the first pitch to open the season in 1910 and established a tradition that continues to this day, to the benefit of both the president and the sport.

"It's a unique relationship," Mead observed, noting, "Can't you just imagine how much the NFL would love to have the president throw out the first pass, or the NHL to have him hit the first puck?"

As a lifelong St. Louis Cardinals fan, Mead noted with amazement the persuasive powers of First Lady Hillary Clinton, who persuaded the president—a longtime Cardinals fan—to switch his allegiance to the Cubs.

In the second inning, the Republicans were the first to draw blood. Kenny Hulshof led off the inning with a hard-hit double down the left-field line, and Donatelli shouted, "Wow, he really knocked that ball!"

Then-Congressman Gerald Ford with an unknown teammate at the annual congressional game in 1949. "I usually play the outfield," said Ford, "but everybody else refuses to catch, so I'm stuck."

Representative Chip Pickering of Mississippi followed with a walk and then John Ensign of Nevada got the second hit, a single to right field, driving in Hulshof.

Steve Largent followed with another base hit, driving in Matt Salmon of Arizona, who was pinch running for Pickering.

Watt got out of the inning without further damage, striking out two batters and throwing a runner out at first base. The Republicans took the lead, 2–0.

In the booth, Donatelli and From continually emphasized to listeners that the game was being played for charity, specifically, to benefit the Metropolitan Police Boys and Girls Clubs of Washington, the Washington Literacy Council, and the Bowie Therapeutic Nursery Center.

The players had asked that the charitable aspect of the game be stressed so that listeners wouldn't get the impression that members of Congress were cavorting at taxpayers' expense, a real concern in a time when the public holds politicians in historically low esteem.

The P.R. problem was brought home vividly by the next guest, Steve Chaconas, program director of Washington radio station WWRC, the flagship station for the broadcast.

"It's nice to see our elected representatives chasing each other around the bases instead of chasing interns around their desks," he observed.

Chaconas later noted approvingly, "It's good to see members of Congress stealing bases, instead of the taxpayers' money."

On to the third inning, and the GOP struck again. Representative John Thune, a Republican from South Dakota, led off with a line drive to left field. Thune took second base on a passed ball, advanced to third on a wild pitch, and came in to score when the Democrats' catcher, Representative Tim Holden, made a wide throw to third.

Senator Rick Santorum of Pennsylvania followed with a double down the left-field line and moved to third on a grounder. Representative Steve Buyer, a Republican from Indiana pinch running for Santorum, then scored the fourth Republican run on another double by Pickering.

Another error and a walk to Largent and the bases were loaded; but the GOP failed to capitalize as Watt, tough under pressure, struck out Representative Todd Tihart of Kansas on a curveball to end the inning. The Republicans led, 4–0.

Both Largent and Watt were in command in the fourth, as both teams went scoreless. Although there was not much excitement on the field, the

highlight of the game came for Donatelli and From when they interviewed
Bob Costas.

The three discussed *Baseketball*, a film in which Costas had a role; the
home run competition underway between Mark McGwire and Sammy
Sosa; and Bud Selig, who would soon become the next Major League
Baseball commissioner.

The chitchat went on for a few more minutes with the hosts enjoying
immensely the opportunity to talk sports on national radio with this great
man.

Down on the field, the Democrats were at last showing some signs of
life as Max Sandlin of Texas and Chris John of Louisiana hit back-to-back
singles. With runners on first and second and only one out, the Democrats
were threatening. But it all came to naught when Sanford Bishop of
Colorado lined a grounder to third baseman Zack Wamp of Tennessee,
who got the force-out at third and fired the ball to first for a double play.

*Congressman Zach Wamp, one of the GOP heroes of the game, and his proud
mama*

Former Speaker of the House Newt Gingrich signs autographs at the 1998 congressional baseball game.

A 5–3 double play is a rarity—certainly in the history of this rivalry—and the crowd enthusiastically applauded the fine effort.

In the stands to the right of the booth, Speaker of the House Newt Gingrich was signing autographs for a crowd of people circling him. Told that the game was being broadcast over the Armed Forces Radio Network, Gingrich expressed his gratitude to those in uniform and the determination of the Republican leadership to enact legislation to improve the pay and material situation of the Armed Forces.

Told that House Majority Leader Dick Armey had accused the Democrats of scuffing the ball and other forms of chicanery in last year's game, the Speaker denied observing any similar trickery.

Gingrich opted instead to accentuate the positive. "It is wonderful," he observed, "to see both parties engage in good clean competition playing the national pastime and raising money for charity." He declined to discuss pending legislation as well, preferring to talk baseball.

As the fifth inning began, Congressman Boswell was in the booth, his Harry Caray glasses in hand. Introduced over the P.A. by the Baysox announcer, Boswell rose effortlessly to the occasion.

"In honor of the memory of one of baseball's greatest announcers, Harry Caray," he intoned, "I invite you all to join in the singing of 'Take Me Out to the Ball Game.' Then, hamming it up, he leaned out the window and bellowed Caray's famous words: "Aw right, let me hear you, a-one, a-two, a-three, take me out to the ballgame. . . ." The crowd loved it and joined in enthusiastically. The congressman also enjoyed his performance immensely.

In the sixth inning, the Democrats rallied again. With one out, freshman Bart Stupak struck out swinging; however, the last pitch got by catcher John Shimkus and Stupak took advantage of the error to run to first. Singles by Sherrod Brown and David Bonior loaded the bases and Adam Smith of Washington flied out to right, enabling Stupak to tag up and score.

Congressman Leonard Boswell does his Harry Caray impersonation during the "fifth-inning stretch."

Taking advantage of a wide throw to Shimkus at the plate, Brown tried to score all the way from second. In a thrilling play, Shimkus grabbed the ball at the backstop and fired it to Largent, who was covering home. Largent tagged Brown out to end the inning. The Republicans still led, 4–1.

In the seventh inning, Donatelli and From interviewed lobbyist "Chinch" Wollerton who, for the better part of two decades, helped coordinate the Republican teams under legendary manager Silvio Conte of Massachusetts. Wollerton regaled listeners with anecdotes from the game's history.

For instance, there's the one about the Republican congressman who broke his jaw one year, a mishap that required him to have it wired shut for the duration of his reelection campaign that fall. Despite the apparent catastrophe of not being able to speak, the congressman won with an increased majority.

The levity in the booth gave way to growing tension on the field as the Democrats loaded the bases with two outs. Skies that had been threatening rain all afternoon gave way to a steady drizzle.

With the game on the line, manager Schaefer allowed Largent to go the distance; his confidence in his ace pitcher was vindicated as Largent struck out freshman Congressman Mike McIntyre to end the game.

Donatelli and From marveled at what a well-played game it had been, with excellent outings by both pitchers, some great fielding efforts, and only two errors over seven innings—an accomplishment that a major league team would be proud of.

Judging by his performance that day, the rumors of Largent developing a curve ball seemed to have been proved true. Said Largent, "I don't know if it was a real curveball or just old age."

Schaefer was carried off the field in triumph by his players, having taken possession of the "coveted *Roll Call* trophy."

Over on the other side of the field, the Democrats were subdued, but gracious, losers.

"We played a good game," said pitcher Mel Watt. "You can't be upset with this. I'm just glad it's over."

Up in the booth, the intrepid broadcasters continued to interview guests, since there was still almost an hour of airtime to fill.

Former Congressman "Vinegar Bend" Mizell came by for a chat and proved to be an inexhaustible source of great stories about his days in the majors. Of particular interest to Pirates fan Donatelli was Mizell's account of the climactic seventh game of the 1960 World Series, in which the Pirates beat the Yankees in the bottom of the ninth on a home run by Bill Mazeroski.

"I'm one of the few people there who missed it," said Mizell, explaining that he had been sent to the bullpen to warm up in case the game went to extra innings. He had turned his back on the field at the crucial moment and missed the historic homer.

From and Donatelli said goodbye to Vinegar Bend and gave a recap of the game, concluding with a drum roll and an announcement that the game had raised over $60,000 for charity—a record. They pronounced the game a great success and signed off. Outside the Baysox stadium, the rain had intensified and the raucous sounds of the postgame party made it increasingly difficult to hear or be heard.

Congressman Boswell's mentor Harry Caray would have summed it up like this: "Ya can't beat fun at the ol' ballpark."

10

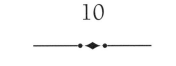

PINCH HITTING FOR SHOELESS JOE

In 1999 the bitterly divided 106th Congress put aside its partisan warfare momentarily to unanimously adopt resolutions in support of a man who had been dead for 50 years. That man was Joseph "Shoeless Joe" Jackson, an illiterate mill worker from Greenville, South Carolina, who went on to become one of the greatest baseball players of all time. Jackson played at the top of his profession from 1908 to 1921 before he was banned from professional baseball for life because of his alleged participation in the "Black Sox" scandal of 1919. Banished, Jackson slipped into obscurity, playing semipro ball in the small towns of the South and operating a liquor store in his hometown of Greenville until the day he died in 1951. Jackson always maintained that he had been innocent of any wrongdoing in the scandal.

Jackson's story is the stuff of epic tragedy, and has assumed the status of myth and legend, fueled by the publication of W. P. Kinsella's novel *Shoeless Joe*, which was made into the blockbuster movie *Field of Dreams*.

The story has a sad ending according to South Carolina Congressman Jim DeMint, "and Americans don't like sad endings."

DeMint was born on September 2, 1951, a mile away from the house in which Shoeless Joe died a month later. He has taken up Jackson's cause as a personal crusade. "It started out as a community thing in West Greenville," DeMint said. "Some of the folks there are trying to revitalize a part of their community around the memory of Shoeless Joe. They've renovated a ballpark where Joe played as a mill worker. They're trying to rebuild a whole section of West Greenville around Shoeless Joe."

DeMint said that he didn't know that much about Shoeless Joe when he was growing up, but that after he was elected to Congress, constituents started asking him to help in clearing the name of a man they considered not only a great ballplayer but also an outstanding member of their community. "When Joe was banned from baseball he came back to Greenville and for the rest of his life he was active in the community. He loved children and spent a lot of time teaching kids to play baseball and to stay out of trouble," commented DeMint.

The congressman was surprised by the powerful constituency that existed for Shoeless Joe across the country. "When I would go up to Dick Armey or other members of the leadership and ask if they could help get a resolution to the floor, many times they would say that they had already heard from their constituents. Some of them even said they had heard from foreigners writing in about Shoeless Joe."

In a speech on the House floor, DeMint said, "It is worthy for this body to take a few minutes to stand for fairness and right an old wrong. . . . No one who has lived the American dream and achieved so much should be stripped of his honor, his dignity."

Although there is some dispute over the details, the essentials of Jackson's story are fairly clear. Joseph Jefferson Jackson was born on July 16, 1889, in Pickens County, South Carolina. He never went to school or learned to read or write and by the age of 13 he was working full time in the Greenville mills with his father. By the age of 15 he was playing semi-pro ball for the Greenville Spinners in the city's mill league.

At some point during that time he got a new set of cleats, which were too tight and left his feet severely blistered. He asked to sit out the next game but was called in as a substitute by the manager. Unable to wear his cleats, he played in his stockings. Nonetheless, he played spectacularly, hitting a triple that prompted a fan of the opposing team to yell out "Joe Jackson, you shoeless son of a gun." He never played in his socks again, but the nickname stuck. In 1908, when Jackson's prodigious talents attracted the notice of the Philadelphia Athletics and the A's offered him a place on the team, the moniker followed him into the major leagues.

For the next 10 years, Shoeless Joe demonstrated a level of excellence on the field that made him famous throughout the country. He was a

Shoeless Joe Jackson in his prime

complete player, excelling in every facet of the game. An offensive powerhouse, during his rookie year Jackson batted an astonishing .408. He
never hit under .300 for a full season and batted .382 his final year. His
lifetime average of .356 is third behind only Ty Cobb and Rogers
Hornsby.

None other than Babe Ruth himself called Jackson "the finest hitter I
ever saw"; he singled Jackson out for study and copied his stance and swing.

Jackson was also a superb outfielder, demonstrating great speed, natural grace, and intuition about the ball's trajectory. His position in left field
became known as "the place triples go to die."

In 1915 Shoeless Joe was acquired by the Chicago White Sox, then
owned by Charles Comiskey, a man who became notorious for his penny-
pinching ways. Comiskey's stinginess in paying his players' laundry bills
won the White Sox the nickname of the "Black Sox," and it is the Black
Sox that were forever linked with the scandal that led to Shoeless Joe
Jackson's downfall.

In 1917 Jackson led the White Sox to a World Series victory over the
New York Giants; in 1919 the Sox again won the American League
Championship and were set to face the Cincinnati Reds in the Series.

By this time the White Sox team was seething with resentment at
Comiskey because of his tight-fisted ways; in this environment they were
easy prey for a New York gambling syndicate. Although the facts are not
entirely clear, most people familiar with the case think that first baseman
Chick Gandil became the ringleader for a group of players who agreed to
take bribes in exchange for throwing the Series.

Jackson was counted among the group of eight but his degree of com-
plicity remains hotly disputed. He certainly knew about the fix but reportedly tried to tell his manager, Kid Gleason, that "something funny was
going on," and that he wanted to sit out the Series. He was told to play.
Joe also accepted $5,000 that was left on his bed in their hotel room by
his roommate, Claude Williams; but, after the series, he tried to return the
money. He also attempted to tell owner Charles Comiskey about the fix
after the Series was over, but was curtly shown the door.

Jackson's partisans maintain, compellingly, that the strongest argument for his innocence is his record in the Series itself. Over eight games
Jackson hit .375, the highest average for both teams; he also hit the only
home run and committed no errors in the field.

When the fix was brought to light in 1920, the eight players associated with it were tried by a Chicago grand jury and were acquitted of the charge that they had tried to fix the 1919 Series.

During the trial, a boy supposedly accosted Shoeless Joe outside the courtroom and cried out, "Say it ain't so, Joe," to which Jackson supposedly replied, "It's so, kid, it's so." The incident is apocryphal, having been invented by a reporter, but it has become one of the most famous lines in baseball history.

Despite the acquittals, the developing scandal threatened to ruin professional baseball. A retired judge by the name of Kenesaw Mountain Landis was named as baseball's first commissioner and given great powers to "act in the best interests of the game." His first action was to banish the eight "Black Sox" players from professional baseball for life, not with-standing their acquittal in a jury trial. Landis stated:

> Regardless of the verdict of juries, no player who throws a ballgame, no player that undertakes or promises to throw a ballgame, no player that sits in conference with a bunch of crooked players and gamblers where the ways and means of throwing a game are discussed, and does not promptly tell his club about it, will ever play professional baseball.

Landis's summary action, undertaken without a formal inquiry or hearing of any kind, stood, despite a second trial, this one held in 1924 in Milwaukee. The jury was asked specific questions called "special interrogatories," including whether Shoeless Joe conspired or participated in a fix of the 1919 Series. Their answer was an unequivocal "No."

Following his ban from professional baseball, Joe Jackson played semipro ball for a while in the 1920s. Later Joe and his wife, Katie, started a liquor store in Greenville and Joe lived there until he died in 1951. Jackson never campaigned to establish his innocence while he was alive and after his death he was largely forgotten.

It was only after the films *Eight Men Out* (1988) and *Field of Dreams* (1989) that a renewed public interest in Jackson's story was sparked. Hall of Famer Ted Williams became interested in Jackson's cause as well. Williams has often been compared to Jackson in appearance and batting style. As a minor league player he asked Jackson's former teammate, Eddie Collins, if Jackson was in on the fix. Collins had answered simply, "No."

Williams is a member of the Hall of Fame Veterans Committee and he persuaded fellow vets Bob Feller and Tommy Lasorda to join him in an effort to get Jackson inducted into the Hall of Fame.

In 1999 Williams persuaded Chicago lawyer and Jackson supporter Louis Hegemon to write a petition on behalf of the three Hall of Famers; on July 2, 1999, a 14-page document was sent to Commissioner Bud Selig. The petition began with a lengthy brief making the case for Jackson's innocence and noted that, in any case, the only sanction levied against him—Landis's lifetime ban from professional baseball—expired in 1951, when Jackson died.

Given this fact, the petitioners argued, the commissioner should waive any further jurisdiction over Jackson and remand his case to the Veterans Committee of the Hall of Fame, a move that would almost certainly result in his induction at the first opportunity.

It wasn't long before Williams and Congressman Jim DeMint joined forces; DeMint's House resolution relied heavily on the Williams/Feller/Lasorda petition. It did not argue for Jackson's exoneration per se, but rather called on the commission to "remove the taint from the memory of Shoeless Joe Jackson" and to ensure that he would be appropriately honored for his contributions to baseball.

"What I've tried to push with the commissioner is: let's not go back and retry Shoeless Joe," said the congressman. "There are those who feel that he was found innocent in court and that he tried to expose the fix, but there are others who argue the other side.

"We're just saying he was banned from baseball for life and he served his term with dignity and he's been dead for 50 years. He was one of the greatest baseball players in history, and shouldn't we take him off the ineligible list and at least let the Hall of Fame vote on it?"

House Resolution 269 passed on a voice vote on November 8, 1999, and a similar resolution was unanimously adapted by the Senate on November 19, 1999.

DeMint next sought to turn up the heat by enlisting the support of a heavy hitter in the Senate, Senator Strom Thurmond. Thurmond, a Washington institution for 50 years, was born only 13 years after Jackson. Commissioner Selig met with Thurmond and DeMint (Williams was unable to attend on short notice). In the meeting both the senator and the congressman pressured Selig for a quick resolution of the matter. Selig explained that he had asked Jerome Holtzman, retired sportswriter

Baseball Commissioner Bud Selig (left) meets with Senator Strom Thurmond (center) and South Carolina Congressman Jim DeMint (right) on the case of Shoeless Joe Jackson.

for the *Chicago Tribune* and official Major League Baseball historian, to conduct a thorough review of the Jackson case—the baseball equivalent of the Washington Presidential Commission as a way to handle a hot potato.

Holtzman's report is still awaited.

"The Commissioner's got a job to do," said DeMint. "He's got to protect the integrity of baseball, but the point I made when we met is that there is only one case we've got where someone was thrown out of baseball without a hearing and that furthermore he served his term.

"I think it's a no-win situation to say that Joe was innocent or guilty. What he should do is say 'The facts of the case are very old. What we do know for sure is that Shoeless Joe served his sentence with dignity and we're taking him off the ineligible list.'"

Sadly, despite petitions, resolutions, reports, and the determined efforts of many individuals, Shoeless Joe Jackson is still waiting to claim his rightful place in the Baseball Hall of Fame. Only time will tell if he will ever be given that honor, which, as one of the greatest baseball players of all time, he so richly deserves. Meanwhile, the congressman pledges to continue his crusade.

In an interesting postscript, in an allusion to the Pete Rose case, DeMint later said, "If there are others who are banned from baseball, let them serve their term, and then if the Hall wants to consider them, that's fine."

11

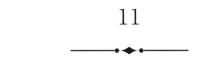

CONGRESSMAN COUNTERS COBB'S CRITICS

Congressman J. D. Hayworth, a Republican from Arizona, has been a guest on Radio America programs numerous times and has on occasion even filled in as a guest host. He's a natural on radio, which is not surprising given the fact that he worked as a radio sportscaster and news anchor before being elected to Congress in 1994.

Hayworth had his first radio gig at age 13, and also did some radio broadcasting as a college student at North Carolina State University. The congressman showed considerable promise as a football player, but an injury ended his playing days, at which point he turned to broadcasting as a career, working through the eighties in a number of cities including Greenville, South Carolina, Cincinnati, and finally Phoenix. From 1987 to 1993 he was a broadcaster for Channel 10 television there, while also doing talk radio on a local station. In 1992 and 1993 the Congressman had one of his favorite assignments, acting as the voice of spring training for the Chicago Cubs on local radio.

A gregarious, outgoing guy, Hayworth likes to talk about most anything—sports, politics, history, you name it—but his favorite topic is reminiscing about his grandfather, Ray Hayworth, a major league baseball player for 15 years and later a manager and scout.

But perhaps the most remarkable fact about Hayworth's grandfather, now 96 years old, is that he is the last living teammate of Ty Cobb. The elder Hayworth played with Cobb on the Detroit Tigers in 1926, the last year that Cobb was a player/manager there.

The congressman says that his grandfather offers some remarkable insights into Cobb's character—much of it contrary to the conventional picture of Cobb as a ruthless, profane, and unscrupulous ballplayer and human being. Hayworth's grandfather remembers him differently.

"He has always said that it's true that Cobb was a tough guy, and that he was not altogether pleasant, but that he was very different than the monster he has been made out to be," the congressman said. "As a manager, my grandfather told me, Cobb had a deep concern for his players, both as players and as people. He remembers that Cobb would take as long as needed to work with his players, especially on hitting."

Hayworth adds that his grandfather said Cobb was a great manager to work for as long as you worked hard. "He loved playing for him," Hayworth said. The elder Hayworth remembered Cobb as an excellent counselor concerned with his men's welfare.

Congressman J. D. Hayworth and his grandfather, Ray Hayworth, on Capitol Hill.
Photo courtesy of Congressman J. D. Hayworth.

"Cobb was a very savvy investor with an excellent stock portfolio," the congressman added. "My grandfather remembers one time in particular when Cobb came into the clubhouse and got the players together for a financial counseling session. He had a $1,000 bill with him and he passed it around to all the players. Then he passed some stock certificates for General Motors and Coca-Cola and some other stocks around." The lesson: "It's not what you make that's most important. It's what you save."

Hayworth says his grandfather had an excellent career as a catcher, playing for 13 years for Detroit and two years for the Dodgers. He was rated the number one defensive catcher for a number of those years.

Following his retirement as a player, Hayworth went on to manage the Fort Worth Cubs in the Texas League, where he coached an outstanding young outfielder named Edwin Snider—later to become better known as "Duke" Snider, a Hall of Fame player for the Brooklyn Dodgers. Hayworth later coached for the Braves, the Dodgers, and the Cubs. As manager of one of the Cubs' farm teams, he coached Smoky Burgess and Stan Hack. He later became director of scouting for the Cubs.

The congressman says his grandfather, now retired in North Carolina, still loves to visit Washington. "He has fond memories of playing here," Hayworth said, "because for one thing, he was one of the few players who could hit Walter Johnson.

"When my grandfather comes to Washington on the train," he added, "he loves to reminisce about Union Station and how he and the other Tigers would hang around the fountain while they waited for the train and some of the good experiences he had here."

In 1995 the congressman brought his grandfather to Washington to throw out the first pitch at the congressional baseball game—a duty he carried out with aplomb at 91 years of age.

"My grandfather is still alert and still very active," Hayworth said. "He was kind of disappointed that Tiger Stadium has been replaced by a new ballpark, but he still roots for the Tigers.

"I love baseball," the Congressman said. "I love the history that's associated with the game."

No wonder. In the Hayworth clan you don't get history from books. If you're talkin' baseball in the twentieth century, you get that history firsthand from the family patriarch. He was there.

12

A Sportsman's Creed

Senator Connie Mack Remembers His Grandfather

Asked if he has any regrets about leaving Congress after 18 years, Florida Senator Connie Mack said without hesitation, "None whatsoever. I feel I've accomplished what I came here to do and there's no sense in hanging on for the sake of hanging on. It's time to do something else with my life."

For the senator and his wife, Priscilla, the next phase of their lives will involve a substantial amount of time devoted to promoting cancer research and treatment. Mack and his wife have both battled cancer themselves and are determined to do their part to help find a cure for the dreaded disease.

Mack is the grandson of the legendary Connie Mack, owner/manager of the Philadelphia Athletics from 1901 to 1950; the retired senator attributes his sense of perspective in part to his famous baseball family.

He illustrates with a story. "When I ran for Congress the first time," he recalled, "I got into a runoff election. The runoff election in Florida takes place during the first week of October, which is, of course, also when the playoff games are under way. . . . And the night of my runoff election, sure enough there was a game. I went up to Sarasota, which is at the northern end of the district, and thanked everybody there for their involvement.

"I got in the car and drove back down to Fort Myers. It was an hour and a half drive. Immediately turned on the radio. There were no returns given by the radio stations, because it was virtually the only race, since it

The great Cornelius McGillicutty (also known as "Connie Mack") catching for the Washington Senators in 1888. The game was played on the old Swampoodle Grounds near present day Union Station, less than a half mile from grandson Senator Connie Mack's office.

was a runoff. So I went an hour and a half with no idea of how the elections had come out. So we get to Fort Myers and I go running into the Holiday Inn, where we had set up our headquarters.

"I go bursting into Mother and Dad's room. Sure enough, Dad was watching television. He was seated at the edge of the bed, and I looked at him with a great deal of anxiety and said, 'How's it going, Dad?' He said, 'Don't worry, Son, the score's 4 to 3.' True story. He was watching the ballgame. It was a very important message to learn at the beginning of a political career, to recognize that there are other things going on in people's lives that are very important and politics is only a portion. And secondly, from the standpoint of messages, this was, 'Connie, don't take this thing too seriously.' It's a great story, and it actually happened."

The senator's father got his own lesson in humility on another occasion, and it's another favorite story of the senator's. "There was an attempt to start a seniors league in Florida . . . men probably in their forties, fifties, and Dad was asked to throw out the first ball in one of these games. He did so. He was excited about it. They sent a limousine to pick him up. My sisters and brothers went with him. The following day I saw the headline in the paper. It said something like, 'Connie Mack, the son of the legendary owner and manager of the Philadelphia Athletics, and father of United States Senator Connie Mack, threw out the first ball.' So I called him. I knew he was going to be excited. He was absolutely glum. I said, 'What's wrong?' He said, 'Son, I've gone through my entire life being known as Connie Mack's son. Now, they're referring to me as Connie Mack's father. I'm having a terrible identity crisis.'"

The name Connie Mack is one of the most famous in baseball and also one of the most unusual. The old man's real name was Cornelius McGillicuddy. Asked if that is the situation with him as well, the senator replied, "It is indeed. It's the name on my driver's license and my voter registration and on all legal documents."

His grandfather was dubbed "Connie Mack" by a Washington sports reporter who grew frustrated grappling with the unwieldy name of "Cornelius McGillicuddy" in his reports and decided on his own to shorten it. The shorthand caught on and there has been a Connie Mack in the family since then. The senator's father bears the name, as does his son.

Interestingly, only men with the name Cornelius use the surname "Mack" in the McGillicuddy family. "Even my wife uses McGillicuddy," Mack said, "and it produces some interesting situations having two names."

The original Connie Mack's incredible career in baseball spanned seven decades. Born in 1862, when baseball was in its infancy, he managed eight World Series teams in his 53 years and is the holder of numerous records as a manager. Among them: number of games (7,755); number of wins (3,731); and number of losses (3,948).

The image Mack retains of his grandfather is the same one that baseball fans have: "An old fella not in a baseball uniform, but in a dark suit, high stiff collar, holding a score card in his hand, and motioning to his players. He wore that same dress, if you will, until the day he died," Mack said. "He would come down to visit us when we moved to Florida in the early '50s. One of my responsibilities as a young fella, probably 12 or 13 years old, was to sit in his room in the morning, about 5:30 in the morning, waiting for him to awaken, and then kind of help him get his day started, and then he put on that same dark suit . . . and . . . out in public he would go. It was just part of who he was."

Connie Mack III campaigning for the House of Representatives with his father, Connie Mack II.

Little League player Connie Mack gets some expert batting instruction from his grandfather in Fort Myers, Florida, in the early 1950s.

The senator was born in Philadelphia in 1940 and remembers spending a lot of time as a boy at Shibe Park (later named Connie Mack Stadium), where his grandfather managed the Athletics. Shibe Park was demolished in 1976 but old timers remember it as one of the most beautiful of all the old parks; Mack has fond memories of the days when his mother would take all her children there, each one with his or her score card, to see games, particularly on weekends. "She was an avid baseball fan," he said, "and she taught us how to keep score."

Baseball then was truly a family affair: Mack's grandfather was an owner and manager; his father, who had played baseball in college, was first base coach; and an uncle, Earle, was also a coach.

Baseball had granted Mack's grandfather a singular exemption from wearing a baseball uniform (a requirement in baseball as in no other sport). Another rule, however, holds that only personnel in uniform can go on the field. This unique combination of circumstances resulted in other odd habits. It is reported, for instance, that when the old man questioned a call by the umpire, he would dispatch Earle to advise the ump of this fact. Such was Connie Mack's stature in the game that the umpire would actually walk over to the Athletics' dugout to discuss the call!

The senator and his siblings all had their favorite players (among his: Bobby Shantz, Elmer Valo, and Sam Chapman) but his parents were adamant that the children not exploit their family connections to fraternize with the players. It is true that the family sat right behind the A's dugout and that players would throw balls to them or set balls on the dugout roof to roll down onto the seats so the children could get them. "But basically," he said "our excitement and love of the game came from watching it like everybody else. I only remember being allowed in the clubhouse two times, once at Shibe Park and once I think in spring training," he said.

In 1951 Mack's father sold his interest in the team and the family moved to Florida. His grandfather would come down to visit them periodically, and the senator recalls those visits as special occasions.

Among the most vivid memories Mack has of his grandfather, or "Pop-Pop," as he called him, is the old man sitting on their lawn in the suit that the boy had helped him put on and acknowledging the greetings of passers-by.

The legacy of baseball's grand old man looms large in the life of Senator Mack, his father, and now his son, who was recently elected to a seat in the Florida House of Representatives from Fort Lauderdale.

The senator was in Philadelphia during the spring of 2000 to attend the Republican National Convention and he took his son with him. "It was really the first time that Connie and I were able to spend some time together in Philadelphia from a baseball point of view," he said. "We visited the old neighborhood and we went to the ballpark to get some memorabilia."

But it was the statue of the elder Connie Mack outside Veterans Stadium that impressed him the most, particularly the old manager's creed that has since come to be known as "The Sportsman's Creed." It reads:

I will promise to play the game to the best of my ability at all times.

I will always play to win. But if I lose, I will never look for excuses which would detract from my opponent's victory.

I will always abide by the rules of the game on the diamond as well as in my daily life.

I will never gloat in victory or pity myself in defeat.

I will judge a teammate as an individual and never on the basis of his race or religion.

"It was 'The Sportsman's Creed' that Connie really took note of," the senator said. "He copied down the words and has used them in his own

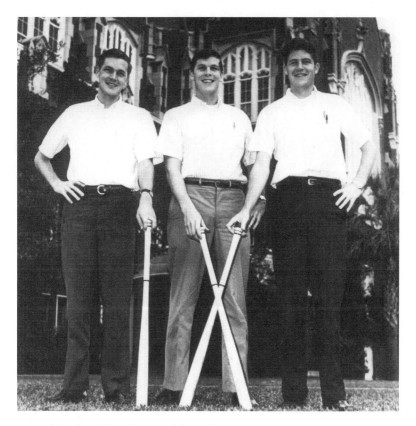

The Mack brothers (from left to right): Michael, Connie, and Dennis at the University of Florida. The bats form the Roman numeral IX—the number of titles that their grandfather Connie Mack won as owner/manager of the Philadelphia Athletics.

campaign as a way of reminding people, not just sportsmen, of how life should be lived."

Great as the elder Connie Mack was in the baseball world, for Senator Mack it's his grandfather's character that is most admirable. "He was a man of honesty, integrity, and great character," Mack said. "I think that 'The Sportsmen's Creed' is really a reflection of the man. Which I think says something else as well. If you're a manager, if you're a leader, there's more to what you're doing than the intricacies of either baseball or politics. It's important as to who you are. What are the principles that guide you? Who are you at your core? And I think that came through in the way he lived his life, and in that creed as well."

13

THE MOUND, THE HILL, AND THE HALL

Jim Bunning Reflects on His Life in Baseball and Politics

Jim Bunning has said that his election to the U.S. Senate is his proudest achievement. That is undoubtedly true at one level, but one suspects that, if sentiment were the criterion, he would have to admit that his heart truly belongs to baseball.

It is certainly the subject he likes to talk about most, as his staff readily acknowledges. His scheduler must wince every time a request comes for a baseball-related interview because, once you're in his office talkin' baseball with Jim Bunning, a vote on the Senate floor is just about your only competition for the senator's time.

And in truth he has lots to talk about. Not only is he one of the few members of Congress to have played major league baseball, he is in the Hall of Fame to boot. Bunning's induction at Cooperstown in 1996 came 25 years after he was first eligible, but by any fair reading of his career stats it was long overdue. Bunning retired in 1971 after a 17-year career with the Detroit Tigers, the Philadelphia Phillies, the Pittsburgh Pirates, and the Los Angeles Dodgers, with a career record of 224 wins, 184 losses, and a 3.27 ERA. When he retired he was second only to Walter Johnson in total strikeouts, with 2,855. He was also only the second pitcher to win 100 games and strike out 1,000 players in both leagues; the second player to throw a perfect game in National League history; the third to throw a no-hitter in both leagues; and an All-Star player for eight years. All this for teams that were, for the most part, below average.

With this record Bunning should have been a shoo-in for the Hall of Fame, but was passed over repeatedly. In 1988, the year he feels he should have been a sure thing, he received 74.2 percent of the 75 percent required for induction, falling only four votes short.

"Nine of the writers turned in blank ballots," he said. "It was obvious that they were doing that to keep people out rather than let them in. I'm the only one that happened to."

When he was inducted in 1996, it was by a vote of the Veterans Committee. Despite this, Bunning is not bitter. "There was nothing I could do about it," he said, "so why worry about it?"

Instead he turned his energies to politics. Following a failed bid for the Kentucky governorship, Bunning was elected to the state legislature as a Republican in a Democratic district. He won election to Congress in 1986 and in 1998 was elected to the Senate, taking office just in time to participate in the Senate Impeachment trial of President Clinton. Bunning voted to convict on two counts, Articles 1 (perjury) and 2 (obstruction of justice). Politically, Bunning is a staunch conservative, supporting tax reductions, limited government, tax relief for small businesses, and opposing wasteful government spending.

Then–U.S. Representative Jim Bunning at the ceremony inducting him into the Baseball Hall of Fame. Photo courtesy of Senator Jim Bunning.

Baseball has been a Bunning passion since he was a small boy growing up in Southgate, Kentucky, a town of about 500 people five miles from Cincinnati across the Ohio River.

"My childhood was a very happy childhood," he said. "I started playing amateur baseball in the second grade, because my church and school that I went to, St. Therese, sponsored a team in the Knothole League, class D Knothole. I started playing even before that in the second grade, because at school picnics the second grade played the third grade. . . . My interest in baseball was always great."

Surprisingly, Bunning excelled more at basketball than baseball at first, making the starting team in basketball as a sixth grader, a year before he made a starting position on the baseball team.

Like many other athletes, Bunning thinks that baseball is a harder sport to master than almost any other, and he attributes his success to the fact that he played constantly as a kid.

"I played baseball in all the spare time that I had," the senator recalled, "and it wasn't organized. It was three on three, or whatever it would be, and I played all the time. We would go down to the field with bat and ball and glove and we played with three guys in, three guys out. The way you got the hit is to throw the ball from wherever you caught it to make the out, and the bat would lay across home plate, and you had to hit the bat with a ball, or else the hitter stayed at the bat.

"I had very good success, except that my teams didn't score many runs," Bunning said, noting a pattern that would follow him through much of his major league career.

Even during high school, this seemed to be a theme for Bunning. One of his losses was 2–1, in extra innings, to the Ohio state championship team, and another was a 1–0 score against the Kentucky state champions.

It was a pattern that the baseball scouts noted at the time. By his senior year, Bunning was being heavily scouted. "Maybe it was the way I threw," he said. "I didn't throw overhand, I threw sidearmed."

In his senior year, Bunning confronted a dilemma. Xavier University had offered him a four-year basketball scholarship, while the Detroit Tigers, the Cleveland Indians, and the Boston Red Sox had all offered him contracts for their farm clubs. He decided to play baseball but this required his parents' permission, since he was only 17. His father said no.

After Bunning played basketball for a year at Xavier, however, his father relented and agreed to sign a contract with the Detroit Tigers, with the stipulation that his son finish college. Both the young man and the Tigers agreed, and Bunning graduated from Xavier in three and a half years.

In the interim he maintained a rare balancing act, reporting to the Tigers' Richmond, Indiana, Class D farm club in June from 1950 to 1952, meaning that he had to miss almost half the baseball season. He graduated from Xavier a half year early, however, and was able to report to spring training in 1953, signing on with the Buffalo Bisons, another of Detroit's minor league franchises.

In the first week of 1955, Bunning was the league's leading pitcher and was called up by the Tigers as a relief pitcher. By his own admission he didn't do too well, chalking up a 3–5 record. And even though his team won the 1956 winterball championship, he did not make the Tigers' cut in spring training.

Bunning was sent back to the minors with the Charleston Triple A franchise and was soon leading the league again. Once again he was called up by the Tigers and sent to the bullpen. This time things clicked and Bunning ended with a 5–1 record.

"Then I got the biggest break of my life," he said. "I went to Havana, Cuba, and played winter ball for the Marienel team. Connie Mareno showed me how to throw a slider and that was the pitch I needed to throw and get over when I was behind the hitters." The addition of the slider gave Bunning the complete repertoire of pitches he needed and he was off and running.

Back with the Tigers, manager Jack Tighe gave Bunning the opportunity to start against the Boston Red Sox at Fenway Park. He pitched a complete game, winning 2–1. His record his rookie year was an impressive 20–8.

Bunning won a reputation as a very hard working and intelligent pitcher. He began compiling stats on every hitter in the American League, a real innovation at the time. "I was the first one, I guess, on the Tigers anyway, that would keep little notes on hitters and key hitters you had to get out if you were going to win, and how to pitch certain hitters, certain ways; and of course now they do it with computers. But I did it in a little book, and kept track of it that way."

The statistics, he said, were particularly important for the lesser-known, weaker hitters. "I thought there were always key hitters you had to get out in key situations in baseball games to be the winning pitcher. In other words, you'd get one of the weak hitters up in the key spot that you

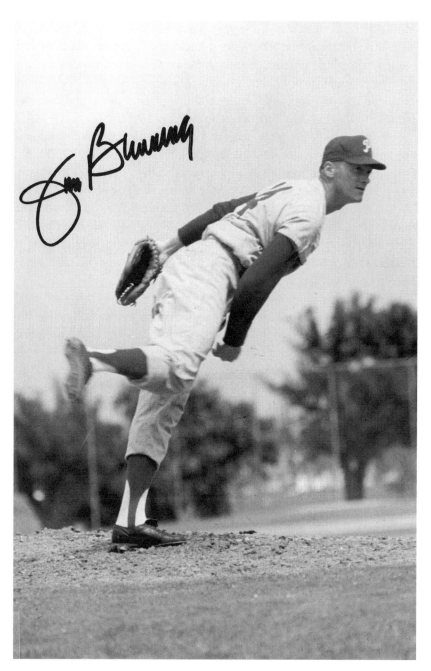

Jim Bunning on the mound for the Philadelphia Phillies. Photo courtesy of
Senator Jim Bunning.

had to get him out or else you were going to lose. So I kept track of those, all . . . the hitters on the other team. I mean, the big hitters got their hits, but it was the little hitters that used to hurt you all the time.

"So I was able to compile a pretty good book on all the American League hitters that way, and then we started to chart pitches and doing all those kinds of things in Detroit that I started in 1957."

By the early 1960s most teams had begun compiling records on their opponents; nowadays this is done routinely by computer. But in 1957, Jim Bunning was a real pioneer as a statistician. Partly due to this new technique, he pitched a no-hitter against the Boston Red Sox on July 20, 1958.

In 1964, with a 103–87 record, Bunning was traded to the Philadelphia Phillies and proceeded to win 19 games in each of the next three years. On June 21, 1964, Bunning pitched a perfect game against the Mets at Shea Stadium—only the second such game in National League history up until that time.

Unlike many pitchers, Bunning was not superstitious, and this stood him in good stead. "I was never very superstitious in baseball, don't walk on the foul lines and stuff. People wore the same sweatshirts, the same hats. I never bought that superstition or any of it."

Along the way—in 1952 to be precise—Bunning got married, and he and his wife, Mary, immediately started a family. They ended up with nine children—including two sets of twins—giving them just enough, appropriately, to field a baseball team.

The senator attributes much of his success to his wife. "I married the perfect gal. She had to be perfect to live with me, and to do all the mothering and fathering that needed to be done when I was absent playing baseball. And she used to love when October came, and she then could turn it back over to me for the discipline and everything that needed to go along. One of those things that baseball has taught my wife, Mary, and myself is that, if you could do things together, do them together. So we do everything together in politics, something we could not do, because of our young children, in baseball."

Faced with the constant travel required of professional baseball, the Bunnings were adamant that their children put down some roots. "We decided very early in baseball that we were going to give our kids some roots in Kentucky. So every year, we'd take the kids to spring training, but they'd come back after and so all nine of our children graduated from the same grade school. Started there and finished there. It was a little different because once they got to high school . . . we didn't have coeducational Catholic high schools. And so we spread out, and before we knew it we had seven different colleges involved. But the fact is that everyone had the opportunity to go to four years of college if they wanted; and baseball was good to me in the respect that I could afford to pay for it." (In his last two years back with the Philadelphia Phillies, Bunning made $110,000 a year—a figure that he believes was the highest paid to any pitcher at that time.)

During his playing career, Bunning was active in the creation of the players' union and the players' pension fund—a fund that features a variable annuity and is now worth more than $1.5 billion.

He continues to be active on behalf of the best interests of baseball, using his 1996 induction speech in Cooperstown to call for reform of the way the game is funded. Addressing the owners, he said, "Get your house in order. Find a way to share revenues without asking players to foot the bill."

Bunning also pressed the baseball writers to vote three players into the Hall of Fame: pitchers Phil Neikro and Don Sutton and first baseman Tony Perez. All three, he notes with satisfaction, have now joined him in the Hall.

Bunning has a real concern about the future of the game. "The new contract coming out—it could all blow up again," he said. "And if it does, I don't care how good the new ballplayers are, the fans will stay away."

The solution, he said, again comes down to revenue sharing. "They've got to solve their problem like football does . . . sharing their revenue better. Whether it's the national contract or the individual club's contract, I'm talking about the local revenues. We can't have one club guarantee $250 million a year in income, and another club $100 million. It doesn't work. Remember, you're only as good as your weakest team."

Asked to reflect on his proudest baseball achievements, Bunning noted that he struck out a ratio of three batters for every one he walked and allowed only 3,400 hits. But the thing that means the most to him, he said, is "Not missing a start in 11 straight seasons; starting off 399 straight games without missing a start."

How about the toughest hitters he faced? "Ted Williams, Jimmy Ray Hart, Nellie Fox, Billy Williams, and Yogi [Berra]—they were the toughest outs for me."

On the other hand, two of the greatest hitters of the time, Hank Aaron and Willie Mays, were ironically not as tough for him. "They got their hits off me," he said, "but they didn't hurt me like most of the pitchers they faced."

Pitchers today are disadvantaged, Bunning believes. "I don't like all the home runs. I don't like the pitchers being disadvantaged by the ballparks as much as the fans do. I think Pedro Martinez and Roger Clemens and Randy Johnson and all those people are exceptional, and would have been exceptional, had they played the same era that I played in. But there is a shortage of pitching because of expansion and the new ballparks, which are smaller."

The home run glut, the smaller ballparks, and the shortage of quality pitchers as a result of expansion are all problems with today's game that worry Bunning.

The pitching/hitting imbalance and the revenue disparity are of abiding concern to Bunning because they are a threat to the game he loves. "I owe everything to baseball," he said. "Everything. My full personality was formed by baseball. My competitiveness, my thick skin, being able to speak and chew gum at the same time, my outlook, my value for family, everything about my life in baseball transferred to my personal life. Talk to my wife about this and you'll understand."

14

BASEBALL IS NOT BANGLADESH

Reclaiming the Future of the Game

Ohio Senator Mike DeWine is a self-professed baseball fanatic. He is a season-ticket holder of the Cincinnati Reds and glories in the proud past of professional baseball's oldest franchise. But DeWine is deeply concerned about the future of the Reds and, indeed, of professional baseball in general.

"The status quo is simply unacceptable," said DeWine. "Unless something is done to correct the payroll and revenue disparities among the teams, baseball as we know it will no longer exist."

The senator is not content to merely talk about the problem, either. He has resolved to use his position as chairman of the Senate Judiciary Subcommittee on Antitrust, Business Rights, and Competition to put the spotlight on the problems that plague today's game.

On November 21, 2000, DeWine held a hearing to discuss professional baseball's difficulties. The hearing's main focus was the report of the blue-ribbon committee established by the commissioner of Major League Baseball, Bud Selig, to conduct a thorough, independent review of the economics of baseball today. Named to the panel were former Senate Majority Leader George Mitchell, syndicated columnist and television commentator George Will, former Federal Reserve Chairman Paul Volker, and Yale President Richard Levin.

Mitchell and Will were called upon to testify, as were commissioner Selig, sportscaster Bob Costas (who has written about reforms needed in the game), Frank Stadius (president of the United Sports Fans of America), and Rodney Fort (professor of economics at Washington State University). Leadoff batter was the commissioner, who opened with some good news:

> We set a new attendance record in 2000, drawing nearly 73 million fans to our ballparks. More fans attended major league baseball games than attended the games of the other three major professional team sports combined. When you add the 35 million fans drawn by minor league baseball, the aggregate number of fans that attended professional baseball is nearly 110 million. In the so-called halcyon days of New York baseball in 1949, the three New York teams—the Yankees, Dodgers, and Giants—drew a combined 5,113,869. Last season, the Yankees and Mets drew 6,027,878.

Selig quickly added, however, that a disturbing trend of growing revenue imbalances, which started in the early 1990s, has rendered fully half of the 30 major league teams uncompetitive. "If not remedied," said the commissioner, this situation "could have a substantial effect on the continued vitality of the game."

In response to this perceived crisis, Selig empowered the panel to investigate whether baseball had a real, as opposed to a perceived, competitive imbalance. They were also asked to consider whether this problem would be alleviated over time, and to recommend specific reforms.

Senator Mitchell made it clear that the panel members were completely independent and that the members should see themselves as representing the fans, rather than the commissioner, the owners, or the players. The commissioner's office had nonetheless provided all staff support and all relevant data including the teams' expenses, revenues, profits, and losses.

Following a year and a half of study and meetings with owners and player representatives, the panel concluded that the revenue imbalance problem was real, structural, and worsening, and that the trend threatened the survival of professional baseball. Said Mitchell:

> Today, high revenue, high payroll clubs completely dominate postseason play. In the last six years, including the 2000 postseason, out of the possible 48 post-

season spots, only four clubs with payrolls in the bottom half of the industry made it to the postseason. Of the 189 postseason games played during this period, only three (or less than two percent) were won by clubs with payrolls in the bottom half of the industry.

These facts lead inescapably to our ultimate conclusion that competitive imbalance does indeed exist and that baseball's economic structure is ultimately responsible. We also concluded that if the current trend of competitive imbalance is not reversed, baseball's status as an accessible, affordable, and competitive spectator sport may be jeopardized.

Mitchell noted that the limited revenue-sharing plan approved by the owners in 1996 had not helped to solve the problem. The limited nature of the revenues involved had convinced some of the larger-revenue clubs that the extra money was insufficient to address their problems, and so they had pocketed the money to help improve their profitability. George Will added that baseball's gross revenues doubled from 1995 to 1999, but that this cascade of cash worsened the revenue disparity between the large and small market clubs from a ratio of 2–1 to 3–1.

The panel's recommendations were as follows:

1. Substantially increase local revenue sharing from the current 20 percent to 40–50 percent. Distribute these funds evenly among the clubs.
2. Establish a "competitive balance tax," which would levy a 50 percent tax on those clubs that exceed a fixed payroll threshold of $84 million, the amount that triggered imposition of a luxury tax in the 1996 agreement.
3. Encourage clubs to maintain a minimum payroll of $40 million.
4. Permit the commissioner to allocate monies from the Major League Central Fund to close the revenue gap for small-market teams.
5. Authorize Major League Baseball to conduct an annual postseason draft in which the eight teams with the worst records in the preceding season would have the opportunity to draft players from the farm clubs of the eight teams with the best records. This would hopefully prevent the top teams from hoarding talented young players in their farm systems.

6. Reform Major League Baseball's entry draft by adding international players; eliminating compensation picks; increasing the likelihood of low-revenue clubs signing top prospects by reducing the number of times a player can make himself eligible for the Rule 4 draft; allocating a disproportionate number of selections to chronically uncompetitive clubs; and allowing the trading of draft selections. By expanding and improving the Rule 4 draft, all clubs should have equal access to talent at the entry level in much the same manner as do teams in other professional sports.

7. Allow selective relocations of franchises to cities with larger revenue bases that can better support them.

George Will used his remarks to provide context for some of the game's problems. According to Will, the whole concept of "local revenues" is a misnomer. "Revenues do not result exclusively from the sale of a local product. It takes two teams to have a game. Any team that doubts that it is selling not just, say, Yankees baseball but major league baseball should imagine what its attendance would be for 162 intrasquad games. Substantially more of the industry's revenues should be just that—the *industry's* revenues." As Will said, a fundamental difference between the sports business and other businesses is that a sports franchise with no competitors is *out* of business.

Will also made the point that baseball's long history, while a great strength of the game, has contributed to its current problems. The economic model on which the game is based predates the modern professional sports market.

One major example of this, Will said, is the advent of broadcasting. Television rights now produce huge revenues for large-market teams such as the New York Yankees, but only small revenue totals for small-market teams such as the Pittsburgh Pirates. For example, as Senator DeWine pointed out in his remarks, in 2000 the Chicago Cubs and the Atlanta Braves earned $55 million and $54 million respectively from broadcasting revenues, while the Cincinnati Reds and the Milwaukee Brewers took in only $6 million and $4.6 million respectively.

Baseball's survival, said Will, is dependent on creating a field of competitive teams so that every season, each team has a reasonable expectation of being competitive. "Baseball is not Bangladesh," Will said. "It is not poverty stricken. And it can get well by deciding to get well."

The panel's recommendations would do a great deal to help professional baseball if adopted; but there are other urgent problems that require attention as well.

Columnist and commentator Fred Barnes has been a severe critic of big league baseball in recent years, but offers some good "tough-love" advice.

"Major league baseball games are much too long," he said. "Who has the time to spend almost four hours at a game on a weeknight?" He adds that umpires are totally undisciplined and are unable or unwilling to set a consistent strike zone, and that "few players today have perfected skills like bunting, stealing home, or making good throws from the outfield. Surely, we can get more complete games than we see today," Barnes groused—and again, he's right.

He's also right about the long-term negative effects of the home-run derby we've seen in recent years. Watching Mac and Sammy has been fun, but with a few more seasons like 2000, the thrill will fade fast. Barnes is also correct that more weekend games should be played in the daytime. Baseball *is* more enjoyable under the sun.

All these concerns pertain to professional baseball at the major-league level. However, at the minor-league level the game is thriving as never before—in part because the owners have gone out of their way to make the games enjoyable for families.

At the opposite end of the spectrum is baseball at the local, Little League level. Here again, the game is plagued with problems. Urban minority populations seem to have tuned out the game completely. This is seen in the absence of kids playing the game in the streets and local parks and in the scarcity of black and brown faces in the stands at major and minor league ballparks. Not only will this result in the gradual elimination of players like Frank Thomas, A-Rod, Ken Griffey Jr., and David Justice from the game, it will totally eliminate baseball as a unifying and stabilizing force in American society.

Organized baseball—from the major leagues all the way to the local T-ball team—has got to do a better job of appealing to young people. It has to market its stars better, get home games on TV when kids can see them, speed the game up, and more generously fund efforts such as the RBI program (Reviving Baseball in the Inner Cities).

Baseball needs innovations like what's going on at Washington's Columbia Lighthouse for the Blind. At Camp Lighthouse, blind children are taught to play beep-ball, a form of baseball in which a beeper is inserted in the ball, allowing batters to swing at it. If they get a hit, they run to sound-activated bases. Baseball needs more of this kind of ingenuity and creative thinking on the part of all of us who love the game and who long to see it become once again a truly national pastime for America.

III

AROUND TOWN AND BEYOND

15

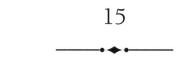

SPOOKS, ODD-LOTS, AND FNU-LNUS

Baseball at the CIA

Moe Berg is probably an unfamiliar name to most people, even historically minded baseball fans, but he is a familiar figure in the intelligence community.

Berg was a journeyman catcher in the majors from 1923 to 1939, playing for three of those years with the Washington Senators (1932–1934). Although he was a solid ballplayer, most of Berg's notoriety comes from his other profession: intelligence work.

"He had two loves: baseball and spying," said Linda McCarthy, who is perhaps the world's leading expert on Moe Berg. McCarthy was the curator of the exhibit on Berg at CIA headquarters. She is a 24-year veteran of the agency, having retired in 1998 to devote herself to a new enterprise called "History Is a Hoot," an organization that provides educational materials and tours of historic sites in the area.

Nine years before she left the CIA, McCarthy founded the agency's Fine Arts Exhibit program; she also served as the curator of the program until she retired. She published a book on her experiences there entitled *Spies, Pop Flies, and French Fries: Stories I Told My Favorite Visitors to the CIA Exhibit Center.* Her favorite story is the tale of Moe Berg, and it is the centerpiece of her book.

Berg had a first-class intellect. He was educated at Princeton, Columbia, and the Sorbonne, and held a Ph.D. as well as a degree in law.

Said Berg expert and author Bill Gilbert, who included Berg's colorful history in his book *They Also Served: Baseball and the Home Front, 1941–1945*, Berg "was interested in anything and everything." He was also fluent in a host of languages, including German and Japanese.

After retiring from baseball in 1939, Berg signed on officially with the OSS—the precursor to the CIA—although it is now known that he was involved in undercover work for the government for some time before that.

In the late 1930s, Berg participated in several baseball barnstorming tours of Japan. He was a hit with the baseball-crazy Japanese, conversing freely with them in their own language; however, teammates recall that he also spent a good deal of time taking home movies of the Tokyo skyline. Later it was revealed that Berg's films were used in composing the aerial maps for Jimmy Doolittle's raid on Tokyo and for the later massive bombing raids on Japan.

In 1944, Berg was smuggled into Germany's nuclear research center headquarters disguised as a Swiss graduate student. His mission was to assess whether Germany's top scientist, Werner Heisenberg, was engaged in the development of atomic weapons. If Berg felt the answer was yes, he was instructed to kill Heisenberg using a Beretta revolver he had strapped

Baseball player and spy Moe Berg (center) on one of his OSS missions

on under his coat. However, given the number of SS agents present, Berg decided—perhaps prudently but not necessarily truthfully—that Heisenberg was not in the atomic weapons business.

Berg was dispatched on many other missions during the war. According to Gilbert, "Berg was known personally by President Roosevelt and had a lot of high-level connections. He was probably the only baseball player in history to keep a tux in his locker for high-level social activities."

Berg remained obsessed with baseball until the day he died, his last words being: "How did the Mets do today?"

Interest in Moe Berg has been growing in recent years. The book *The Catcher Was a Spy* by Nicholas Dawidoff was published in 1995 and in July of 2000 ESPN aired a documentary on his life in which both Gilbert and McCarthy were featured.

Moe Berg aside, baseball is a recurrent theme at the CIA. The year before McCarthy's exhibit, Mark Benbow and four other colleagues staged an exhibit called "Baseball in the Heartland," which was profiled in *Baseball Weekly*.

"We had all seen Ken Burns's series on PBS," Benbow said, "and were disappointed by the New York, New York, New York, focus." Benbow and some of his coworkers started talking about putting on a baseball exhibit that would highlight the sport's Midwestern history. Meeting at lunch, they put together a prospectus and submitted it to the Fine Arts Committee, which approved the exhibit.

The resulting display, set up over a weekend in the spring of 1996, contained a section on baseball cards organized by William Fulkerson, a display of major league uniform replicas donated by Carl Thomas, equipment and memorabilia, tapes of some broadcasts, and a computer game that allowed employees to match up teams from different eras.

There was also an empty display case available for CIA workers who wanted to donate their own items for display. "Security was never a problem," Benbow said, "since there are cameras covering the area 24 hours a day. So many people gladly put stuff in the case."

One of the sections featured memorabilia donated by Victoria Malsz, which had been given to her by her late father, George McQuinn, a first baseman for four major league teams from 1936 to 1948. In 1944, McQuinn was MVP for the St. Louis Browns in the World Series against the Cardinals. He hit a home run to win Game 1 and led the team with seven hits, five RBIs, and a batting average of .438. A native of the Washington suburb of Arlington, McQuinn was a scout for the Senators for several years after his retirement as a player.

"He was a Washingtonian through and though" said daughter and CIA-employee Malsz. "He loved baseball and had the bad luck to have two lame-brained daughters who knew nothing about the game."

Every year, Malsz said, "The Topps baseball card company would send us a free box of cards and, of course, they contained chewing gum. Well, my sister and I would throw away those annoying cards and keep the gum." The thought of all those cards—many now very valuable—still drives her husband crazy, Malsz said. He is a baseball fanatic, as are her two sons.

"The baseball gene skipped a generation," Malsz said, but all ended well. "I'm glad to say that my father lived to see his grandsons play Little League."

Mark Benbow can attest that baseball in all its forms is perennially popular at the agency. There are numerous rotisserie leagues at the CIA as well as a large, agency-wide softball league for both men and women.

Given the agency's line of work, security considerations give the CIA's league its own unique set of challenges. Schedules and field sites are classified, for instance, lest terrorists wait in ambush or foreign agents and spies lurk about seeking classified information. According to one reliable source in the agency, keeping up-to-date and accurate rosters can also be a problem, due to erratic travel schedules, spur-of-the-moment overseas assignments, undercover missions, agency aliases, and other special considerations that confront the volunteer team managers. Yet the game goes on, played, of course, during time off, and in a league funded by the employees' recreation fund.

Not surprisingly, some of the team names reflect inside-the-agency humor. The team of former public affairs director Herb Hetu, for instance, was "The Spooks." "We played for beer, pizza, and honor—in that order," he said.

Another former team was the "Odd-Lots," a double-entendre involving a Communist Chinese radar system as well as the team's own reflections on the players. Team member Craig Gralley remembers the games he played at the Washington Navy Yard back in the 1980s. More memorable than the games themselves, he said, were the postgame get-togethers at the Tune Inn, a renowned Capitol Hill joint with an eclectic clientele. The gathering place featured country-western music, an amazing display of condom dispensers in the men's room, and a kick-ass old waitress named Vi who served food with the deadly delivery of Dennis Eckersley's side-armed slider.

One of the strangest and most amusing team names was owned by the women's team called the "Fnu-Lnus." As McCarthy explained, the women were mostly clerks who tracked reports from informants—who were often identified as "first name unknown" (FNU) or "last name unknown" (LNU). "They were awesome," said McCarthy.

CIA baseball isn't limited to Washington, D.C., either. It goes with agents and embassy personnel around the world. Larry Strawderman, now retired in New Market, Virginia, has vivid memories of baseball in the Dominican Republic during the 1960s, when he was assigned to the American embassy there. "Winter baseball in the Dominican Republic had its own special flavor," he said. "There were meringue bands playing at the field and the crowds were always in a festive mood."

During that time Strawderman coached 13- to 16-year-olds in the Manny Mota League, which received help from the Dodgers Organization. "We had Tommy Lasorda giving clinics and Charlie Hough, Jim Beauchamp, and Reggie Cleveland helping out. Let me tell you," he said, "you haven't lived until you've heard Tommy Lasorda speaking broken Spanish."

16

Exit Emil

*The Emil Verban Memorial Society Holds Its Last
Washington Luncheon*

"Any team can have a bad century" was the late Chicago Cubs announcer
Jack Brickhouse's sardonic assessment of his team's performance over the
last 100 years. The comment is a reflection on the fact that the Cubs
haven't been in a World Series since 1945 and haven't won one since
1908, a performance so dismal and improbable that it defies the law of
averages by a factor of one million to one. (This figure was calculated by
George Castle and is the basis for the title of his book *The Million to One
Team.*)

Uncountable miseries have been inflicted upon long-suffering Cubs
fans ("long-suffering" is automatically paired with "Cubs fan") through the
years by the "hapless" Cubs (the word *hapless* is so often used to describe
the Cubs that the casual reader could be excused for thinking that
"Hapless," rather than Chicago, is the home town of the team). The Cubs
are notorious for blowing opportunities on the rare occasions when they
present themselves. They blew a nine-and-a-half-game lead over the New
York Mets in 1969 and a two-to-nothing lead in a five-game National
League Playoff Series with the San Diego Padres in 1984—but these are
just two of the many painful examples that could be cited.

This suffering was embedded in the minds of the 350-plus Cubs fans
who attended the 11th biennial luncheon of the Emil Verban Memorial
Society in April of 2000. The society is the Washington, D.C.–based Cubs

fan club founded in 1976 by Bruce Ladd and a small group of fellow Cubs expatriates in Washington, including new Vice President Dick Cheney (who has membership number four).

The society has become a renowned and unique Washington institution over the past 24 years. It has no officers (although Ladd conferred the title of "historian" upon himself), no elections, dues, charter, by-laws, regular meetings (except the luncheon), or membership criteria. Nomination is made by the members, who are all assigned a number, and approval is subject to the caprice of the historian.

Then there is the club's name. Unlike the Stan Musial Club, the Washington-based fan club for Cardinals fans, most people, including most longtime baseball fans, have no clue as to who Emil Verban was. This is understandable, since Verban was an unremarkable journeyman second baseman who compiled a solid but unspectacular career while playing for the Cubs, the St. Louis Cardinals, the Philadelphia Phillies, and the Boston Braves from 1944 to 1950.

Finally, there is the matter of it being a "memorial" society—a description that came as a shock to Verban himself when he heard about in 1975, since he was still very much alive and would remain so for another 14 years.

"It all started out as something of a lark," said historian Ladd, speaking by phone from the new "world headquarters" of the society in Chapel Hill, North Carolina (also, coincidentally, Ladd's retirement home address).

"I was trying to come up with something more creative than Cubs "fan club," and then I thought of Emil. The memorial part was thrown in for a little humor." The members got a kick out of it and the name stuck, Ladd said, "Because we had all seen Emil play and because his solid, steady play sort of symbolized those solid Midwestern values that we grew up with."

It also goes without saying that Verban's record is far more reflective of the Cubs' performance over the last 50 years than that of Hall of Fame players such as Ernie Banks or Ferguson Jenkins. Ladd cautioned against characterizing Verban as mediocre, however, noting that "he was a good contact hitter, chalking up 793 career hits, and he was an excellent fielder, twice making the All-Star Team."

Out in Lincoln, Illinois, his hometown, Verban was surprised to learn of the society's existence. "I have a son who is a dentist," he said, "and one day a patient told him, 'I'm so sorry to hear about your father.' He said, 'What do you mean?' and she said, 'I read that they set up a memorial society for him. I didn't even know he had died.' We both got a laugh out of that."

Emil Verban with young Cubs fan Bruce Ladd III. Photo courtesy of Bruce Ladd.

"Emil didn't like the idea of the society being named for him at first," said "Verbanite" Hal Bruno, a longtime political correspondent for ABC, "but then he and his wife and children came to realize that it was really an honor and that we really loved him very much. Then they felt good toward us."

The turning point in Verban's attitude came in 1984, when he and his family attended a society luncheon in Washington, D.C. Following the event Bruce took them to the White House for a meeting with President Reagan.

"The meeting was scheduled for 10 minutes," Ladd said, "but once we got into the Oval Office the president didn't want to let us leave. Lincoln, Illinois, isn't very far from his hometown of Dixon, and he and Emil found out they had friends in common and they started reminiscing about baseball."

When they left the Oval Office a half hour later, Ladd recalled, they ran into Senator Bob Dole, Pete McCloskey (president of the Telecommunications Association), and Ladd's boss, Travis Marshall, a senior vice president at Motorola—all of whom had been forced to cool their heels for 20 minutes while the President talked baseball with Emil Verban. Verban and his wife came to the next two luncheons in 1986 and 1988 and enjoyed them immensely.

The year 1988 provided another highlight for Verban. Ladd recalled that one society member at that time was the head of a P.R. agency that represented the Borden Company. One of Borden's products was Cracker Jack and in 1984, as a promotional vehicle for the product, the agency organized an old-timers game featuring retired major league players.

The game was held at Washington's RFK Stadium, and Ladd persuaded the agency to put Verban in the lineup, which included a host of Hall of Fame names. When Emil was brought in as a pinch hitter late in the game, the Verbanite contingent of about 50 people hoisted a giant banner and began cheering. "Pretty soon the rest of the crowd got into it," Ladd said. The old man hit a grounder to third, which was fielded by Ed Yost for the out, but it was still a great experience for him.

The next year, 1989, Emil Verban died at 73 of a heart attack; but his widow, Annette, and the children continued attending the biennial luncheons until Annette's death in 1999.

Emil Verban Memorial Society founder Bruce Ladd applauds as former Cubs announcer Jack Brickhouse takes a call from a fellow Verbanite, President Ronald Reagan. Photo courtesy of Bruce Ladd.

In any case, Ladd recalled, "The thing just sort of mushroomed and people from all over were begging to join."

Initially, a membership cap of 400 was set, but that has been systematically breached to accommodate VIPs seeking entry, including congressmen (Bob Michel and Henry Hyde); senators (Allan Dixon, Dan Coats, Paul Simon, and Peter Fitzgerald); cabinet secretaries (Ed Madigan, Bill Daley, and Lynn Martin); Supreme Court justices (Harry Blackmun, Antonin Scalia, and John Paul Stevens); columnists and broadcasters (Bob Novak, George Will, Hal Bruno, David Broder, and Bryant Gumbel); retired players (Ernie Banks and Ron Santo); two Major League Baseball commissioners (Bud Selig and Bowie Kuhn); one first lady (Hillary Clinton); one vice president (Dick Cheney); and one president (Ronald Reagan). Most of the ranks, however, are filled by Washington lobbyists, lawyers, and other "regular folks" toiling away in a variety of professions in the environs of the capital.

The society's biennial luncheons were eagerly anticipated by members. They fulfilled a support group function for Verbanites, allowing the attendees to focus on selective happy memories of Cubs games and players while ignoring the darker side of the Cubs' record over the last 100 years or so.

They were held at the beginning of the baseball season—almost always the high point of the season for Cubs fans, a time when hope fills the air and before the inevitable gloom sets in. Ladd noted that the 2000 Cubs season, like many with the team, started off with a bang and ended with a whimper. In their opening game with the Mets, played in Tokyo, the Cubs won the first regular-season game played outside the United States or Canada, scoring the first hit, the first home run, and the first win of the new year in the process. But the first game was the high point of the season, which the Cubs ended with a 65–97 record and a last place finish.

These luncheons typically drew 300–400 people. The guests of honor always included a number of ex-Cubs players, with perennial favorites including Randy Hundley, Andy Pafko, Ron Santo, and Joe Pepitone. Hundley and Pepitone are a particularly amusing combination. Friends and former teammates, they are very different personalities—Hundley the plain-talking good ol' boy from West Virginia, Pepitone the dapper, fast-talking Brooklynite and party animal.

Another popular feature was the "Brock for Broglio Bad Judgment Award," named to commemorate the infamous 1964 trade of Cubs outfielder

Cubs great Ernie Banks presents The Ernie Banks Award to former First Lady Hillary Clinton. Photo courtesy of Bruce Ladd.

Lou Brock for St. Louis Cardinals pitcher Ernie Broglio. Brock went on to a 19-year, Hall of Fame career, while Broglio pitched only 59 games for the Cubs (winning 7 and losing 19) and retired two years later. Past award recipients include ice skater Tonya Harding, the infamous Saddam Hussein, and deposed Cubs General Manager Larry Himes, "honored" for his refusal to re-sign pitcher Greg Maddux. Maddux won a Cy Young award during his last year with the Cubs (1992) and has since won four more.

The "Ernie Banks Positivism Award" was also presented at each luncheon, with winners including Ronald Reagan, Joe Garagiola, Harry Caray, and Hillary Clinton. Reagan's acceptance remarks were sent in on videotape, but both Harry Caray and Hillary Clinton came in person to accept their awards; they both hit home runs with their remarks.

Clinton talked eloquently and off the cuff about her memories of attending Cubs games as a girl growing up in the Chicago suburbs, and showed surprising recall and knowledge of Cubs history. She also displayed a sense of humor, noting how coping with Cubs misfortune had prepared her for life in Washington, and giving a hilarious account of her adventure in entering the announcer's booth to sing "Take Me Out to the Ball Game," with Harry Caray.

Caray gave a vintage stream-of-consciousness monologue, noting among other things that "despite the stupidity of players, despite the stupidity of managers, despite the stupidity of owners, the game goes on." Some members couldn't help but recall those remarks when George Will, noting that the Cubs were in their 55th rebuilding year, introduced Cubs President and General Manager Andy MacPhail, another year's Ernie Banks Positivism Award winner.

It was with sadness that many Verbanites reacted to historian Ladd's 2000 announcement that this would be the last biennial luncheon. Instead, the meetings will henceforth be replaced by biennial society weekends in Chicago. These weekends will feature Cubs games at Wrigley Field and dinners at Harry Caray's restaurants, and will no doubt be enjoyable. But for many Verbanites they will never replace the biennial luncheons—those unique occasions of fun and fellowship, sentiment and much humor.

The whole Verbanite gestalt was summed up in the invocation by Rabbi Jack Moline at the society's last luncheon:

Creator of the universe, author of blue skies and green grass, poet of the ivy, watch over the young men who carry our dreams through summer days and nights. Save them from arthritis, bursitis, and arbitration. Give them consistent strike zones, true hops on their fielding chances, and, most of all, the thrill of the game that they knew when they first picked up a ball.

Show us a sign. Justify our faith. Give Kerry's arm a future. Give Sammy's bat a present record. And validate the triumphs of our past by seeing that Ron Santo is admitted to Cooperstown, where he has long deserved to be.

Do these things not for our sake, Lord, but for Your own. For we promise that if You will but enable us to fly a World Series flag at the top of the pole throughout the season, many more will come to believe in you, and many more will demand from Bruce Ladd a reconsideration of the suspension of these gatherings.

As your prophet said, "Let's play two."

Amen, rabbi. As the rabbi and his fellow Jews say of Passover ("Next year in Jerusalem"), Verbanites will dutifully say "Next year in Chicago." But it won't be the same.

17

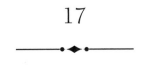

Matzo Balls

The B'nai B'rith Sports Hall of Fame, located in the Philip Klutznick B'nai B'rith Center in downtown Washington, D.C., recently celebrated its 10th anniversary, and has moved into a larger new space to accommodate its growing collections. Many people may not be familiar with the Jewish presence in American sports, but Elizabeth Kessin Berman, the curator, disabuses the doubts of skeptical visitors with cheerful determination.

"There is a strong Jewish athletic tradition going back to the Old Testament," Ms. Berman said, "and Jews have been well represented in sports since the sports world as we know it began in the nineteenth century."

Take, for instance, Sandy Koufax, the legendary Hall of Fame pitcher shown on the museum brochure's cover. In fact, there have been prominent Jewish athletes in many sports over the last 100 years, from football great Sid Luckman to Olympic Gold Medal–winning swimmer Mark Spitz. However it is baseball that boasts, by far, the largest number of Jewish sports heroes.

Given its unique status as America's national pastime, baseball offered the waves of Jewish immigrants in the late nineteenth and early twentieth centuries a passage into the American mainstream. In lower Manhattan, Brooklyn, the Bronx, Philadelphia, Boston, and other cities, including Washington, D.C., thousands of Jewish boys grew up playing baseball.

Dodgers pitcher Sandy Koufax, featured on the brochure cover for Washington's B'nai B'rith Jewish Sports Hall of Fame

Seven Jewish baseball players have been inducted into the B'nai B'rith Hall of Fame thus far: Dodgers pitcher Koufax; Hank Greenberg, Hall of Fame slugger for the Detroit Tigers; New York Giants catcher Harry Danning; Ken Holtzman, pitcher for the Chicago Cubs and Oakland Athletics; Al Rosen, third baseman for the Cleveland Indians in the 1940s and 1950s; and Steve Stone, Cy Young Award–winning pitcher for the Baltimore Orioles. Other inductees in the baseball section are Mel Allen, legendary announcer for the New York Yankees; longtime *Chicago Tribune* columnist Jerome Holtzman (who invented the concept of "saves" as a distinct statistical category); and Shirley Povich, a reporter and columnist for the *Washington Post* for seven decades and longtime president of the Baseball Writers Association of America.

Many other players are mentioned in the Hall's displays, including George Stone, an outfielder for the Boston Red Sox and St. Louis Browns from 1903 to 1910 who won the American League batting title in 1906. Others include Jimmy Reese (born James Solomon), who played for the Yankees and St. Louis Cardinals in the 1930s and was a longtime major league coach; Buddy Myer of the Washington Senators, who won the American League batting title in 1935; and Ron Blomberg and Elliot Maddox, who played on the Yankees' pennant-winning team along with Ken Holtzman in 1976.

Of all the Jewish sports heroes enshrined in the museum, it is Hank Greenberg who occupies the highest pedestal. Born in the Bronx in 1911 of Romanian Jewish parents, Greenberg went on to play first base and outfield for the Detroit Tigers in the 1930s and 1940s, becoming the first nationally acclaimed Jewish sports star. A towering baseball figure, both literally and figuratively, Greenberg became a symbol of pride for Jews from coast to coast during the depression and post-war years, a time when anti-Semitism was widespread.

It seemed a perfect irony that Greenberg should rise to fame in Detroit, a city in which the two other most famous citizens were industrialist Henry Ford and radio personality Father Charles Coughlin, both known for their undisguised anti-Semitism.

Greenberg faced a certain degree of prejudice throughout his career, but he won over the people of Detroit with his Herculean achievements with the bat. "Hammerin' Hank" had a lifetime batting average of .313, accounting for 1,628 hits, 1,276 RBIs, and 331 homers—incredible numbers for a career of only thirteen years, during which he lost four years at the peak of his powers because of service in World War II. In 1935 Greenberg hit 36 home runs and drove in an incredible 170 runs, earning him the American League MVP award. In 1937 he drove in 183 runs and in 1938 he racked up 58 home runs, falling just short of Babe Ruth's record of 60. He was inducted into the Baseball Hall of Fame in 1956.

Washington film producer Aviva Kempner explored Greenberg's fabled baseball career, as well as his importance off the field, in her documentary *The Life and Times of Hank Greenberg*. A native of Detroit, Kempner never actually saw Greenberg play; but he was a hero to her father, who often talked about his idol.

The critically acclaimed film was the realization of a longtime dream for Kempner. She pursued that dream for 10 frustrating years while she scraped together the $1 million necessary to produce the film. The result was well worth the effort, however.

It begins brilliantly, with Mandy Patinkin singing "Take Me Out to the Ball Game" in Yiddish over a film of Jewish kids playing baseball in New York City in the 1920s. Interspersed with archival film footage are con-

Aviva Kempner, producer/director of The Life and Times of Hank Greenberg, *with a poster of "Hammerin' Hank"*

temporary interviews with teammates of Greenberg's, as well as other ballplayers, fans, and acquaintances from that era, and the star's family members. The documentary also draws on a few filmed interviews with Greenberg, as well as extensive reminiscences that his family persuaded him to tape-record toward the end of his life. The result is an award-winning documentary that vindicates the faith, vision, and perseverance of its producer, as well as its subject.

Kempner is pleased with her handiwork but expresses her frustration, like most Washington-area baseball fans, about the lack of a major league baseball team in the area. "It's ironic," she commented. "The most commercially successful documentary about baseball was produced in a town with no baseball."

Today it is almost impossible to imagine the pride that American Jews felt in Greenberg. Attorney Alan Dershowitz has called him, "The most important Jew of the 1930s," and thought he might become the first Jewish president.

Senator Joseph Lieberman evoked comparisons with Greenberg when Al Gore chose him as the first Jewish vice-presidential nominee. Suzanne Fields, a Jewish columnist for *The Washington Times*, titled a column about Lieberman "Bursting with Pride," and compared the breakthrough importance of his nomination to that of Greenberg's contribution, noting that both proved it was possible to preserve one's Jewish identity and still be a part of mainstream American life.

Barry Steelman, a navy shipmate of mine 30 years ago and now a local attorney, also described himself as bursting with pride ("kvelling" in Yiddish) about the Lieberman nomination. He in turn compared it with his great pride in the legendary Sandy Koufax, who Steelman idolized while he was growing up in Los Angeles. "We used to play hooky from Hebrew school when Koufax pitched," Steelman said. "He was a tremendous hero to every Jewish kid in L.A., and probably in America."

Another Jewish baseball player was the subject of a documentary in 2000—Moe Berg, catcher for the Washington Senators in the pre–World War II years. Berg was also a spy for the OSS during that period, and his double life makes a compelling story. The documentary was produced by the History Channel and featured two Washington-area authors, Bill Gilbert and Linda McCarthy, as its main on-camera experts.

Among the journalists enshrined in the museum is the late Shirley Povich, a sports reporter and columnist for the *Washington Post* for 75

"Hammerin'" Hank Greenberg

years. Povich was also one of the founders of the Baseball Writers Association and served as its president. Babe Ruth, Lou Gehrig, Ty Cobb, Mickey Mantle—he knew them all personally.

Asked to pick the Shirley Povich all-time baseball all-star team, Povich chose the following:

Pitcher: "Easy. Walter Johnson, the best pitcher of all-time, period."

Catcher: "A three-way tie between Yogi Berra, Bill Dickey, and Mickey Cochrane."

Infield: "First base. Lou Gehrig; second base, Rogers Hornsby; short-stop, Honus Wagner; third base, Brooks Robinson."

Outfield: "Ty Cobb, Babe Ruth, and either Joe DiMaggio or Ted Williams." Between DiMaggio and Williams, Povich said, "You have to make a choice, because both were great. Williams was a better hitter, probably the most scientific hitter of all time, but then you have to say that DiMaggio was the better ballplayer."

As the *Washington Post*'s leading sports reporter for 75 years, Povich witnessed many, if not most, of the great sports highlights of the twentieth century: Babe Ruth's called shot, Don Larsen's perfect game, Bobby Thomson's shot heard 'round the world, Mickey Mantle's tape measure home run, Lou Gehrig's farewell address, and every president since Taft throwing out the first ball. His was a perspective that no one else alive in 1998 could claim.

Povich's columns were a powerful attraction for sports fans, as Richard Nixon demonstrated. According to a story told by Povich to his friend Bill Gilbert, Nixon once told Philip Graham, the liberal owner of the *Post*, "Shirley Povich is the only reason I read your goddamned paper."

The author with the late, legendary sportswriter Shirley Povich, one-time president of the Baseball Writers Association and an honoree in the B'Nai B'rith Jewish Sports Hall of Fame

Shirley Povich was much more than a sportswriter. He was a major force in the Washington, D.C., community, helping to stay the departure of the Senators for several years, maintaining an extensive speaking schedule for charitable and civic organizations, and raising funds for worthy causes. Bob Wolff, former Senators announcer, tells of the time in 1942 when Povich turned impresario and organized a fund-raising extravaganza at Griffith Stadium featuring Kate Smith, Babe Ruth, and numerous other celebrities. The event drew 37,000 people and raised $2 million in war bonds—enough to build a navy cruiser and to make it the second largest fund-raiser of the war.

Nor was Povich's influence confined to Washington. He was a key figure in the Baseball Writers Association—the group that now approves candidates for the Baseball Hall of Fame—and was known by the unofficial title of the "dean of American sportswriters."

He did all this, mind you, while shouldering the burden of his first name—Shirley. The name caused some confusion among the ill informed. He made the roster of *Who's Who in American Women*, for instance, and replied to the publication's questionnaire inquiry about sex with "Occasionally."

Writing, however, was more than an occasional activity for Shirley Povich. It was a craft at which he labored diligently all his life, filing his last copy with the *Washington Post* just before his death on June 4, 1998, at age 92.

It's a shame that he couldn't have lived another six months to see the groundbreaking for Shirley Povich Field in Bethesda, Maryland. About 100 people attended the ceremony and Shirley's son, Maury, (now a nationally known broadcaster) said that although his father normally avoided accolades, he had looked forward to participating in that ceremony.

He must have loved the fact that the field is the home of the "Big Train" team, named for his old friend, the legendary pitcher Walter Johnson. The team itself is a member of the Clark Griffith League—named for another friend. And—the icing on the cake—the Big Train's general manager is Henry Thomas, grandson of the Big Train himself.

18

SHENANDOAH

Baseball in the Valley League

It's a muggy July evening at Rebel Field in New Market, Virginia, and haze partially obscures the mountains just beyond the baseball diamond.

Rain fell about an hour before the game and perhaps because of this there are only about 400 people present—down from the 600 or so that normally attend. But given the fact that New Market's population is only 1,500 people, 400 is still pretty impressive.

The crowd is here to cheer on their team, the New Market Rebels, one of the six teams in the Shenandoah Valley League, which is itself one of 11 college wooden bat leagues sanctioned by Major League Baseball. The other teams are the Winchester Royals, the Front Royal Cardinals, the Harrisburg Turks, the Staunton Braves, and the Waynesboro Generals, all only one to two hours away from Washington, D.C.

New Market itself is a little more than an hour away from the beltway but, culturally speaking, it's in another world. The "time warp" atmosphere of Valley League baseball has caught the attention of media from around the country, including ABC, the *Washington Post*, and the *Atlanta Journal-Constitution*, all of which have done features on the towns and their teams. It's easy to see why on this July evening out at the ballgame.

As each Rebel player walks onto the field, he is accompanied by a local Little League player. All doff their caps when announcer Dick Powell says that Patty Kinkaid will lead the singing of the national anthem.

The bleachers are largely full, as are the green plastic chairs of the Grandstand Managers Club behind home plate. The locals rent their chairs for $75 per season and enjoy their proximity to cheer on the Rebels and harass the umpire on bad calls.

Twilight edges into darkness and, as if on cue, the moon rises through the notch in Massanutten Mountain. Bugs swarm in the lights that illuminate the field and a pack of kids waits on the embankment behind the home plate stands to chase after foul balls. Balls that are turned in are redeemed for a free pack of baseball cards. Other children tramp through someone's yard to get to the sundaes at Pack's frozen custard stand.

On the field, things are going well for the Rebels, who enjoy a 4–2 lead in the middle of the seventh inning, at which time retired FBI agent Sol Quinn cranks up his accordion to accompany the crowd in their singing of "Take Me Out to the Ball Game."

In the eighth inning the situation starts to deteriorate for the Rebels as the Turks tie up the game. Things get really exciting, however, when a disputed call produces a shouting match between the managers, which degenerates into a brawl that empties both teams' benches.

The melee finally ends with the Turks manager being ejected from the field accompanied by a deafening chorus of boos and insults from the crowd. He swaggers away, muttering curses, and watches the rest of the game from outside, down the right-field line. The children are thrilled. The brawl makes for an exciting ending to a great evening, even though the Rebels lost.

New Market is special. The town itself lies just east of Interstate 81 at the foot of Massanutten Mountain and dates back to the late eighteenth century. A major Civil War battle was fought there and the well-preserved battlefield and museum lie just outside the town limits. Main Street is lined with antique shops and boasts one of the country's most unusual museums, known as "Bedrooms of America." Another famous landmark is the Southern Kitchen restaurant, which offers cheap wine and home-style cooking, both at good prices. The Bryce Mountain and Massanutten resorts are also nearby, to the north and south respectively.

The area's population has grown in recent years. An increasing number of Washington residents have moved into the valley, seeking to escape the rat race of the city while remaining close enough to drive in whenever they like.

Boys of summer: Rebel players (left to right) Taylor Wood, Brad Zieglar, Patrick Choate, Charlie Wentsky, and Steve Bondurant relax before a game at Rebel Park.

Baseball has been part of New Market's community life at least as far back as 1865, when the New Market *Bicentennial Gazette* reported on games played between the New Market and Harrisonburg Lone Star clubs. Many other towns fielded teams, including Lurray, Harrisburg, Staunton, and Front Royal. These semipro teams of local ballplayers were active for about 80 years, but by the 1950s they were dying out.

In 1947 they were replaced by the incorporation of the six Shenandoah Valley League teams, all comprised of college ballplayers. Each team receives a subsidy from Major League Baseball. The players are selected from colleges around the country.

Unlike the other five teams in the league, whose franchises are privately owned, the Rebels are owned by the citizens of New Market; the whole town supports the team.

"It's like Mayberry," said Charlie Wentsky, a sophomore from the College of Charleston who is spending his second summer playing for the Rebels. "Everybody knows everybody else and everything they're doing."

All of the team's players are emphatic that it's been a positive experience, although for some it's been a big adjustment. "San Jose is a city of over a million people," said Patrick Choate, a student at San Jose State, "and there are only 1,500 here, so it was quite a shock at first. But this has been a big break for me. I'm able to get away from school and all those problems and just concentrate on baseball."

Wentsky said the experience has been a huge boost for his pitching. "I never had much help on pitching in college. But Kevin [Kevin Anderson, the Rebels' manager] is a super pitching instructor. I've learned a lot of things, like better support under the ball, better balance, that I never worked on before, and more about strategy. This is my second year with the Rebels and I wasn't even three quarters as good when I came as I am now."

Taylor Wood, a junior at the University of Florida, said his hitting stats have improved. "In college you use aluminum bats and if you just keep a . . . steady swing you'll get a hit, but using these wooden bats is a lot more difficult. The ball doesn't come off the bat as easy and it doesn't go as far. In college a lot of guys just try to hit home runs; here you have to create your own offense, sacrifice, bunts, moving runners along, that kind of thing. Another difference is that here you're facing good pitchers every game."

Wentsky said pitchers have the same problem in reverse. "When you throw in college you see five or six good hitters a night . . . and you come here and there's nine hitters in the line-up that are capable of hitting the ball, and to me that's the most overwhelming thing."

All the players agreed that the sheer intensity of the schedule is also a major factor in improving their skills. Unlike the college season, in which they might play three games a week, in New Market they play every day.

In addition, several have part-time jobs. For instance, Brad Zieglar, a pitcher from Southwestern Missouri State, works mornings at the New Market battlefield museum.

"It's been fun," he said. "I've always loved history, so having to memorize a lot of details about the Battle of New Market was not a problem for me. I've also learned a lot about the Civil War, which has been interesting."

The job, however, doesn't leave him much spare time. Zieglar—and all the players—report to the field every day at 5:00 P.M. They do calisthenics, take fielding and batting practice, and rake and line the field, all before the game starts at 7:30. Following the game there is a team meeting, so they don't get home much before 11:00 P.M. If it's an away game, there's also an hour or two of travel time.

"It takes tremendous discipline and dedication on the part of these players," said Maynard "Mo" Weber, the Rebels' batting coach. "That's why

I love coaching players at this age. They are all totally focused on their game and improving their skills."

Weber, who is something of a local legend, just turned 77. He has been coaching baseball off and on for more than 50 years, including two stints as head coach at the College of William and Mary, and he has no plans to retire. "Why should I," he said. "I'm doing what I love to do best, and I even get paid for it."

In addition to his coaching experience, Weber has accumulated a vast number of quips and one-liners in his 77 years, for instance:

Meet our newest player, Willy Doit, and his girlfriend Betty Dont.

I'm a lowball hitter and a highball drinker.

My wife and I used to be in the iron and steel business. She used to iron and I used to steal.

Weber has also accumulated a great wealth of experience, as well as incredible insight into the game.

"Many of the boys come here with some really bad habits," he said. "Their athletic ability has allowed them to get by up to now, but at this level that doesn't work anymore."

Adjusting to wooden bats and strong pitching can also be a real blow to their pride, he said. "In college most of these guys were MVP players who hit 15 or more home runs and batted over .400," he pointed out. "Here only one or two hit over .300 and there are several players—and I mean starters—who are under .200."

Like Weber, manager Kevin Anderson also loves coaching baseball today. "From the college level up, the game is in great shape," he said. "Every one of the players are in great shape. They all lift weights and are very hard workers."

Mo agreed. "They're flat out better. They're much stronger than they were when I was a kid, and the coaching is much better in the colleges. Baseball is a nonrevenue sport and a lot of colleges would have the foot-ball coach take the baseball team as his second job—or they would even get a volunteer from the community in some cases." But now, Weber said, most colleges have well-trained baseball coaches and many have beautiful new facilities.

However, both Weber and Anderson agreed that it's at the local level that the game is suffering. "In most of the communities around here," Anderson said, "the Little League season ends in early June. When I was a kid it was just starting, and we would play ball on our own, too, all summer long. Now you rarely see kids out playing ball."

Still, the community spirit is strong here. For example, a local couple gifted Anderson and his wife with a home-baked cake while his wife was "expecting." An old-fashioned gesture—for an old-fashioned place. "It's amazing," said Choate. "It's like this whole town is one big family."

Families are in fact what make the Rebels possible. Local residents house players and give them a home away from home during the league's season. Although the families are officially responsible only for housing the players, in practice most end up cheerfully spending large sums on extra groceries for them as well.

"Our ballplayer drinks gallons of milk," said Glenda Ekey, who is Choate's local host, "and he eats anything and everything I put on the table for him. We just love having Patrick with us. He is such a gentleman, and he gets along really well with our 12-year-old grandson." Indeed, the 21-year-old athlete enjoys throwing around the football with his young friend.

Rebels announcer Dick Powell was similarly enthusiastic. "We've had ballplayers stay with us for six years," he said, "and if they are a reflection of the young generation, then our country is in good shape."

Powell admits that he had his doubts in the beginning. "The first two players we had were brothers from the Citadel and they were party boys who were coming and going at all hours of the night. We didn't know what to do." Fortunately for the Powells, the brothers dropped off the team. "Then we got Brian Menino and he was terrific," Powell said, "and we've had good luck since then."

Almost all of the host families have said that the conduct of the players who stayed with them was excellent. "They're typical messy teenagers," said local Barbara Frye, "but our daughters were worse."

One reason for these glowing reviews is probably that the players lack any time for fooling around. But how about romance?

"It's kind of funny," said Wentsky. "When we get here at the beginning of the season all the 12- and 13-year-old girls are lined up along the fence, all made up like they were 16 or 17." Unfortunately, he observed, "There just aren't many girls 18 or over around. I guess they are in college or away working." But then, Wentsky said, "Three-fourths of the guys on the team have girlfriends back home, and they don't cheat on them."

How about drinking? "Anybody who thinks college boys don't drink beer is naïve," said Jean Morse. Morse and her husband, Everett, have hosted players for six years. "Some of the players are 21 and can drink legally," she said, "and I say no problem. The only rule is if you drink, you don't drive." On many occasions players have handed her their car keys and spent the night.

Morse doesn't mind cooking for these overnight guests. "It might be pizza, barbecue, lasagna, ham, fried chicken, pot roast, you name it," she said. "We even fired up the grill at midnight to cook hamburgers, hot dogs, and sausages. And there have been times when I cooked breakfast for the team."

In addition to the players, coaches and other volunteers frequently come along for the late evening dinners. There are frequently 30 or more mouths to feed—a crowd that most people would find a burden several times a week. But Morse thrives on it. "I love having the players here," she said. "The next morning I never know how many bodies I'll find laying around. I just tell them leave the furniture where you found it. And they do. I've never had a piece of furniture damaged in six years."

"Mama" Jean and the players stay close even after the season is over. "We had one player, Brian Farcas, who lived with us for three years. And he became like a son to us," she said. "When Everett (they call him 'Big E') retired, Brian and his parents came to the retirement party. A lot of other players called or sent cards or presents."

Mama Jean is a hero to the players, just as is Jay Zuspan, the owner of the Christmas tree farm outside of town. By common consent, Zuspan had the main responsibility for redesigning and rebuilding the field and for its ongoing maintenance. "It's just unbelievable what he does," said Wentsky. "He must put in 60 hours a week on the field."

In addition, Zuspan and his wife host one or more players in their home each season. And, as if all of that wasn't enough, he also attends every home game and "at least 80 percent of the away games." He also pays for the team's meals on the road.

Zuspan and Mama Jean are two of the most prominent individuals among the dozens of people who volunteer time and funds to sustain the Rebels organization. The keystone of this remarkable volunteer structure is Larry Strawderman, the president of the Rebels organization for the past two years. Strawderman grew up in New Market and played on Rebel Field as a kid. Following a career with the CIA, he retired in 1992 and he and his wife moved back to New Market.

In the Rebels' organization, said Strawderman, "If you ask what your job description is you're in the wrong organization. Here we depend on volunteers to do whatever needs to be done."

President Strawderman's duties are many. Foremost among them is fund-raising, since the Major League Baseball subsidy covers only $8,000 out of a $40,000 budget. So, he works with local merchants to wheedle display advertising for the field, supervises the operators of the concession and souvenir stands, makes sure the players have housing, oversees field maintenance and equipment purchases, and works with the coaches. In addition, he and his wife house four players. But, like the many volunteers working under him, he finds his job tremendously rewarding.

Part of the appeal of the job for Strawderman, as it is for many of the other volunteers, is the knowledge that they are playing a small part in developing some of the major league stars of tomorrow. Rebel Field's sign says "Gateway to the Majors," and approximately 20 Rebel players have gone on to play in the big leagues. *Baseball America's* most promising rookie selection for 2000, Jon Rauch, played for the Harrisburg Turks in 1998. But Strawderman also realizes that making "the show" (the major leagues) is a long shot for these players. On average, only 25 percent of the Rebels will make it to even the minor leagues.

For Strawderman, the greatest thrill in his job is the chance to have a positive impact on the lives of some outstanding young men. "Playing for the Rebels really tests their mettle," he said. "It shows players within a few weeks how good they really are. Some realize that they have hit the wall. They play out the season and may do well in college baseball for the rest of the time they are in school, but they know they should be looking at other careers." Others, Strawderman said, "Say, 'Hey, I'm doing pretty well. I know now I can compete in the minors.' Others, like Brad Ziegler, who lives with us, decide that if they don't make it as players they want to go into coaching."

They are a diverse lot, these Rebels players, coming from all over the country to play baseball in this small town in Virginia. "But whatever happens to them," said Strawderman, "this experience will always be with them. They never forget their summer in the valley."

IV

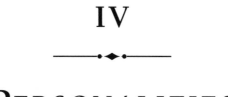

PERSONALITIES

19

A TEXAS RANGER COMES TO WASHINGTON

The playoff tiebreaker took 36 days to complete, but when it was all over George W. Bush had won the pennant. On January 20, 2001, a Texas Ranger took the oath of office as president of the United States.

In George W. Bush, the country gets a president steeped in three generations of baseball lore and history. His great uncle, Herbert Walker, was one of the first co-owners of the New York Mets and took young George to see the team's first spring training. Laura Bush says that George, "Always wanted to buy a baseball team and to be an owner like his uncle Herbie."

His father was the star first baseman for the Yale team, a man who met Babe Ruth and sought out the company of players like Joe DiMaggio and Ted Williams, a man who, as president, kept his college baseball glove in his desk drawer in the Oval Office.

George W. also grew up loving the game. He was an average Little League player but made the freshman team at Yale and later coached Little League in Midland, Texas. He has collected autographed baseballs since he was a kid and now has over 250 balls signed by players from Stan Musial to Mark McGwire. Moreover, his five-year tenure as co–managing partner for the Texas Rangers proved to be the formative experience of his life.

It may not be true of Bush, as Ronald Reagan said of himself, that he "owes everything to baseball," (inheriting the name Bush didn't hurt, after all), but clearly, he owes a great deal to the game. Summing up Bush's five-year tenure with the Rangers, the *Washington Post's* Dana Milbank wrote, "Baseball has arguably been the most important thing in Bush's life. . . . It made him a success after a series of business failures, it made him rich, and it launched his political career. Baseball also gave Bush a powerful, if intangible, asset: it made him a regular guy, not a president's son from Andover, Yale, and Harvard, but a guy who spit sunflower shells while hobnobbing with the on-deck batter."

When Bush emerged as the front runner for the Republican presidential nomination in 2000, reporters rushed to examine his record with the Rangers, researching his tenure there for clues as to how he would govern as president. Bush's time with the Rangers became the subject of cover stories in *The Weekly Standard* and *Harper's* magazine and of in-depth analyses in *Time*, the *Washington Post*, the *Philadelphia Daily News*, and other publications.

And, in truth, there is much to be gleaned from Bush's record as co–managing partner of the Rangers—much that provides clues as to what his management style will be like as president.

When he turned 40 in 1986, George W. Bush did not have much to show for his life. He had sought to follow in his father's footsteps as a successful Texas oil man, but bad luck, bad business decisions, and bad economic times in the oil industry had combined to render him a failure. He had also tried to emulate his father in 1978 by running for Congress but failed there as well. Worse, his marriage was shaky, due mainly to his heavy drinking. In 1986, however, George W. Bush showed his true character. Waking up with a hangover after his fortieth birthday party, he said, "I've had my last drink," and quit, cold turkey.

With that decision, his life began to turn around. His marriage grew stronger and his energies more focused. In 1987 he became a key player in his father's campaign for president and in 1989, acting on a tip that the Texas Rangers were for sale, he put together a consortium of investors to buy the team.

Of the total of $86 million invested, Bush contributed only $606,000, most of it borrowed money, but he quickly became a key player in the organization. Tom Schieffer was made president of the team and co–managing partner. Rusty Rose was given the responsibility for handling the financial side of the operation. Bush, however, was made co–managing partner, and became the public face of the team. By all accounts, he threw himself into the job with all the energy and enthusiasm he had.

George W. Bush at the ballpark with his father and Tom Schieffer, co–managing partner of the Rangers. Photo courtesy of the Texas Rangers.

Journalist David Brooks wrote a cover story for the *Weekly Standard* on Bush's record with the Rangers, the product of an exhaustive study on the subject. At the outset, said Brooks, Bush wisely decided to leave the details of running the team to others and to concentrate his energy where his strengths lay: relations with the fans, press, and players; building up a good community image for the team; and working out a strategic vision for the franchise's future.

Brooks noted that Bush achieved his first bipartisan success of sorts in his relationship with president and co-owner Schieffer. The brother of Bob Schieffer, host of *Face the Nation*, and a former Democratic state legislator, Tom Schieffer had made many enemies due to his abrasive style. Yet Bush was able to persuade him to invest $1.4 million of his own money in the team, and the two established an effective, harmonious working relationship, with Schieffer as the inside man, running the team's operations, and Bush as the outside man, selling the team to the public.

Bush and his partners had their work cut out for them. The Rangers had been in the doldrums for most of the 18 years they had been in Texas, failing to make the playoffs a single time. Attendance was lousy, and there was a good deal of talk about the franchise moving to another state.

Bush and his partners saw that a total overhaul, a new image, and an expanded fan base were necessary. The key here was the ability to draw fans from both Dallas and Fort Worth, two cities with a long and intense rivalry. The owners settled on the community of Arlington, midway between the two cities, as the preferred site. Bush demonstrated his powers of persuasion by getting the mayor of Arlington to sign off on the project and to do so, moreover, in a way that had the Arlington taxpayers footing 70 percent of the bill. (The owners of the Rangers eventually came up with their share of that $60 million by levying a surcharge on ticket sales at the new ballpark.)

But Arlington's approval hardly meant the deal was closed. Raising the required revenues meant getting voter approval and here again, Bush took the lead. He toured the community relentlessly, speaking to Kiwanis clubs and other civic and fraternal groups, and met one-on-one with reporters from the local media to sell them on the project.

The effort was successful. The voters approved the construction referendum by a margin of 65 percent to 35 percent. Richard Green, the mayor of Arlington at the time, gave Bush the lion's share of the credit for the success. "I'm not sure how else to explain the phenomenon," he told the *Washington Post*.

Tracy Ringolsby, now a reporter for *The Rocky Mountain News*, covered the referendum for the *Dallas Morning News*, and agreed with this assessment. "I remember that, at the time, the polls were really close on the referendum," he said. "In addition, the vote took place the Saturday that Desert Storm began, and I remember thinking that Bush would get crushed. But he ended up winning hands down."

In Ringolsby's view, Bush not only pushed the new stadium through, he saved the franchise. "The team is in Texas because of George W. Bush," he said. "It would have been moved otherwise." George W. Bush had demonstrated his abundant political skills by winning, in effect, his first successful political campaign.

Nor did his efforts stop there. Bush was very active in the design of the ballpark, the commission for which had been given to the Architectural Services P.C. firm of Washington, D.C. According to David Schwartz, the firm's managing partner, Bush insisted on a ballpark with all the latest amenities, but with an old-fashioned look and feel and a lot of idiosyncratic details that would give the stadium its own identity. Thus, Texas longhorns became one of the ballpark's motifs, as did Texas lone stars.

In his many speeches at commencement exercises and other ceremonies, Bush has always cited a number of "fixed stars to live by." Star No. 4 holds in part that "baseball should be played on real grass and out in the open." This belief was also honored in the stadium's design.

One of the keys to success in modern sports stadiums is the luxury box, which is essential to attracting big bucks from wealthy individuals and corporations. The ballpark at Arlington has 120 of them but, according to Schwartz, Bush insisted that they be as inconspicuous as possible in order to diminish class distinctions. "George has the view that baseball is a great common denominator of the American people," Schwartz said. "The chairman of the board talks about it and the guy on the assembly line talks about it. He wanted a ballpark where the common man did not feel out of place. He wanted a place that was great for the whole family."

Bush also insisted that the stands be built as close to the ground as possible (in this case, 18 inches) to increase the sense of immediacy for the fans. And he showed a keen appreciation for the value of season ticket holders, personally lobbying local companies to buy tickets and providing special events and other perks for them.

Bush himself could usually be found in the first row of the stands at virtually every home game in the new ballpark. Eschewing the team's

George and Laura Bush with their twin daughters. Photo courtesy of the Texas Rangers.

luxury suites, he preferred to be among the fans: talking with them, signing autographs, listening to complaints and suggestions—working to establish a rapport between the fans and the ownership. Family members also joined Bush frequently at the ballpark, and he often escorted celebrities such as Roger Staubach to the games as his guest, gaining more publicity for the team and himself in the process.

Bush also showed himself to be a very savvy operator with the press. He insisted on building a first-class press box with an elevator connecting it directly to the clubhouse level, and he frequently visited the press box and broadcast booths during the games to talk with reporters. Bush also made himself available to the media during batting practice and worked hard one-on-one to win over hostile reporters.

"I remember his first press conference," recalled Ringolsby. "There was one columnist there who was really hostile, and I was very impressed with the way that Bush focused the discussion on him. He spent a lot of time dealing with his concerns and was able to calm the situation down."

Ringolsby remembered Bush as being always accessible. "I talked with him in the press box, on the field, in the dugout, in hotels, wherever he happened to be, and he was always down to earth and friendly, just really personable," he said. "He's a normal guy, totally without pretensions—not at all what you'd expect from a man whose father was the president."

According to reporters who covered him then, Bush was also deeply involved in the effort to rebuild the Rangers from the ground up, designing an approach to acquiring new players that weighted character along with talent. He made his share of mistakes—the decision to trade Sammy Sosa and a junior pitcher to the White Sox in return for Harold Baines, a player well past his prime, being foremost among them—but the Rangers also brought along a host of outstanding new players, including Rafael Palmeiro and Juan Gonzalez. Bush and his partners decided to concentrate their investments in the team's farm system rather than in acquiring expensive, big-name free agents. But when circumstances warranted it, as with pitching ace Nolan Ryan, they were willing to spend the big money. Bush established a close friendship with Ryan and made it clear to all the players that they were appreciated and would be well compensated.

When asked what his toughest decision with the Rangers was, Bush has said that it was firing Bobby Valentine as manager. After three years, the team's condition was stagnating in 1992. When it was decided to let

Valentine go, Bush was given the unpleasant job of telling him. He did the deed so tactfully, however, that Valentine left holding no grudge against him. The same situation repeated itself two years later when Bush fired general manager Tom Grieve. Grieve has nothing but praise for Bush, and said that both he and Valentine voted for Bush for president.

The plan put in place by Bush and his partners worked. The "Ballpark at Arlington," as it became known, was an instant hit with critics and fans alike. The 49,000-seat stadium boosted attendance by over 700,000 per year, and the luxury boxes helped bring in a revenue bonanza catapulting the Rangers to large-market status and enabling the team to become competitive. Franchise revenues grew from $28.8 million in 1988, the year before Bush and his partners bought the team, to $116 million in 1998. In 1996, the Rangers made the playoffs for the first time, and they repeated in 1998 and 1999.

According to Carl Lubsdorf, Washington bureau chief for the *Dallas Morning News* and a veteran Bush watcher, Bush took great pride in what he had built. "I remember scheduling an interview with him in 1994," when Bush was running for governor of Texas, Lubsdorf recalled, "and he asked me to meet with him at the ballpark. What he wanted to talk about most was the Rangers. It was obvious that he was very proud of what he accomplished." Lubsdorf also recalled that his wife, Susan Page, Washington bureau chief for *USA Today*, and a number of other reporters met with Bush at about that same time. They had some extra time before going back to the airport and Bush took them all out to see the ballpark.

In addition to his key role with the Rangers, Bush was given the added responsibility of working with his fellow owners in Major League Baseball. Here again, he proved to be well liked and respected by his peers. This proved to be the case even in the vote to fire commissioner Fay Vincent in 1992. Vincent was an old family friend of the Bushes, and George W. defended him vigorously, the only owner to do so.

In the disastrous labor dispute of 1994, Bush steered a moderate course between owners like George Steinbrenner, who wanted to give the players' union whatever they demanded, and those such as Jerry Reinsdorf, owner of the Chicago White Sox, who wanted to see the game shut down for as long as necessary to break the union's back. In this select company of large checkbooks and even larger egos, Bush was able to navigate skillfully, bringing to bear his charm and diplomatic skills.

In his *Weekly Standard* profile of Bush, Brooks related an amusing and illuminating incident:

> *In the early 1990s, the owners of Major League Baseball held a meeting in Denver. Jerry McMorris, the owner of the new Colorado Rockies, decided to host a lunch not at a restaurant near the meeting site but at a country club in suburban Castle Rock. It was a mistake. These men are imperious types with the attention span of a four-year-old child. They are not used to being herded onto buses for long drives.*
>
> *Things went from bad to worse when the bus got lost. The driver circled round and round. The mood got ugly.*
>
> *Gene Autry, the owner of the California Angels, needed to relieve himself. His wife went up front and said something to the driver. The bus pulled over to the side of the highway, where an embarrassed Autry got out and urinated. It was an awkward moment for everybody. Then, when Autry had stiffly hoisted himself back onto the bus, George W. Bush's voice rang out: "Hey Gene, you still got a great spray for a guy your age." A smile opened up on Autry's face and the bus exploded with laughter. Bush had once again said just the right thing to improve everyone's mood and remind them of how much fun it is to be around him.*

According to Ringolsby, Bush got along well with the owners because, "He's a consensus builder who is excellent at working with people." At the same time, Ringolsby finds Bush to be "a man of principle who sets a course and follows it. He will not be dissuaded if he thinks he's right." Ringolsby cited Bush's strenuous opposition to interleague play and his stubborn defense of Vincent, whom the other owners wanted to fire. "In both cases, he was a minority of one," Ringolsby said, "but he is not a trend follower if he thinks he's doing the right thing."

In 1997, Bush and his partners sold the Texas Rangers franchise to wealthy businessman Tim Hicks for $250 million. In recognition of his contributions to the team, the other partners increased Bush's ownership share from 2 percent to 12 percent, giving him a profit of almost $15 million on the deal. The sale made Bush a wealthy man and gave him a compelling success story to put on his resume.

What can we distill from George W. Bush's five-year tenure with the Rangers that will enable us to predict his conduct in the White House? Well, actually, a good deal. We can say that the new president is a man who honors tradition, values loyalty, and hates to fire employees, but who also recognizes when it's necessary and carries out the task tactfully but firmly. He is a man who focuses on the big picture and delegates the details to good managers, then holds them accountable; a man with vision who sets a course and then follows through on it; a man with ample political skills, personal charm, and powers of persuasion.

Lubsdorf and others have speculated that Bush will use his skills and the prestige of his office to make it known, unofficially but firmly, that he would like to see major league baseball back in Washington, D.C. We'll see.

Meanwhile, we should take note of Mr. Dooley's observation that "politics ain't beanbag." It ain't baseball, either, although reporters who covered Bush's success with the Texas Rangers expect to see many of his winning tactics brought to bear in the White House.

With Congress split almost 50-50 between Republicans and Democrats, the words of Ringolsby should be encouraging to Bush. Ringolsby's grandfather was vice president of the firmly Democratic United Mine Workers under John L. Lewis, and Ringolsby admits to being a lifelong Democrat. Yet he himself said of Bush, "I've told him, 'You're so down to earth, you must have been born a Democrat and adopted by a Republican family.' I just really like Bush and I have a ton of respect for the man."

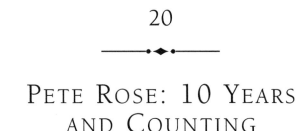

20

PETE ROSE: 10 YEARS AND COUNTING

John Dowd is one of Washington's "superlawyers," but he is not one to hide behind legalese. Gruff-spoken and as blunt as his bulldog appearance would suggest, his opinion regarding Pete Rose is simple: "Pete Rose is a liar."

In 1989 Dowd was hired by Major League Baseball commissioner Bart Giamatti to conduct an investigation into allegations that Cincinnati Reds manager Pete Rose had violated baseball's Rule 21, which forbids gambling. According to Rule 21, illegal gambling is grounds for suspension from baseball for an indeterminate time. Gambling on baseball is grounds for a lifetime ban. Pete Rose was accused of violating both provisions and, even worse, of betting on his own team.

The incendiary nature of these charges against one of baseball's most famous names created a crisis that threatened to throw major league baseball into turmoil. The problem was tossed to the new commissioner, Bart Giamatti, by his predecessor, Peter Ueberroth. Giamatti, a renaissance scholar and former president of Yale University, was a passionate baseball fan and regarded the commissioner's job as a dream come true. Instead, it quickly became a nightmare as the Rose crisis consumed him. A quick resolution was imperative. Giamatti turned to John Dowd of the prominent Washington law firm of Akin, Gump, Strauss, Hauer, and Feld. Dowd had considerable experience dealing with gambling problems in baseball.

Giamatti wanted to give Rose a chance to deal with his problems and stay in professional baseball, Dowd said. "He was given so many opportunities to present his case—at least seven chances—but our attempts to settle were taken as a sign of weakness."

According to Dowd, "Pete Rose is not an attractive human being. He had women problems, customs problems, all kinds of problems, and he had always swept them under the rug. He thought he could do the same with baseball, but he misjudged Giamatti." The commissioner was left with no choice but to investigate, Dowd said, and Rose was forced to cooperate because his contract required him to submit to the authority of the commissioner.

Giamatti gave Dowd and his assisting attorneys a few guidelines:

1. Let the chips fall where they may.
2. The world will see what you do, so it had better be perfect.
3. Examine him; don't cross-examine him.
4. Disclose to Rose's lawyers the information you have.

Giamatti cautioned Dowd and his colleagues to "Remember, Pete's not the legend. The game's the legend."

But in fact, Pete Rose is, and remains, a living legend.

Pete Rose is one of the most famous (or in the minds of some, infamous) names in the history of baseball. In the course of a career playing for the Cincinnati Reds, the Philadelphia Phillies, and the Montreal Expos, Rose built a legacy that in some particulars is unlikely to be surpassed. He was elected an All-Star 16 times. He was National League rookie of the year in 1963 and won back-to-back batting titles in 1968 and 1969. He was the National League MVP in 1973 and was World Series MVP for the Reds in 1975. In 1978 he had a 44-game hitting streak that still stands as a National League record and puts him second only to Joe DiMaggio's 56-game, major league record–holding streak. The next year he signed with the Philadelphia Phillies for $800,000, a record salary at that time. Rose led the Phillies to a World Series Championship in 1980 and retired in 1986 with a .303 career batting average. He is still in first place in both hits (4,256) and games played (3,562).

Such was Rose's stature and so great was the turmoil created by his gambling controversy that there was, in Dowd's words, "a real cloud over the game." Resolution of the crisis required a thorough investigation, including face-to-face sessions with Rose. These were conducted over two days in the spring of 1989 at a Catholic convent near Dayton, Ohio, a location chosen by Rose's lawyer.

"Rose is not well educated, but he is street smart," Dowd said, adding, "I was surprised how unprepared he was and I was surprised at how poorly represented he was." Dowd said that, to his amazement, "One of his lawyers slept most of the time and the other one spent most of his time eating the donuts and other foods that the nuns had made for us."

In preparation for the sessions with Rose, Dowd and his assisting attorneys interviewed approximately 100 witnesses. Unlike Rose, most of

Pete Rose, banned for life

these people were not required to cooperate with the investigation, since it was not a government-sanctioned legal proceeding.

But, according to Dowd, this didn't present a problem. "It's amazing," Dowd said. "I would tell them I'm working for baseball and I need your help and they all willingly participated. It's something about the force of the game. People care about it."

With the cooperation of the witnesses, Dowd and company compiled a devastating indictment against Rose. The summary report, which has come to be known as the "Dowd Report," totals 225 pages and is supplemented by 2,000 exhibits, including transcripts of tape recordings, phone messages, betting slips, payment records, and complaints from bookies that Rose had stiffed. Most importantly, said Dowd, "We had eight to ten people who pinned the rose on Rose, who said that they heard him or overheard him betting on the Reds."

Dowd regrets that he was not able to have the interviews with Rose videotaped so that the public could have seen his reactions. "You could tell plainly when Pete was lying and when he was telling the truth," said Dowd.

As he was exposed to the testimony of the witnesses, Dowd said Rose "acted stunned. Sometimes he would just say, 'I don't know what to think.'"

Rose clearly felt betrayed at times as well. This was the case with the testimony of Paul Janszen and Mike Bertolini, two longtime intimates and middlemen who testified that Rose had accumulated an enormous debt to the "wise guys"—the New York City Mafia. "He had housed Michael Bertolini and Paul Janszen, trusted them, and they had made a lot of money off of him," said Dowd. "He felt betrayed."

According to Dowd, Rose's gambling addiction was damaging to himself, to the Reds, and most of all to baseball itself.

"The magnitude of Pete's debts was just enormous," he said. "He was using three bookies a day and betting on five games a day, football, hockey, basketball, baseball, you name it, and each bet was for $2,000 and up." The debt owed to the New York mob alone was half a million dollars. "This debt was so destructive," the attorney said. "It was like battery acid. Guys were coming into the manager's office and into the dugout to collect their money and the players saw this, of course. It's telling," he continued, "that the Reds are universally conceded to have had the best team in baseball, man-for-man, in both 1987 and 1988, but they came in second both years," partly because Rose was so engrossed in his gambling debts.

Washington lawyer John Dowd, nemesis of Pete Rose

All the while Rose continued betting on his own team—or, in some cases, not betting on it. "When certain pitchers such as Mario Soto pitched," Dowd stated, "Rose wouldn't bet on the Reds—sending a signal to the bookies that he thought they would lose."

Asked whether or not he thinks Rose was throwing games, Dowd declines to say yes. "I will not say what I cannot prove three ways," he said. But then he added, "You don't have to be a rocket scientist to see what was going on."

Dowd's report is thorough but hardly comprehensive. Other alleged gambling connections of Rose's—including those with the Chicago Mafia—were not investigated, because to do so would have taken another six months, and early resolution was imperative to Major League Baseball. But the report stands unchallenged by Rose, noted Dowd.

Based on its findings, Major League Baseball banned Pete Rose from professional baseball for life. This ban also makes him ineligible for induction into the Hall of Fame. Meanwhile, commissioner Bart Giamatti died of a massive heart attack in 1989, a death that Dowd attributes in part to the toll taken on Giamatti by the Pete Rose crisis.

Now, close to ten years after his ban from baseball, Rose has asked the new commissioner to reinstate him. But Dowd doesn't think it will happen. "Pete had a chance at one time," he said, "but it's too late now."

21

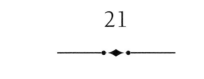

THE LONELY QUEST OF
PETE ROSE JR.

On Father's Day of 1999, Tiger Woods won the U.S. Open with a record score of 12 under par. At the press conference following this historic feat, Tiger noted the holiday and stated that he was dedicating his trophy to his father, the man he felt had been key to his success in golf.

That same day, 3,000 miles away in Reading, Pennsylvania, Pete Rose Jr. called his father to wish him a happy Father's Day. The younger Rose didn't have to say it, for his father surely knows: Pete Jr. has dedicated his whole life to his dad, his "idol."

For the young Rose it has been a long, lonely, and frustrating quest. For 12 years he has endured the privations of minor league life: the long bus rides between towns, the cheap hotels, fast food, and meager salary, the long absences from wife and family, and all the rest. The love of the game and the hope of making it to "the show"—the major leagues—make this life exciting to the younger players but, at 30, Pete Rose is no longer young by baseball standards.

It isn't that Rose isn't good. He has a career batting average of .255, and no player survives for 12 years in the minor leagues unless he's an excellent ballplayer. He is like a runner falling inches before the finish line. The knowledge of how close he gets is both a source of frustration and a motivation to keep him going.

Pete Rose Jr. idolizes his father and has also studied his career carefully. In doing so, he came to understand that Pete Sr.'s Herculean accomplishments are all the more remarkable given his relatively small size (only 5'10" and 155 lbs in his rookie year) and the fact that he is generally believed to have limited natural ability (the Reds' initial scouting report on Rose read "Can't make a double play, can't throw, can't hit left-handed, and can't run.").

Pete Rose Sr. became a star because of steel willpower, relentless work and study of the game, hustle, courage, and belief in himself. One suspects that it is the knowledge of these facts, as much as a desire to equal his father's greatness, that fuels the equally determined efforts of Pete Jr. There has always been talk in the stands of the young man's dogged determination to follow in his father's footsteps and play in the major leagues—and also skepticism about whether he would ever make it.

Actually, he did make it, however briefly. In 1997, Rose Jr. had his best season in the minors, batting .308 and hitting 25 home runs for the Chattanooga Double A farm team of the Cincinnati Reds. The Cincinnati organization, wallowing in the doldrums, called Rose up to the major leagues on Labor Day of that year. Over 34,000 fans showed up for his first game, three times the average turnout for the season.

Pete Sr. has remarked with some bitterness that the Reds called up his son merely to increase gate receipts and that they never gave him a fair shot, nor intended to do so. Nonetheless, Rose played in 11 games, hitting only .148 in 14 trips to the plate. He was sent back to the minors and is still there three years later. In 1999, he was playing for the Reading Phillies, a Double A farm club for the Philadelphia Phillies. Washington-area baseball fans have had many opportunities to see Rose Jr. play ball over the past decade, during which he played both for and against two local teams—the Prince William Cannons and the Frederick Keys—as well as against the Bowie Baysox.

Although Pete Jr. bears a definite family resemblance to the old man, it is quickly apparent that there are some major differences between father and son. Where Pete Sr. has achieved notoriety for being loud, volatile, profane, and crude, the son is a perfect gentleman, soft spoken, polite, and patient, with nary a cuss word uttered.

He is also larger than his father (6'2" and 230 lbs vs. 5'10" and 190 lbs). The younger Rose eventually decided to use his greater size and strength to change his game. "For years I tried to copy my dad's style, slap-

Pete Rose Jr. playing for the Reading, Pennsylvania, Phillies.

ping singles all over the field," he said, "but then I decided to build up and try to hit for power. It worked. In 1997 my career really turned around." In that year young Rose hit 25 home runs and had 98 RBIs, which won him a call-up to Triple A and then (briefly) to the majors.

Why did it take him years to make the change? "Well, I've always idolized my dad and I wanted to be like him," he replied.

George Will has written that "Pete Rose Sr. has baseball in his chromosomes." The son echoed the sentiment. "Baseball is in my blood," he said. "It's the only career I've ever thought about pursuing. If you think about anything else, you should be in another business." It's a genetic trait that the son has inherited undiminished. From the time he could walk, Pete Sr. took his son to the baseball park with him every day for home games and "Petey" (a nickname he still carries) even had his own locker.

When he was 10 years old, however, his parents went through a bitter divorce and his mother won custody. Pete Sr. even had to get a court injunction in order to take his son to the World Series in 1980.

Petey saw much less of his father after that and reports circulated for years that Pete Sr., disappointed with his son's failure to make the major leagues, had written Petey off. Both Pete Sr. and Pete Jr. have denied this. Pete Jr. has said that his father has often been helpful to him along the way.

The record would seem to bear that out. In the spring of 1999, for instance, Pete Sr. persuaded then–Philadelphia Phillies manager Terry Francona to let Petey report to spring training with the team, although Francona expressed his opinion at the time that Rose would not make the roster. The prediction proved correct and at the end of spring training Rose was cut, although Francona said that he had improved since he had last seen him.

For his part, young Rose is determined to continue improving and expresses relentless confidence that he will succeed. "I'm absolutely convinced that I'll play in the major leagues," he said.

Pete Rose and his son, Pete Rose Jr., meet President Gerald Ford at the 1976 All-Star Game. Photo courtesy of the Gerald Ford Library.

But the clock continues ticking. Rose, now 30, is the oldest player on the Reading team—10 years older than some of the players. The age question dogs him relentlessly, but he handles it with a weary patience. "Playing with the younger guys helps keep me young," he said. "I work out all year round to keep in shape and I'm blessed to have a wonderful wife who is totally supportive."

How much longer will he go on before he calls it quits? "My dad played until he was 45," Rose replied firmly. "I have a lot of years left ahead of me and I intend to make it. Nobody can stop me from following my dream."

22

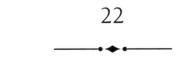

HARRY CARAY CAPTURES
WASHINGTON . . .
AND AMERICA'S HEART

In the summer of 1992, baseball author Curt Smith persuaded the Smithsonian Institution to hold a series of retrospectives on great baseball announcers entitled "Voices of the Game" (also the title of a very fine book by Smith).

Cubs announcer Harry Caray agreed to participate—although "participation" doesn't really do justice to his involvement. "Invasion" is more like it. He landed at National Airport in the style of the marines landing at Guadalcanal, crossed the Potomac River, and took Washington by storm. Accompanied by P.R. escort Matt Amadeo (whose name Caray consistently, and characteristically, mispronounced), he went from radio station to TV station, conducting cell phone interviews en route. It seemed as if every news organization in the news capital of the world wanted the Caray treatment, and they got it. Bombastic, irreverent, outrageous, provocative, he crisscrossed the city, glad-handing fans, complimenting (and frequently kissing) any pretty girl within reach, before stopping by his hotel room late in the afternoon for a serious raid on the minibar in his suite.

That evening, the 1,000 fans jamming the Smithsonian's auditorium were treated to a Caray tour de force. Unlike the other speakers in the series, who waited for Curt Smith's carefully scripted introductions, Harry took over immediately, launching into a stream-of-consciousness narrative that covered his childhood as an orphan, how he got into baseball, all the beer brands he had endorsed, his stock portfolio, Stan Musial, Bill Veeck, the Cardinals, the Cubs defying the law of averages, and on and on, the crowd egging him on all the way.

By the time Smith finally managed to get Caray introduced 30 minutes later, much of his story had already been covered; Smith plowed ahead nonetheless, showing slides and old film footage of some of the many great moments and great figures in Caray's life.

Caray, true to form, constantly interrupted this presentation with stories, humorous asides, and pithy commentary. On Pete Rose:

> I gotta tell you . . . you know people are saying Robin Yount's got 3,000 hits and George Brett's going to get 3,000 hits. Big deal. Pete Rose has 4,226 hits. You know how many years you would have to get 200 hits to do that? . . . Yet they say he's banned from baseball. Well who banned him? . . . I think it's the worst thing that ever happened.

On heroes:

> People ask why we don't have heroes any more. Well I'll tell you why— because we have stupid people running sports. That's why.

After the applause died down, Harry chuckled and said to Smith, "You know, Curt, those are the kind of things you can say when you bought Anheuser-Busch stock at $4.00 a share."

Later, reflecting on the "tornado" that had careened through Washington, Smith said, "What John Wayne was to the movies, what Ethel Merman was to the stage, what Louis Armstrong was to jazz, Harry Caray was to baseball."

Offering an important insight, Smith noted, "He knew baseball isn't *War and Peace*; its not a clash of armies; it's not Armageddon. It's fun, and he made it fun. He was the most beloved baseball announcer who ever lived."

Amen, brother Smith.

That June day nine years ago, flying around Washington, Caray seemed like a force of nature. Even though he was in his late seventies (he always lied about his age), he seemed indestructible. But, of course, no human being is, and he was no exception.

The next year, while traveling with the Cubs in Miami (at 79 he was still traveling with the team—that's 81 road games a year!), Caray collapsed and was taken to the hospital. He was later diagnosed with an irregular heartbeat. Characteristically, he was soon back in the booth, but things were never quite the same. He was on medication from then on and most notably he had to quit drinking.

To put things in perspective, you have to realize that before Caray suffered a stroke in 1987, his daily consumption of alcohol, as he described it in his autobiography *Holy Cow!*, was as follows:

> I'd have a few Budweisers at the ballpark during the day, then maybe four or six drinks after the game, then I'd go home and have a few more, and then I'd go out for a late dinner and have a few more. I never got high, it never impaired my judgment. . . . I never got drunk. I just got happier.

Following his stroke, Harry adopted a new daily routine that was "a lot more reserved":

> I'd have maybe a beer before dinner, maybe a gin martini or two with dinner, and an after dinner drink.

Now that's moderation!

"It's amazing," his longtime friend and drinking buddy Pete Vonachen said. "He quit just like that."

He did it because Dutchie begged him to. His third wife ("I hit a home run with my third marriage" he said) was the love of his life, and he would do anything to make her happy. Although he bitterly condemned his doctors for refusing to relax the ban, he never had another drop.

Staying on the wagon bought him and Dutchie some time, but in February 1998 his picture appeared on the TV screen and we all knew his time had come.

That night he made the national news in a way normally associated with the deaths of presidents and popes. The outpouring of emotion across the nation was astonishing and all of Chicago seemed to be in mourning. A tearful fan interviewed on WGN summed it up for all of us: "We're not mourning for Harry," he said. "He's doing fine. We're mourning for ourselves."

It was the eve of spring training, and Harry wouldn't be there. Six weeks from Opening Day, and Harry wouldn't be there.

For the past 10 years, day in and day out during the baseball season, he came into our homes and became part of our families. Like the chatty

The author interviewing Harry Caray at the Cubs convention in Chicago, January 1996

relative who never stops talking, he reminisced, opined, complained, joked, bantered, and clowned around, all the while calling the baseball game. For millions of people, Harry Caray was the voice of summer.

For 13 years he held forth from the announcer's booth at Chicago's Wrigley Field, entertaining Cubs fans from coast to coast via superstation WGN. As America's best-known and most-beloved baseball broadcaster, Caray's antics, distinctive voice, and love of the game were fixed in the national consciousness.

There was his trademark exclamation, "Holy cow!"; his joyful "It might be; it could be; it is—a home run!" And of course the "Cubs win! Cubs win! Cubs win!" shout at the end of those few games when they actually were victorious.

His incessant chatter between pitches ("Visiting today are Don and Lois Lewandowski of Racine, Wisconsin, here to root for the Cubs") made thousands of people celebrities for a day in their hometowns. And his standard sign off—"So long everybody"—will long be remembered.

Then there were his mangled pronunciations of names. NBA superstar Michael Jordan—an enthusiastic Cubs fan—reportedly declined to be interviewed by Caray because he didn't want to be introduced to the world as "Michael Jackson."

Steve Stone, Caray's sidekick in the booth for 13 years and, as you might imagine, an endless fountain of Caray stories, remembers this propensity to mangle names well. He noted that Caray had particular trouble with Hispanic names. "In one inning he pronounced Hector Villaneuva's name seven different ways. He called him Valanzuela, Villanova, Venezuela."

Then there was his tendency to forget names—even Stone's. "One day, at the beginning of the game, he turned to me and referred to me on the air as 'Ben Stein,' but then he realized that that was his business partner who was in Thorek Hospital, so that couldn't be right. So then he said, 'Dave Stone,' but he knew that was wrong too, so he turned to me and said, 'What is your name anyway?' and I said 'Steve Stone' and he said, 'Yeah, that's right,' and went on."

Stone is one of the best baseball commentators in the business. A Cy Young Award–winning pitcher, his experience in the field, his intelligence, and his intense study of the game over the years combine to make him one of the most knowledgeable and insightful analysts of the game—and made him a perfect complement to Caray, the consummate showman who had lost some of his sharpness as a play-by-play announcer in his last years.

Other Caray signatures included the oversized, black-rimmed glasses he wore (his optician said they were listed as the "Goliath" brand and that no one before or since has ordered them), the butterfly net he used to catch foul balls, and the Budweiser beer can or bottle that he brandished with gusto for half a century.

Another tradition that was very popular with the fans was his enthusiastic, if less than tuneful, rendition of "Take Me Out to the Ball Game" during the seventh-inning stretch.

But most of all there was his love of the game. For 53 continuous years as a broadcaster, he transmitted that infectious enthusiasm—first as the voice of the St. Louis Cardinals for 25 years, then for a year with the Oakland A's, followed by 11 years with the Chicago White Sox, and finally for 16 years with the Cubs.

Fifty-three years as a broadcaster is a remarkable achievement—especially given Harry's lifestyle. He ate and drank in great quantity and his all-night pub-crawling exploits in Chicago and the other cities of the National and American Leagues is the stuff of legend.

Former Cubs first baseman Mark Grace, one of Caray's favorite players and a frequent drinking buddy in the days before Caray got on the wagon, has many tales about his friend's partying days.

"I've seen the sun come up with Harry many times," Grace said, adding, "Some of my worst mistakes have been having just one more drink with Harry."

Caray's friend Pete Vonachen has lots of stories like that to tell as well. "I remember one time back in St. Louis," he said, "at the end of a game, Harry said, 'Let's go over to East St. Louis for a drink.'"

East St. Louis was a bad part of town, but they hung out there a lot anyway; in fact, on this occasion they stayed out all night.

"The next day the Cardinals played a double header," Pete said. "There we were, with no sleep. It got over a hundred degrees in that old ballpark and there was no air conditioning in the booth. Harry was just in agony. Sweat was pouring off him. He had his son Skip in the booth and he kept yelling, 'Daddy, daddy, are you all right?'

"Well, somehow he got through it, and I was heading home to get some sleep, which I desperately needed, and Harry yells, 'Pete, let's have just one drink before we go home,' and would you believe it, we ended up in East St. Louis all night again!"

At 84, Caray was still going strong, although a stroke, heart problems, and several falls had forced him to curtail road trips with the Cubs and—most onerous—to give up the sauce.

Finally, on Valentine's Day, 1998, Caray took Dutchie out to a Palm Springs nightclub to celebrate and, rising to greet a fan who had approached his table, he collapsed of a heart attack. He died four days later.

Outside Chicago's Holy Name Cathedral, people began queuing up nine hours ahead of time for Caray's funeral. All day long and into the night they filed by his casket—cops, nuns, elderly people with walkers, executives with briefcases, young and old, black and white—Harry's people. His appeal was universal.

What was it about this little old man in the oversized glasses that inspired such love on the part of his fans? Very simply, it was love requited.

Harry never tired of saying that it's the fans who make baseball possible, stating an obvious truth ignored by many of today's millionaire players. He was always accessible. His number was listed in the phone book and he gladly acceded to every autograph request. Over the years, people called him at home for interviews, interrupted his meals to introduce themselves, and bugged him for autographs for their kids, and he responded graciously every time.

Matching his kindness was his generosity. Orphaned as a boy, he was lavish in the financial and fund-raising support he gave to Chicago orphanages and many other charities.

Mindful of his humble origins, he never lost the common touch. At the end of his life—rich, famous, honored by the Smithsonian Institution and feted at the White House—he was still good old Harry.

Once, for instance, Caray happened to pass two odd-looking middle-aged men with navel-length beards and long hair sitting near the Cubs' dugout.

Harry was obviously perplexed.

"Hey, you guys Rabbis?" he shouted.

"No," one answered, "we're ZZ Top."

"ZZ Top!" he exclaimed, shuffling on by and chuckling. "What kind of religion is that?"

Caray's funeral was just the way he wanted it—attended by both the mighty and the lowly, filled with baseball jargon, irreverent reminiscences, laughter, applause, and a few tears, the great pipe organ playing a variation on "Take Me Out to the Ball Game" as his coffin was carried out of the cathedral, and all capped by a raucous party at his restaurant.

Dutchie Caray has said that she was staggered by the depth of the fans' love for her husband. "I've got boxes of cards and letters piled up to the ceiling at home," she said. "There must be tens, maybe hundreds of thousands of them. There is just no way I can ever get through them."

Dutchie is no stranger to the fans herself, as was proved by the warm welcome they gave her on Opening Day, 1998, the first game after Harry's death and a day designated as a tribute to him. This was perhaps one of the greatest moments in baseball history, one that ranks alongside Lou Gehrig's farewell speech and Bobby Thomson's "shot heard 'round the world."

Dutchie was invited to sing "Take Me Out to the Ball Game" during the seventh-inning stretch, joining Harry's grandson, Chip, now Harry's successor, in the broadcast booth. As the middle of the seventh inning approached, emotions started to build in the sellout crowd, with chants of "Har-ee! Har-ee!" getting louder and louder. A tumultuous ovation greeted Dutchie, who somehow got through the song—singing it appropriately off key.

When it was over, the crowd refused to settle down and the chanting and cheering continued for 10 minutes while hundreds of black balloons floated skyward and a bagpiper played "Amazing Grace."

"I'll never forget it as long as I live," Dutchie said. "The crowd just kept cheering and yelling. Chip and I just hung on to each other for strength. It was so emotional. It's like they didn't want to let him go."

Three years later they still don't. "I still get letters from fans telling me they miss him," Steve Stone said. "Well, I miss him too."

So do we all.

V

ON AND OFF THE FIELD

23

TALKIN' T-BALL

Adventures and Misadventures in Great Falls's Little League

On a mid-June evening, I drove by the home of Robin Marusin, the tireless "queen bee" of Great Falls baseball, and dropped off the helmets, balls, bats, first aid packs, and a rubber five-sided plate and adjustable rubber pipe—the "tee." This was the equipment I had used for the past two and a half months as manager of the Cubs T-ball team.

It was the last time I would do this. My fourth and final season as a T-ball manager had come to an end, and I admit that I felt a little sad as I parked in the Marusin driveway. I had some wonderful experiences coaching the almost 50 kids (including 3 of my own) who had been on my teams. But I don't want to seem maudlin. I was also more than ready to leave behind the special challenges of this unique game and trade up to being a manager at the "minor-league" level, which more closely resembles baseball, a sport with which T-ball has only the most tenuous connection (more about this later). And besides, I plan to be available as a part-time assistant coach for my daughter Melissa's T-ball team next year. After all, all I had wanted to be four years ago was an assistant coach.

It all started in March of 1993 at a meeting of the Mohegan Indian Guides Tribe in the tipi of Thundering Buffalo, also known as Tadeus Zubricki. Indian Guides, the father-son bonding experience, is another of those only-in-America phenomena, one in which the members take on

Native American names. "Plodding Turtle," "Flushing Water," and "Puking Panther" are a few of the more distinctive ones that I recall. But let's not digress.

Jeff Baker (excuse me: "Brave Eagle") announced that there was a critical shortage of assistant coaches for the T-ball league and asked if I would help out. Since my oldest son, Andrew, was signed up to play, I agreed, figuring that while I had never seen a T-ball game, I could pick up the basics from the manager.

Imagine my surprise a few days later when a letter arrived informing me that I *was* the manager.

"But Jeff," I protested to Brave Eagle, "I've never even seen a T-ball game."

"Don't worry," he repeated serenely, "you'll do fine and besides, there's nobody else available."

I reluctantly agreed, thinking that I could get a crash course at the league's coaching clinic. Wrong. There was no clinic. Coach's manual? "Nope." Rule book? "Sorry." The Great Falls baseball program was only a few years old and guidance was in short supply. Jeff did say that he would be happy to answer any questions I had. Panic was setting in, but I was stuck. The draft was upon me.

In the draft, the managers sit around a table poring over a list of 150 or so names of kids, grouped by age, from five to seven. There are a few general criteria used in picking T-ball players for each team:

1. your own kid(s)
2. kids who live near you (to facilitate car pooling)
3. parent's requests ("Johnny is best friends with Billy Jones and will be traumatized for life if he can't be on Billy's team.")
4. age (Seven year olds have a two-year advantage in coordination and attention span over the five year olds. The difference can be critical to your success—even survival—as a manager.)
5. gender (Girls are outnumbered by about five-to-one in T-ball. Thus, to avoid the emotionally—and possibly physically—crippling experience of being outnumbered twelve-to-one, each girl must have at least one other girl on her team.)
6. kids whose dads have volunteered to be assistant coaches (the more of these, the greater your chance of success as a manager)

Most managers and coaches are men although, strangely, this is not the case at higher levels. Marilyn Quayle, for instance, is still a legendary

The Roberts's T-ball titans (left to right): Andrew, Timmy, and Melissa

figure in McLean Little League lore, and two of the ten managers of Great Falls minor league teams are women.

Once the roster is complete, the manager can exercise his or her pre-rogative and pick the team name. As a loyal and long-suffering Cubs fan, that was an easy one.

That done, I called all the parents to introduce myself and to announce casually that I was looking for a "team mom." This is a critical position to fill, as the team mom activates the phone tree to inform other parents of cancelled practices and other info and also coordinates the cru-cially important snack rotation among the parents. The key here is the more sugar, the better. Ho Hos, Hostess Cupcakes, and Twinkies are rel-ished and consumed with gusto. "Healthy" snacks such as fruit, however, are bitterly rejected or, worse yet, thrown out on the field and stomped on, adding to the cleanup woes of the manager and the team mom.

These tasks out of the way, I now contemplated the first weekly prac-tice and the first weekend game. I scheduled our practice for a day late in the week so I could observe other coaches running practices and seek their advice.

I'd played in or watched hundreds of baseball games, but it soon became clear that, while there were superficial similarities between base-ball and T-ball, there were also some major differences.

For one thing, T-ball has only three innings. However, every player bats and fields in all three innings. A soft version of a baseball is set on top of a rubber tee and the batter swings at the ball until he or she hits it.

211

There are no strikeouts in T-ball. Since the ball isn't pitched, there isn't any need for a pitcher. In practice, however, most balls are hit in the vicinity of where the pitcher's mound would be, so a player is stationed on this spot. There is also a player between first and second base. The remaining players are all assigned to the outfield and, in the case of our teams, there were frequently 13 players on the field instead of the usual 9.

If anyone actually did keep score, the games were close, since every batter hits the ball and few of the fielders can field it. The most common play in T-ball, in fact, is the overthrown ball at first base. (Memo to Little League Baseball: create two additional official T-ball positions—players situated past the foul line in back of first base to retrieve overthrown balls.)

Our team had a resident statistician, my seven-year-old son Timmy, who ranks every activity (favorite activities at school: 1. dismissal, 2. recess, 3. gym, and 4. lunch) and every player on the team, number one naturally being himself. Timmy was able to produce precise (if dubious) scores at the end of each game—28–18, 21–11, etc., which was helpful to his teammates and entertaining to the parents, who consulted him at the end of every game. Best of all, the Cubs always won.

I soon learned that the key to successful T-ball managing is to keep it simple, keep 'em busy, and keep it fun. There is no place for tactical brilliance—double steals, pitchouts, the hit and run, etc.—in T-ball. We're talking basics here. Rudimentary basics such as how to stand (crouch like you're going to duck walk), catch a fly ball ("look" the ball into your glove), and field a grounder (keep your glove touching the ground, open your other hand above it like an alligator's mouth, and shut the mouth as soon as the ball is in the glove).

Basics start with the bases—as in where they are. Many beginners don't know first base from home plate. If a ball is hit to the outfield, the tendency of most of the team is to pursue it in a thundering herd. Therefore, a very important lesson to teach early on is that infielders play in the dirt part of the field; outfielders play in the grass. Only players in the grass should chase balls hit onto the grass. I've found that the distinction between a force-out (in which a fielder with the ball just has to tag a base) and a putout (in which it is necessary to tag the runner) is a major source of confusion for T-ball players. Solution: if you're in doubt, just do both.

Batting is the most fun part of the game for the players, but ability and technique vary widely. Again, you start with rudimentary basics—such as "squash the bug." A batter should pivot on his or her back foot as though there were a bug underfoot when swinging. By the end of the season, the "get-the-bat-back-bend-your-knees-take-a-level-swing-keep-your-eyes-on-the-ball" mantra is one that most coaches are saying in their sleep.

Bat safety is another high priority. Helmets are a must, the on-deck circle has wisely been eliminated, and bats are doled out very cautiously, as if they were as lethal as Uzis, which is true in some cases, especially with those kids who throw them after they've hit the ball. Once my son Timmy and the opposing manager's son got into a fight, and Timmy hit him in the stomach with the bat, sending the kid sprawling and screaming into the dirt, his mother into a fit of hysteria, and his father into a rage. "He's lucky," said Tim on his way home and to confinement in his room. "I could have hit him in the knees."

T-ball games are contests of primitive baseball with overtones of demolition derby, capture the flag, bird watching, and transcendental meditation. On one end of the spectrum the more hyper kids fidget, squirm, jump, do cartwheels, anything to keep them tumbling yet stationary and playing a position. On the other end are the kids who pick daisies in the outfield or squat in the infield sifting dirt through their fingers, oblivious to the world. Put two girls in proximity on the field and they enter a little-girl "talk zone," discussing dolls, clothes, and boys. Put three on a team and they may become a mini cheerleading squad, working up coordinated routines that totally overshadow what's going on in the game.

There are only three innings in T-ball, but these can easily last the allotted two hours. Each side bats through the entire order each inning, which, with 13 players, can take a long, long time, and produce a lot of fidgeting on the bench. During one practice, when I was working with a kid at the tee, I looked back to discover that my whole team was gone. They had all left the field and were playing in the woods nearby.

One of the best things about tee ball is the lack of parental pressure, second-guessing, and interference. Every kid plays every inning and rotates through every position, so there's not much room to complain about unfair treatment. And since the kids are just beginners, nobody takes the game seriously. Instead they just relax and enjoy the entertainment on the field.

They say that given the age of these children, a coach should count himself a success if the kid merely wants to play again next year. With the bar set that low, I've been pretty successful.

Everyone certainly seemed to be in a good mood at our end-of-the-season party. The season, which had begun in the snow flurries of early April, ended in the 90° heat of early June. I asked for a show of hands from the kids who were planning to play next year, and every hand went up. That made me feel good.

Not all of them will, of course. Some will defect to soccer or lacrosse or whatever, but some will stick with it and discover that, as they get older and more coordinated, baseball becomes more and more fun to play. It becomes more exciting to coach too, which is why, despite four years of spills and chills with the tee, I'm ready to move on.

24

QUEST FOR THE CUP

If writer W. P. Kinsella is right that baseball is our national pastime because its fans literally reckon the passage of time by its rhythms and great moments, then the spring of 1996 will forever be know in Great Falls as "the season of the cup."

"Baseball is serious business," Tony Porto said to me as the season was getting underway. Porto was the manager of the Cardinals Little League team, and you could tell that he was serious about baseball by the mere fact that he was watching a game played by the Orioles (for which my son Andrew was a pitcher) to scout the opposition. Little League players are nine and ten year olds, and scouting that age group is, to put it mildly, extremely rare.

But hell, I knew Porto was a fanatic two years ago when I managed the Cubs T-ball team (five to seven year olds) and he managed the Yankees. Before every game he gave his players Big League Chew (shredded bubble gum), applied black greasepaint under their eyes, and led the team in calisthenics to the tune of a team song played on a boom box.

Porto is also an impresario of great flair. For instance, all those in attendance at the Little League opening ceremonies of 1995 will recall him anticipating the spectacle of the opening ceremonies of the Olympics by giving his team purple flags to wave as they marched by the reviewing stand.

Despite his penchant for theatrics, Porto has developed a reputation as an excellent, if demanding, coach during his six years with the league. "My philosophy is simple," he said. "Play by the rules, play fair, and play to win." As an illustration, he added, "I'm not above intentionally walking a player." It would prove to be a fateful statement, foreshadowing a titanic battle between the Orioles and the Cardinals that would rage throughout the spring.

The manager of the Orioles was Jennifer Sabri, a sophisticated, elegant blonde whose stylish appearance belies intense mental toughness and a fierce determination to win. Sabri, whose two sons (Chris and Michael) were on her team, spent much of the season in telephone conversations with other team parents and managers. Porto, a successful, self-employed businessman, nonetheless has a sixties counterculture look: shoulder length hair, mustache, and earring. Though the contrast between their appearances could not be starker, both managers share a passion for baseball and make time to indulge in it.

Although the mothers of Great Falls spend a great deal of time carting their children to sporting events, women are still relatively rare as coaches. So it was unusual that two of the league's teams were managed by women, the other being Dena Kranis, manager of the Yankees. (Kranis, a Southerner, is married to a Greek-born gentleman and speaks fluent Greek, albeit with a Southern accent.) Some of the male managers resented the female intrusion on their turf, although Tony Porto was not one of them. In fact, according to Sabri, Porto became a good friend and her strongest supporter—even as their rivalry heated up during the season.

In their first game with the Cardinals, the Orioles took the lead and had runners on first and second. Porto's ace pitcher, Anthony Lazaro, was on the mound. (Anthony is the son of Great Falls dentist Ralph Lazaro, assistant manager of the Cardinals and the sponsor of the team, whose jerseys read "Dr. Lazaro's Mighty Molars.") The Orioles' ace pitcher, Chris Sabri (son of the manager), was at the plate. Porto told Lazaro to walk Sabri.

Jennifer Sabri said later that she had heard of a similar ploy attempted by Porto during a previous game and had shifted her batting lineup in anticipation of a repeat, placing some of her stronger hitters after her son. The upshot was that three runs scored.

However, if the Porto ploy was a tactical failure, it was a great success as psychological warfare. The move set off an incredible eruption of howls, screams, and epithets in the Orioles' stands, with two Orioles moms brusquely informing the pitcher's father, Dr. Lazaro, that they would be taking their dental business elsewhere. The intentional walk, although allowed under National Little League rules, violated the local league's unofficial code of propriety and fair play. The Orioles won but Porto had become an icon of enmity among the enraged Orioles parents—which was fine with Porto.

The next week the Orioles played the Yankees, managed by Dena Kranis. Hoping the Yankees would knock the Orioles out of first place, Tony Porto appeared in the Yankees' dugout and then on the field itself, where he gave advice on strategy and tactics to manager Kranis. Growing anger in the Orioles' stands peaked when Kranis, on Porto's advice, protested a ruling by the umpire, causing a delay in the game. The Yankees were ahead by this time and the delay fueled suspicions on the part of manager Sabri and the Orioles fans that the Yankees were trying to run out the clock. (Little League rules specify a maximum playing time of two hours.) The rising waves of protest from the Orioles fans began to take their toll on the Yankees manager, who was by this time speaking loudly to her husband in Greek. Soon thereafter, Tony Porto left the dugout.

The Yankees victory intensified the anger of the Orioles fans; phone lines sizzled between outraged parents. The Orioles filed a protest with the league.

The animosity had reached a fever pitch on June 19, when the Orioles faced the Cardinals again. "You'd better know your rule book," Porto had told Sabri the day before, an ominous warning that had kept the Orioles manager up late poring over Little League regulations. As game time approached, the stands filled up—mostly with players' mothers. In the Cardinals' dugout Dr. Lazaro, who had rushed in from his office, was still in his dental togs. Several officials from the league were present to mediate the anticipated disputes. In the Orioles' stands, the moms, well fortified with wine coolers, were in a combative mood.

The Orioles drew first blood, scoring four runs in the first inning. The Orioles moms, their need for vengeance assuaged, were cheering lustily. The euphoria was short-lived, however; in the second inning Porto sent his ace pitcher, Anthony Lazaro, to the mound. The Orioles were stopped in their tracks, not to score another run for the rest of the game.

The Cardinals, meanwhile, came on strong, scoring six runs in the fourth inning. In the fifth, Porto sent in a relief pitcher, his son Chris, and accompanied him to the mound with a blaring rendition of "Wild Thing" played over the P.A. system. (This move was taken from the movie *Wild Thing*, in which the Indians tried to unnerve the opposing team by introducing their dominating, but totally reckless, reliever with the song.) The Orioles fans took the razzing in stride but, as the Cardinals' runs began to pile up, a mood of resignation settled in on the Orioles ranks. Among the moms in the stands, talk had shifted from Tony Porto to comparisons of delivery-room travails.

However, as the Orioles prepared to bat in the bottom of the sixth, the game came to an abrupt halt. It just so happened that two Cardinals catchers had to leave the game early and that the kid tapped to fill in did not have a protective cup, as required by league rules. Despite Porto's pleas, Sabri summarily rejected providing a replacement on grounds of hygiene. In the Orioles' stands talk of C-sections, fetal monitoring, birth weights, and postpartum depression had turned to snarling accusations that Porto had reached a new low in game-delaying practices. The Orioles threatened to lodge a protest with the league.

Tony protested his innocence and, in desperation, raced off in the direction of the neighboring field, where a girls softball game was in progress, bellowing, "Does anyone have an extra cup?" Getting no help from the bewildered players and fans there, he raced back to his own field to confront an indignant Sabri, who was furious that Porto seemed to be employing another game-delaying gambit. Now an expert on the rules because of her crash course before the game, Sabri informed Porto that, according to official regulations, a manager was required to field nine players *with the required equipment.* "You have defaulted on your obligation," Sabri told Porto, "so forfeit the game."

Things remained at an impasse for another 10 minutes until a Cardinals mom appeared at the top of the hill yelling, "I've got one!" holding the protective cup triumphantly aloft.

Lost in all the confusion was the boy tapped to fill in as catcher. Never having played the position before, he was struggling to put on the catcher's gear. Unfortunately, the umpire had lost patience by this time and bellowed, "If he's not out here in one minute, you forfeit the game." It was clear to everyone that it would take the lad five minutes to get all the gear off, put on the cup, and put the gear back on. It was a moment of intense, tooth-grinding drama. Fortunately, a dentist was on hand.

Quickly sizing up the situation, in a game-saving snap decision Lazaro said, "Step into this thing right here." With all spectators' eyes fixed upon him and the umpire's merciless eyes on his watch, the mortified young catcher maneuvered the device's straps over his shoes and shin guards and into place over his uniform. He then clanked, shin guards askew, to home plate, looking like a character out of *A Clockwork Orange*.

Both stands dissolved into laughter and applause and play resumed. Although the Cardinals went on to win, the hostility between the two teams had totally subsided, erased by the hilarity of the "cup incident."

At an end-of-season party at Jerry's Pizza, the Orioles gave manager Sabri a dozen roses and a bottle of fine wine. Meanwhile, at the home of Dr. Lazaro, the Cardinals presented Tony Porto with an athletic cup inscribed with a bogus message from Jennifer Sabri.

The teams then dispersed and the baseball season of 1996 came to an end for the Orioles and the Cardinals. Talk of their rivalry had spread far beyond the two teams, however. Throughout Great Falls—from the Safeway to the 7-Eleven, from the Saddlery to the Silk Purse and Sow's Ear Boutique—people were trading stories of the climactic playoff game.

Like Babe Ruth's "called shot," Tony Porto's "quest for the cup" had quickly assumed the status of legend in the sports lore of Great Falls, Virginia.

25

FOR THE LOVE OF THE GAME

Each year baseball fans eagerly anticipate the World Series in late October. But for Victor Price of Great Falls, Virginia, the real World Series—the one he'll always remember—is already over.

The annual Little League World Series is held every August at Little League world headquarters in Williamsport, Pennsylvania. In 2000, from August 26–28, Vic Price, his wife, Tracy, and their sons Mickey, 12, and Timmy, 10, were all-expense-paid guests of the League in Williamsport, where Price was presented with the "Volunteer of the Year" award during the Series.

"There are almost a million adults doing volunteer work for Little League," said Scott Rosenberg, assistant to the president of Little League Baseball. "We also receive many hundreds of nominations for Volunteer of the Year. Winning the award is a real honor and it means that Vic has done something really significant."

In the case of Vic Price, the Great Falls nomination citation succinctly summed up what that achievement was:

After a major drought destroyed the sod on our two main fields last fall, Vic initiated a league campaign to replace the sod and improve the fields. Using his own time and equipment Vic put in new sod on our two main fields. He installed fence tops around the outfield fences for safety and put in warning tracks with crushed rock on both fields. In addition, he installed a new scoreboard for one of the fields, put in a flagpole beyond the centerfield fence on our main field, and put in a batting cage. Vic also built equipment boxes for helmets, bats, hats, and gloves and installed them in each dugout. Since we don't have an irrigation systems on our fields, Vic is at the fields at 5 A.M. every day to water the fields before heading to work.

Great Falls's Little League program is only 10 years old; residents were amazed that one of their own would be singled out for such a coveted national award. None who know Vic Price, however, had the slightest doubt that it was well deserved.

During the spring months, faculty and parents arriving early at Forestville elementary school in Great Falls grew accustomed to seeing a van labeled "Vic's Tree Service" in the parking lot behind the school.

Gazing into the distance, the same people could observe the van's owner, Vic Price, going about his morning routine: watering the two baseball fields with a 500-foot-long hose and raising the American flag.

It's a routine that had Price at the fields at 5:00 A.M. so the two-hour watering job could be finished in time for him to get his two boys up and off to school by 7:00 (his wife Tracy is a teacher and has already left by then) and still get to work himself by 8:30. Saturdays, Price was at the fields at 6:00 A.M. supervising the watering, raking, and lining of the fields for the day's games, and he could be found there most evenings as well.

The results of Price's handiwork were so spectacular that he was unanimously selected for the Volunteer of the Year award by the Great Falls Little League board, following a flood of supportive letters from parents, coaches, and board members. "Given what Vic's done, the award was a given," said one board member. Nor were many surprised when he won the Volunteer of the Year award for the state of Virginia a few weeks later.

However, there were gasps aplenty in Great Falls when word was received in June from Little League headquarters that Vic Price had been selected as Volunteer of the Year for the *entire United States of America.*

Great Falls's Nike Park was put in 10 years ago on an abandoned missile site—hence the name "Nike" (not because, as most people think, of a connection with the shoe company). The missile base infrastructure is still intact below the surface, which gives the field a certain cachet, but on the

Little League volunteer of the year Vic Price. Photo courtesy of the *Washington Post.*

ground conditions had long been abysmal as a result of a policy of benign neglect by Fairfax County, which controls the property.

It all got to be too much for Vic Price and last year he (with the support of the Great Falls Little League Board) took matters into his own hands. By prodding a skeptical board, Price won permission to negotiate with the Fairfax County government officials in order to gain permission to completely overhaul the fields.

Price soon became a familiar presence at county headquarters and eventually won the confidence of the proper officials, who came to believe that he would actually see the ambitious project through to completion. And see it through he did.

The effects of the daily work are readily apparent. Though lacking the built-in irrigation system of many local fields, the Nike Park fields are lush and green. "It's the 'Field of Dreams' without the corn," according to the local newspaper, the *Great Falls Connection.*

The *real* field of dreams for Vic Price, however, is the one he installed on his own property in 1998. The sign at the entrance to the field reads "Vic's Field, Home of the Astros" (Astros being the name of the Little League team he coaches).

The field is a regulation-size Little League field complete with bleachers, batting cage, its own generator, and other amenities. This summer, Price enlarged the dimensions of the infield to make it usable for Babe Ruth League as well as Little League baseball. The only drawback is a briar patch that runs down most of the left field line, a baseball graveyard for dozens of balls that go unretrieved by players and coaches who are loath to hack their way through the brambles.

Price is the coach for both of his boys' Little League teams and the field gives him a place to hold daily practices during the season and to operate a more or less permanent baseball clinic for players and parents who drop by frequently, invited or not.

With his sunburned face, moustache, and Astros uniform, Vic Price looks like one of the Ragtime-era baseball players of days gone by. His reverence for the game and its traditions seem equally old-fashioned. Umpires, for instance, are addressed as "Mr. Ump," and players are urged to treat them—as well as opposing players and coaches—with respect. Vic

Vic Price instructs catcher Phil Acoria. Photo courtesy of the *Washington Post.*

also tries to instill in his players a respect for the traditions of the game, for the national anthem, and for patriotic symbols.

What comes through more clearly, however, is his sheer love of the game—demonstrated by example. Practices are tough workouts, but also fast-paced and fun. Teamwork and mutual support are stressed and in games players are urged to maintain a constant chatter in support of team-mates at the plate, with Vic himself leading the way. Every batter is given his own moniker for this purpose, for example: "Hum little Tim Bub, Tim hum batter batter hum Tim Bub."

A particularly popular feature of the practices and scrimmages held at Vic's field are the impromptu chalk talks Price gives, based on reminis-cences of his five years in the minor leagues playing in the farm systems of the Kansas City Royals and Pittsburgh Pirates.

The result, as Great Falls Little League President Buddy Eller said, is that "kids love to play for Vic and parents love to have their kids on his team. We always have far more kids who want to be on his team than we can put on it."

Joe Kennedy, a fellow manager and board member, said, "I've seen Vic have teams at the top of the standings and at the bottom, and it makes no difference in how he treats the kids."

Price attributes his love of baseball largely to his father, Dr. Neel Price, a much-decorated medic during World War II and a well-known OB-GYN in the Washington area for more than three decades. "I look out at the spectators in the stands during our games," Price said, "and I think to myself, gee, Dad probably delivered half of them.

"Dad just loved baseball," said Price, and one manifestation of that love was a field that he built on the family's Fairfax farm when Vic was six. "It was for my brothers and me but also for all the neighborhood kids in the area too."

Price played Little League baseball in Fairfax until he was 12, when the family moved to McLean. There he quickly became a star in the local Babe Ruth League, helping his team win the state championship.

Price attended Langley High School, where he lettered in baseball all four years as well as excelling at football. In 1969 he was named athlete of the year at Langley and to his great surprise received an offer from the Kansas City Royals organization to play in their minor-league system.

Despite the thrill of playing professional baseball, it was a tough deci-sion for the Price family. Accepting the offer meant not going to college

Shortstop Ross Kelly casts a long shadow during a late afternoon practice on Vic's Field. Photo courtesy of the Washington Post.

with his peers and a real risk of failure. "Once you played professional ball for one day," Price said, "you couldn't play any competitive sport in college—not even badminton."

Price took the gamble, however, and for the next five years experienced the joys and frustrations, the thrills and the tedium, of minor league baseball. "The scouts promise you the world," he said, "but you soon find out it's not what you expected."

In Price's case it meant checking into the Homestead Hotel in Kingsport, Tennessee, a fleabag joint soon to be demolished. "There was no air-conditioning," he said, "which meant keeping the windows open. The problem there was that there was a paper mill nearby and the stench was so bad it almost made you gag." And as if that weren't enough, there was construction underway next door that meant the sound of jackhammers at the crack of dawn every day.

Away games meant long nights careening down mountain roads on an old bus and crawling into the baggage bins above the seats in order to stretch out and get a little sleep.

The truncated minor-league season required playing nine games a week, including doubleheaders on Wednesdays and Saturdays. Bruises, soreness, and stiffness were constant companions, and injuries were commonplace as well. "I remember one in particular," said Price. "I was playing center field and charging after a fly ball and I hit the fence. The next thing I knew, I was on the ground with three broken ribs, fighting to breathe."

Nonetheless, Price looks back on his minor-league career with satisfaction. He was player of the month once, set a couple of home run records, and played on two all-star teams in his five-year stint.

On the other hand, he said that the system "tested every value that I held dear." He found the system "very dehumanizing. Players are treated like animals with no regard to their feelings or pride." It was not unusual, he said, to report to camp, be assigned to a room with three other players, and find at the end of the first day that the other three were all gone—released and sent home. "Their hopes and dreams, their whole world collapsed around them."

Price decries this aspect of the minors and he did so very vocally as a player—a fact that he feels probably shortened his career and possibly prevented his making it to the majors. Nonetheless, he has never lost his love of the game.

"Baseball is a contagious thing," he said, "if you make it fun."

Under Price's prodding the Great Falls League has re-introduced an opening day parade and home run contest and has also added a concession stand.

"This makes it more fun for families to hang around the ballpark," he said. "Little kids see their older brothers and sisters playing and they start saying, 'I want to play baseball.' That's the way you make fans and build up the game."

Even though his existing commitments keep him on the field for 30 to 40 hours some weeks, now is not the time for Vic Price to slacken the pace. He is already hard at work pushing new projects, including a new practice field and a field for Babe Ruth baseball, both scheduled for completion by next spring near the existing Nike Park fields and, the centerpiece of the whole complex, a monument to all Great Falls residents who have served in the armed forces.

For Price, locating a monument on the baseball field is a logical move. "Baseball is a game, but it's more than that, too," he said. "It's part of our heritage."

26

IT ALL BEGINS

January 28, 2000. I look out the window at 6:30 A.M. and Great Falls, Virginia, is a winter wonderland.

The weather bureau has figurative egg all over its figurative face. Here in the Washington, D.C., area we have several inches of snow on the ground. It will total more than a foot before it's all over.

Unbelievably, the big storm was totally unforeseen by the "pros" until just hours before it hit, leaving millions of people with no time to descend on the area supermarkets for emergency stocks of milk, bread, and toilet paper.

Fortunately my wife, Patti, happened to go to the store yesterday so we're well stocked with all three of those critical commodities. More importantly, there is popcorn for the kids in the pantry and Jack Daniel's for me in the liquor cabinet.

I call into Radio America, the news/talk network I founded and that I direct as president (or "head cheese" as one of our producers puts it), to make sure we're still broadcasting. Doug Stephan, our morning host, is on the air from Oxford, England, and is having a fine time talking with Roberta Facinelli, also known as the "weather babe," and chatting about what wimps and pantywaists Washingtonians are to let a few flakes of snow shut the place down.

On the spur of the moment he puts me on the air for an on-scene report. I retaliate by telling Roberta about the remark Doug has allegedly made about her: "She's pure as the driven snow, but she's drifted." They both get a laugh out of that one and I sign off.

Outside the snow is coming down like crazy, making it futile to shovel the driveway. Going to work is also out of the question, so I kick back in my study to enjoy that rare pleasure—a day to relax.

On my desk are registration forms for both the Northern Virginia Baseball Academy (NVBA) and the Faris Baseball Camp. I've been asking Andrew, my 13-year-old son, to make a decision about which one he wants to attend for two weeks. Faris offers excellent instruction in pitching and hitting while NVBA offers an indoor infield with Babe Ruth League dimensions—the kind of field he'll be playing on for the first time in the spring. I think he should do NVBA. He leans towards Faris. We've got to decide soon.

Opening my briefcase, I take out the January 26–February 1 issue of *Baseball Weekly* with Braves outfielder Andruw Jones on the cover. I bought it at the newsstand yesterday, the first issue I've bought in a couple of months. The item that caught my eye was the "Fan's Guide to Spring Training: Pitchers Report to Camp on February 14." Hey, that's just three weeks away!

Also in my briefcase is the new issue of the newsletter of the Emil Verban Society, the Chicago Cubs fan club founded in Washington, D.C., by Bruce Ladd 24 years ago. Ladd is very excited about a number of acquisitions the Cubs have made in the wake of the disastrous 2000 season, particularly pitcher Ismael Valdez (acquired from the Dodgers); catcher Joe Girardi (from the Yankees); Eric Young (from the Dodgers); and Ricky Gutierrez (from the Astros). "Hooray!" Ladd editorialized. I agree. They're excellent additions.

More good news: *Baseball Weekly* reports that Cubs phenom Kerry Wood is throwing fastballs every day and hopes to be back in the rotation come Opening Day. Kerry missed the entire previous season with a torn rotator cuff and had "Tommy John" surgery a year ago. His absence was a disaster for the Cubs. With him back and healthy, plus Valdez and veterans Kevin Tapani and Jon Lieber . . . hey! The Cubs could be in the thick of the pennant race this year.

Amazing. Here I sit in my study, housebound in a blizzard, and I'm thinking of baseball.

Dormant for four months, the baseball world is beginning to stir. Spring training starts in just three weeks. It all begins.

The months ahead mean a flight south to Fort Lauderdale for Baltimore Orioles spring training, several trips to Baltimore (an hour away) to see some Orioles regular-season games, a "business trip" to Chicago to see the Cubbies play, and a few games in random cities when I happen to be there on business.

Also in store are a couple of minor league games at the Frederick, Maryland, Keys ballpark; broadcasting the congressional baseball game at Baysox Stadium in nearby Bowie, Maryland; and a few college all-star games with the Reston, Virginia, Hawks of the Clark Griffith League and the New Market, Virginia, Rebels of the Shenandoah Valley League. Then there are televised Cubs games on WGN and Orioles games on WTOP radio. And finally, the year 2001 will end with the "Salute to Baseball Heroes of World War II" conference, sponsored in mid-November by the World War II Veterans Committee, which I head.

My wife, who is a rabid basketball fan but, alas, an indifferent baseball fan, is a good sport. She is patient with, if bemused by, this wall-to-wall baseball.

But this is only spectator baseball. For me, the "rubber hits the cleats," so to speak, on the baseball fields of Great Falls, Virginia, where I've coached youth baseball and T-ball for the past 10 years.

Great Falls is a community of around 10,000 people located about 15 miles northwest of Washington, D.C. Given its proximity to Washington and the Dulles high-tech corridor, it has one of the highest average incomes of any community in the country. My family is surely a drag on its national standing.

Our location makes us unique in other ways, too. For instance, you can see the son of the deposed shah of Iran at the neighborhood super-market, Senator Rick Santorum and Supreme Court Justice Antonin Scalia at the local Catholic church, and Washington Redskins players at the corner 7-Eleven. House Minority Leader Richard Gephardt's wife is the receptionist at our local pediatrician, former Attorney General Ed Meese hangs out at the friendly Irish pub, and Winston Churchill's granddaughter throws out the first ball at the community Little League field.

That field, by the way, is itself symbolic of the unique nature of suburban Washington baseball. Its called Nike Field, not, as I'd initially assumed, because the Nike shoe company donated money to pay for it, but because it was built on an abandoned Nike missile site. The ground under the field is honeycombed with missile storage areas and abandoned command facilities, and access shafts are boarded over and walled off to prevent curious kids from getting into them.

Action on the field and in the bleachers also reflects a Washington sort of tone. In the aftermath of the Republican takeover of Congress in 1994, for instance, new Speaker of the House Newt Gingrich's press secretary, Tony Blankley, could be seen, cell phone in hand and discussing strategy with the Speaker, prowling the sidelines of the T-ball and Little League fields where his sons, Trevor and Spencer, played for teams I coached. Blankley is now a columnist and prominent television commentator and can be seen these days in the bleachers, talking politics with political consultants, lawyers, and congressional aides.

Another unique experience was coaching two of FBI Director Louis Freeh's sons on T-ball teams. Freeh has made Herculean efforts to be a good father to his (six!) sons over the years, despite the intense demands and restrictions his sensitive position imposes. The director always attended games wearing the required belly pack, which contained a gun, presumably, and accompanied by a security officer similarly outfitted. They always stood off to the side of the field, trying to be inconspicuous.

This attempt—never very successful—became even more difficult in 1995 following the Oklahoma City bombing. No one knew whether some large terrorist network was responsible for this horrible atrocity, and security measures went to "Defcon 5" in government agencies. On the T-ball field this meant that Freeh's security agent was augmented by a SWAT team in an unmarked van standing watch while the FBI director's son ran the basepaths.

Another interesting feature of Great Falls life is the number of foreign-born people who live here. Many of their kids want to play baseball, and so names such as Ramadan, Kwan, Kao, and Ortiz are nearly as common on the team rosters as Smith and Jones.

Bahetti is one of these names that I will always remember, mostly with a smile, but occasionally with a wince. The Bahetti family arrived in Great Falls a few years ago from India. Mrs. Bahetti—Padma—wore the traditional Indian sari and a *bindi* on her forehead and was, like her husband, polite and deferential to a fault. Their son Rajiv, 10, was a good deal more rambunctious.

Rajiv had never before used a baseball, bat, or glove, which meant that working him onto the team was going to take some effort. Essentially, this meant individual instruction. Luckily, I had a number of dads helping out that year and one of them, Russ Rieling, basically became Rajiv's personal trainer, giving him a crash course in baseball basics.

Once the season started, Rajiv, quite predictably, struggled at the plate. His outlook brightened measurably, however, when he discovered you could get on base by walking. Meanwhile, I had told Rajiv—and all my other players—that a good way to calm your nerves was to step out of the batter's box in between pitches and take a practice swing. Rajiv did this with enthusiasm. His teammates, however, were yelling at him not to swing at pitches. This pattern of Rajiv standing rooted like a tree in the batter's box during every pitch, followed by backing out of the box and taking a full cut *between* pitches, thoroughly confused Rajiv's parents.

Not wanting to bother me, Padma approached my wife during a game and discreetly asked for advice. "My husband and I have noticed," she remarked, "that Rajiv is swinging his bat long after the ball has been thrown. Is he doing the right thing?"

When told that he was, Padma returned to her seat reassured, but still confused.

Rajiv's strategy worked, however. He got his share of walks and, despite some confusing and amusing moments on the basepaths, he scored some runs.

Moreover, Rajiv's enthusiasm for the game grew. He learned the names of all the major league teams and many of the players, and continues to play the game. His parents are always profuse in their thanks to me. To a coach, that means a lot.

In fact, there is no greater thrill for me after almost 10 years of coaching than to run into a kid that I coached years ago in T-ball or Little League and to have him or her say, "Hi coach Roberts."

Some of the kids I coached in T-ball are now teenagers playing Babe Ruth all-star baseball. Most are not, of course. At the end of Little League at age 13, most stop playing organized baseball. But hopefully they will never lose interest in the game. Thirty years from now, in fact, I hope some kid stops Rajiv on the street and says, "Hi coach Bahetti, remember me?"

Epilogue

————— •◆• —————

The Legacy of Jimmy Trimble

At the 2000 World War II Veterans Committee conference "Salute to Baseball Heroes of World War II," Hall of Fame pitcher Bob Feller said, "The real heroes were the ones that didn't come back." One such hero, a young man named James Trimble III, certainly deserves a place in this volume. More than 50 years after his death on Iwo Jima, Trimble is still recognized as one of the greatest athletes ever produced in the Washington area.

Jimmy Trimble was a star athlete at St. Albans prep school in Washington, D.C. During his years at the school, located on the grounds of Washington National Cathedral, he was the captain of the basketball team and a leading scorer on the football team.

But baseball was Trimble's true passion, and he excelled on the mound as has no pitcher before or since at St. Albans, a school noted as a baseball powerhouse for most of the century. He enjoyed spectacular success as the school's leading pitcher, throwing three no-hitters. Fittingly, one of his heroes was Bob Feller.

"Jimmy Trimble is still a legend at St. Albans," said Don Swagart, the school's director of alumni affairs. Swagart's father was a classmate of Trimble's, and said Trimble was considered by many to be the next Walter Johnson. His coach, Bill Shaw, a member of the 1932 U.S. Olympic baseball squad, considered him to be one of the finest baseball prospects he had ever seen.

Private James Trimble III, USMC. Photo courtesy of Christine White.

Earle Elliott was Jimmy Trimble's best friend and a teammate on the school's basketball, football, and baseball squads. He remembers Trimble as "a solid basketball player, an excellent football player, and an outstanding baseball player—the best high school baseball player I ever saw by far." St. Albans never lost a baseball game with Trimble on the mound, and only tied one, against Woodrow Wilson High.

"He threw hard and he threw nothing but strikes—fastballs and curveballs," said Elliott, adding, "He was very intimidating on the mound, even though he never tried to brush anybody back from the plate." It is reported that Trimble threw so hard that his catcher, Buddy Cromelin, had to put extra padding in his glove.

Trimble acquired his baseball skills on the streets of Chevy Chase, Maryland, a Washington suburb. "We kids played ball of some kind every spare minute we had," said Elliott. During baseball season the two boys, like thousands all over the Washington area, took the streetcar to Griffith Stadium to watch the Senators play. A number of the ballplayers lived in the area, and Elliott remembered one time in particular when Senators outfielder Jesse Hill took the two to the ballpark as his guests.

Even though the team was rarely competitive during those years, the boys were rabid Senators fans. "Jimmy was a big fan of Stan Spence, who played the outfield, and Earl Whitehill and Dutch Leonard, who were pitchers," said Elliott.

One special memory for Elliott was the 1937 All-Star Game, which was played in Washington. The two boys attended and got autographs from many of the players, including Carl Hubbel, Johnny Vander Meer, and Dizzy Dean.

Another vivid memory is of the first time the two saw Bob Feller pitch. "He wasn't even in the lineup. They brought him in as a reliever," remembered Elliott. "I still remember hearing the incredible pop, pop, pop sound as the ball hit the catcher's mitt. We said, 'Who in the world is that?' And we found out it was Bobby Feller. We had never heard of him."

By his senior year at St. Albans, Trimble had caught the attention of Washington's sports reporters. An April 18, 1943, article by Joe Holman in the *Washington Times-Herald* reported:

> Out at St. Albans School for boys . . . they are singing the praises of 17-year-old Jimmy Trimble, a three-sport star with a splendid record. . . .
>
> Trimble, a five-foot, 11-1/2 inch, 155-pound boy who is spreading out all the time, says he enjoys all sports and is considering several scholarship offers by major colleges, but admits that he is hopeful of eventually qualifying for professional baseball.
>
> "Ever since I can remember, I've played baseball with older boys," Jimmy tells you. "My buddies all say I'd make a better shortstop than pitcher, but I'm not kidding myself—I don't hit very well."
>
> One of our staff members, Maury Fitzgerald, who accidentally scouted Trimble recently, says that the youngster has all the action and ability of a seasoned ballplayer.
>
> Fitzgerald saw the youngster strike out 14 Wilson [High School] batsmen, exhibit a blazing fastball, good change of pace and surprising control, and also saw him field his position flawlessly. Maury also saw nothing wrong with Trimble's hitting, recalling that he met the ball well and figured in the scoring.

The article obviously reached the right circles, because Jimmy soon received a letter from Clark Griffith, owner of the Washington Senators:

> My dear Sir:
>
> Joe Holman of the Times-Herald and several of my friends have been calling my attention to your good work as a pitcher this spring. I would like very

much to have you come and work out with the Washington club, which would allow manager Bluege and myself to pass opinion as to your capabilities. These are times when we may have to use quite a number of the 17-year-old boys who are not yet subject to the army draft, so it naturally would be a good opportunity for you to get yourself a good job. The ballclub leaves Washington tomorrow night and will not be back until the 27th of April. If you could come out and see me at that time, I would greatly appreciate it. Just bring your glove, shoes, and sweatshirt, and we can furnish you with a uniform.

Trusting to have a favorable reply from you and wishing you all success, I beg to remain,

Yours most sincerely,
Clark Griffith
President

The natural: Jimmy Trimble pitching for St. Albans School circa 1942. He never lost a game pitching for the Saints. Photo courtesy of the Washington Times-Herald.

Trimble was called to Griffith Stadium for a tryout on May 29, 1943. His parents were divorced and his dad wasn't around, so, Elliott recalled, "My dad went with him to Griffith Stadium. Clark Griffith was there to watch him, and Jimmy did very well." Heinie Manush, a 17-year veteran of six major league teams and later a coach for the Senators, saw Trimble pitch and called him "one of the finest prospects he had ever seen."

Clark Griffith wanted to sign Trimble up for the Senators' farm system, Elliott recalled, but his mother insisted that he first finish school. So Griffith gave the young player a $5,000 signing bonus and agreed to pay for a four-year scholarship at Duke University in the hope that at some point Trimble would elect to put college off until later and join the Senators.

In another article about Trimble, Holman wrote:

> *Conservatively speaking, the happiest boy in Washington, D.C., today is Jimmy Trimble, St. Albans School's right-handed pitching ace, who yesterday signed a contract with the Washington Baseball Club and its president, Clark Griffith.*
>
> *The 17-year-old youngster . . . enters Duke University, where he hopes to become eligible for a Navy V-8, which will enable him to study for a naval commission.*
>
> *After the war is over Trimble, who has been scouted by several major league clubs other than Washington, plans on attending school in the winter and playing with the Nationals [Senators] in the summer.*
>
> *Jimmy Trimble was an all-around athlete at St. Albans, being a basketball forward and football end. He plans passing up football hereafter, although he will play some basketball if granted the necessary permission by his benefactor, Griffith.*

In those days Duke was a baseball powerhouse. The team's outstanding coach, Jack Coombs, was a retired major league pitcher. Trimble played fall baseball for him in 1943 and, according to Elliott, would have been Duke's best pitcher if he'd played the following spring.

While at Duke, Trimble was disqualified from officer training because of defective sight in one eye. He declined to use his political contacts in Washington to get a waiver, and instead opted to enter the Marine Corps as an enlisted man.

Concluded Elliott, "There is absolutely no doubt in my mind that Jimmy would have been a major-league star." But, of course, that was not to be.

Early in 1944, Trimble enlisted in the marines and headed off for basic training at Parris Island, South Carolina. Before shipping out to the Pacific, Trimble and his girlfriend, Christine White, agreed to get married when he returned. The two had met while White was a student at nearby Woodrow Wilson High School. Exceptionally popular at Wilson, she was also voted "prettiest blonde" at the school. White later went on to become a successful actress, starring in a number of movies, including *Magnum Force*, and several TV series, including *Bonanza*, *The Fugitive*, and *Perry Mason*.

White remembered that although Trimble was "handsome in a rugged way," she hadn't liked him at first. She knew nothing about baseball, and he was pitching against her school. "I couldn't understand it," she recalled. "He wouldn't let our boys hit the ball. It seemed so unfair." White hastened to add that she soon learned what a rare achievement a no-hitter was.

In late 1943, a friend arranged a double date for the two girls, and the friend's date was Trimble. White recollected that when she opened the door and introduced herself, Trimble just stared at her, unable to remove his eyes. For young James Trimble, it was love at first sight.

"He told me, 'I want you and baseball,'" remembered White. "I never knew which was first, but it didn't matter."

During his basic training on Parris Island, Trimble was given an opportunity to stay for two additional months and play baseball for the base. At the end of this time he could have entered a special program that would have given him the rank of corporal. Had he done so, he would not have arrived in the Pacific until almost the end of the war. In a fateful—but typical—decision, he declined.

"I would not stay on this island unless forced," he wrote his mother. "After all, I got in the marines to kill Japs." In July 1944 Trimble shipped out to join the Third Marine Division in the South Pacific.

Trimble saw combat on Guam as part of patrols mopping up the remaining Japanese. He was a member of the division's Amphibious Reconnaissance Company, assigned directly to division headquarters. In another fateful decision, he next volunteered to serve in an elite scouting platoon that would put him ahead of the front lines on Iwo Jima.

While on Guam, Trimble showed his C.O. a letter from Clark Griffith, which won him a tryout as a pitcher for the Third Marine Division baseball team. At a time when baseball truly reigned supreme as America's national game, the sport was a major factor in maintaining the morale of the men in uniform. Baseball leagues and exhibition games were organized whenever conditions permitted, and Guam became a baseball hub in the Pacific.

Soon Trimble was spending a lot of time playing baseball. He compiled a superb record on the mound, racking up 21 straight victories in one stretch. He pitched in the "Little World Series" held on Guam in

CLARK C. GRIFFITH
President

CALVIN R. GRIFFITH
Vice President

EDWARD B. EYNON, JR.
Secretary

GEORGE M. RICHARDSON
Treasurer

WASHINGTON AMERICAN LEAGUE
BASE BALL CLUB

OFFICES: 7th ST. AND FLORIDA AVE. N. W.
WASHINGTON 1, D. C.

TELEPHONES: DUPONT {6333 / 6334

February 21st, 1944

Private James Trimble-822783
Platoon 23, Recruit Depot
Marine Barracks
Parris Island, South Carolina

Dear Friend Jimmy:

I received your letter this morning and was very glad indeed to hear from you. I will have your name placed on the National Defense List of the Washington Club. I hope you will be back with us some of these days and that that day will not be far away.

I was glad to hear that your physical training had straightened you up and had made a big strong boy out of you. No doubt, this will serve you in good stead when you again enter your baseball career. It would be nice if you could be stationed at Quantico where you could get in some baseball playing this spring before you get your overseas assignment. If you do, please let me know and I will drop down and see you in action.

With all good wishes for your success in the service and with the hope that everything will turn out fine and dandy for you, I am,

Yours most sincerely,

Clark Griffith

President

CCG:mmh

A letter from Clark Griffith, owner of the Washington Senators, to Jimmy Trimble. Trimble carried the letter with him for the last year of his life. Photo courtesy of Christine White.

1944, and achieved considerable notoriety in military circles for his pitching skills. In a letter to his mother, Trimble reported that he was pitching for the all-star team. His record for them was 6–2, which made him quite happy, since many of the players he was pitching against were former pros.

During this time he got to know someone involved with the New York Yankees operation, who told him that he would be able to get Trimble a spot on the Yankees' pitching staff. In another letter to his mother, Trimble asked her to check the contract she had signed for him with the Senators to see if there was any escape clause. She replied that the contract was binding and that he was morally as well as legally bound to honor his commitment to Griffith. He wrote back that he would of course keep his word.

Jimmy Trimble pitching for the Third Marine Division All-Stars on the island of Guam in late 1944. USMC Photo.

The marine who knew Trimble best, the man who saw him on a daily basis and watched him die in combat, was Donald Mates, now retired in Palm Beach, Florida. Mates was Trimble's tentmate for three and a half months on Guam, from November 1944 to mid-February 1945. Although Guam was officially pacified in early August of 1944, there were still isolated pockets of Japanese resistance until 1946. The marines stationed on Guam thus spent much of their time on patrols chasing after Japanese guerillas. Trimble spent some time on these patrols, Mates said, but he was often called away to pitch.

Mates was awed by Trimble's fastball. A native of the Cleveland, Ohio, area, Mates recalled that "I thought he was the next Bob Feller."

At night, the two men often talked baseball. "I had seen the game where DiMaggio's streak ended," Mates recalled, "and Jimmy wanted me to replay the game over and over and over.

"Jimmy would drive me crazy asking all these technical questions like, 'How would you pitch to [Indians third baseman] Ken Keltner? Fastballs, curve balls, low and outside, high and inside?' That kind of thing. He made me go over Cleveland's pitching rotation—Al Milnar, Mel Harder, Al Smith, and of course Bob Feller—and describe how each one pitched. He was just insatiable for this kind of information.

"Trimble was a cut above everybody else. Most of the marines had never even thought about going to college, but he had already had a year of college. Also, he'd gone to a fancy prep school in Washington, and he would toss off the names of congressmen and other famous people left and right.

"Jimmy was a celebrity in camp; he carried himself like a movie star, but he was liked by everybody, officers and enlisted men alike."

Jim White, another friend in Trimble's platoon, recalled that Trimble "was always optimistic, always laughing and joking and trying to buck people up."

He also had a sentimental side, White said. "One day," he recalled, "Trimble threw a wild pitch and killed one of the little stray dogs that had become a platoon pet. He was pretty broken up about it and wouldn't pitch any more that day."

When baseball wasn't the topic of conversation, Trimble's fiancée, Christine White, was. "He talked about her constantly," Mates recalled. "He was always showing me pictures of her and talking about how beautiful she was, which you could see from the pictures she obviously was.

He would hold up the picture and say, 'This is what's waiting for me when I get home.' It was all wholesome 1940s talk about love for his girl back home. There was none of the raunchy talk like you hear today."

During the eight months he spent in the Pacific, Private Trimble kept up a furious correspondence with White. "Thank God for God, you, and baseball in this dark wilderness," he wrote. "Taps is sounding. I will sign off with my love." Many of his letters were playfully signed "Private Jim."

"He wrote more than 70 letters," said White. "By the end he was 19 going on 35. The letters showed an incredible maturity for someone his age."

Trimble's religious faith was also growing during this trying time. In a letter to the headmaster of St. Albans, he wrote:

> Dr. Lucas, I have a confession to make. Excuse my language, but I was a lousy Christian while in school, and it took a war to reveal my lack of faithfulness. I believe now that I understand a little what God stands for. I know that if a man didn't have faith out here, he would go crazy.

In his last letter to White, Trimble quoted Shakespeare: "Mine honor is my life. The two grow in one. Take honor from me and my life is done."

In a letter written to his mother on February 18, 1945, en route to Iwo Jima on the USS *Harry Lee*, Trimble wrote:

> Yes, Mom, I am going into combat, but don't let that worry you. We have just finished divine services and this afternoon I am taking communion. It's funny how much faith one develops in prayer under these circumstances. I know everything is going to be all right, so promise not to worry—just pray as I know you have been doing. . . .
>
> Just back from communion, Mother, and feel better for having partaken. Yes, dear, in some ways you won't recognize your irresponsible offspring. Thank you so much for obtaining another St. Christopher Medal, Mom. I'm sorry to have caused you the trouble.
>
> It's getting colder, Mom, and believe it or not I am glad for once to get away from the heat.
>
> The weather is beautiful, a clear sky and bright sun shining on the water. What scenic beauty for the tourist!
>
> Mom, will you get some flowers for Chris, Easter lilies if possible? . . .

Well, Mom, I'll leave you now as my limited information has exhausted itself. Always thinking of you and thankful that you are my mother. My love to the whole family. Until then,

Your Loving Son,

Jimmie

Despite the growing faith evidenced by this letter, Trimble was certainly not above taking a drink and having a good time. Recalled Mates, "The last two days before we shipped out to Iwo we were bivouacked in tents in a field. A young Guamanian boy came by selling bottles of 150-proof grain alcohol. Jimmy bought two gallons of the stuff and we drank it all and got sick as dogs. We were definitely not feeling well when we boarded the ship for Iwo."

Trimble and his buddies were headed into one of the most hellish operations of World War II.

The small island of Iwo Jima, a volcanic speck in the Pacific, is only two miles wide and four miles long. Yet its position, only 600 miles south of Japan, placed it along the bombing route from the Marianas to Japan. The Japanese had constructed two airfields on the island, from which their fighters attacked American bombers en route to Tokyo and other cities. Although the planes had been knocked out, the island was still an important early-warning station for the Japanese. It would also provide a useful emergency landing field for crippled U.S. planes. It had to be taken.

U.S. military planners estimated that it would take four days to quell Japanese resistance. In fact, the battle lasted more than a month. At its end nearly 7,000 Americans were dead, and more than 20,000 were wounded. Japanese dead totaled 21,000—out of 22,000 men.

With the 500-foot-high Mount Surabachi on the southern end of the island, one marine called Iwo "an ugly wart on the face of the Pacific." Stripped of almost all of its sparse vegetation by the U.S. bombardment, the island resembled a lunar landscape, covered with coarse black sand and volcanic ash. Steam rose from the porous lava rocks, and the burning sulfur escaping from pits bombed by U.S. planes made the whole place smell like rotten eggs. "It looked like hell with the fires out, but still smoking," said one marine.

Moreover, it was February; the weather was cold and rainy and the volcanic ash had become cementlike mud. It was on this desolate, barren island that the U.S. Marines fought their bloodiest engagement of the war in the Pacific.

The landings were preceded by three days and nights of naval bombardment supplemented by daytime carpet-bombing by B-29s. (Unbeknownst to Trimble, the battleship *Alabama* was one of the ships supplying this gunfire support. Trimble's hero, Bob Feller, was a gunnery crew director onboard the *Alabama*.) It was the most intensive bombardment of the Pacific war up to that time. For Mates, Trimble, and the other marines on the ship, it must have seemed impossible that any Japanese soldiers could have lived through it. But, in fact, so entrenched were the 22,000 Japanese troops in their deep tunnels and fortifications that almost all of them survived and lay in readiness awaiting the marines.

On February 19 the Fifth Marine Division landed on the southernmost beaches at the foot of Mount Surabachi. The Fourth Marine Division went ashore farther north. Except for the mined beaches, which took their toll in casualties, the marines faced little opposition until almost 50,000 of them were ashore. Then the doors of the fortified Japanese gun emplacements opened and the heavy artillery poured a merciless rain of bullets on the massed forces of men and equipment. Totally out in the open, the marines took huge casualties on the beaches and, lacking protection, had no other option but to move forward foot by foot.

On February 24 the Third Division went ashore in the wake of the landings by the Fourth and Fifth Divisions. The scene that Mates and Trimble saw upon landing was one of carnage: bodies and body parts on the beach and in the water, with burned-out equipment strewn about on all sides. "The burning sulfur created an eerie haze that hung over everything," Mates said, adding, "All I could think of was Basil Rathbone in *The Hound of the Baskervilles* with that thick fog. The only difference is that it was Japs, not dogs, running at us through the haze."

During the first three days Mates and Trimble's Fourth Reconnaissance Platoon saw little combat, as they were assigned as personal bodyguards to the Third Marine Division's commanding officer, Major General Graves Erskine. "Erskine knew Jimmy personally, because he was the star pitcher for the division," Mates said.

During the day the hulking mound of Mount Surabachi dominated the scene. On February 26 the Fifth Marine Division took Mount Surabachi and raised the American flag there. The moment was photographed by Joe Rosenthal in what would become the most famous image

Jimmy Trimble (kneeling on the left) with his marine buddies on the island of Guam. This was the last photo taken of him. Photo courtesy of Christine White.

of World War II. Don Mates recalled that he and Trimble had seen the flag and took heart, thinking the worst was over. In fact, the battle was just beginning.

The battle plan for Iwo Jima was for the Fourth and Fifth Divisions to move across the island, cutting it in half. After the capture of Mount Surabachi, the Fifth Division was to move up the western side of the island. The Fourth would move up the eastern side. The Third was to move between the two divisions and head north through the center of the island. By day the marines inched forward, taking ridges and hills, only to have Japanese soldiers emerge from tunnels behind them and engage in hand-to-hand combat.

Following the landings, the Third Marine Division took heavy casualties from Japanese rocket attacks launched from the hill that came to be known as Hill No. 362. On February 27 the Fourth Platoon commander asked for eight volunteers to find the location of the rocket sites and to call in artillery to destroy them. Mates recalled that "Trimble's and White's hands were the first to go up." Mates also volunteered.

The next night, four two-man reconnaissance teams were deployed forward of the rest of their platoon in four foxholes running up a ridge, all connected by radio wire. Said Mates, "As we started out, I told Jimmy, 'If there are guardian angels, I hope they are with us here.' He made the sign of the cross."

At midnight Mates and Trimble were in the second foxhole from the bottom, preparing to trade places with the men in the next one up the ridge. Then the attack came. Mates described what ensued:

At about midnight I woke up, could have been a tug on the wire, and I was ready to get up and switch holes when a Jap flare went off (not bright like ours). Peering into our hole was a Jap. He was on his knees so he could reach Jim, sitting up. I was still stretched out in the bottom. He struck Jim in his back, right shoulder blade, leaving him with a bayonet wound. It did not seem deep. Not a word out of Jim. I threw a hand grenade from my prone position and Jim was firing from a sitting position.

Then all hell broke loose. I could hear McCloskey on the radio, "Green Tiger calling Red Circle." Flares lighting up the sky. Grenades exploding, rifle shots, Jap officers screaming orders, marines cursing, and then two clicks, and Jim screams "grenades" as he fired his rifle. (Jap grenades are ignited by hitting them on something solid, usually their helmets.) One grenade landed between my thighs and exploded and the other along Jim. Because he was sitting up he caught the full blast of both grenades, the rising shrapnel. The grenade between my legs ripped off 20 percent of my left thigh, 5 percent of my right thigh, and fractured both legs.

Jim's back, upper arms, and the back of his head were a mass of wounds, but he was alive. I pulled myself out of the hole and turned to Jim and he reached out his arm and hand to have some help to get out with. At the same time a Jap jumped into the hole with a mine strapped to his stomach and proceeded to wrap himself around Jim. The Jap blew himself into a thousand pieces and blew a hole into Jim's back bigger than a basketball.

It took a bayonet, two grenades, and a Jap suicide attack to kill James Trimble III.

By this time, a tank and a marine platoon had joined the battle and turned the tide. The fighting raged for over three hours and when morning came, there were over 60 Japanese bodies found lying on the ground.

But the marines took a heavy toll as well. Of the eight scouts in the foxholes, two were missing. One was later found in a cave where he had been dragged by the Japanese, tortured, and hacked to pieces. Mates, badly wounded, escaped by rolling down the hill, yelling out the names of presidents (the code of the day) until he was near another foxhole.

Jimmy Trimble lay dead in the foxhole. In the breast pocket of his uniform was his wallet, containing the picture of Christine White that he always carried with him.

When told of Trimble's death, General Erskine was reported to have been "moist-eyed." Two months later, at a ceremony on Guam, the Third Division baseball field was named in memory of Jimmy Trimble by the personal order of Erskine, who was also wounded on Iwo Jima. The general himself attended the ceremony, a highly unusual honor rendered to a

The dedication of Trimble Field on the island of Guam, spring of 1945. The field was named in honor of James Trimble at the direction of The Third Marine Division's commanding officer, General Graves B. Erskine.

deceased private, and wrote the citation that was read to those attending. It said in part:

Private Trimble was an outstanding member of the Third Marine Division All-Star baseball team. Private Trimble's unswerving courage, loyalty, devotion to duty, and high ideals on and off the battlefield will long be remembered by his colleagues.

Trimble's death and the dedication of Trimble Field were reported in articles in all three of Washington's daily newspapers as well as in U.S. military publications throughout the world. A memorial service was held in the Great Choir of the Washington Cathedral. Trimble was buried in Rockcreek Cemetery in Washington, D.C.

James Trimble remains a vivid memory to the dwindling number of people who knew him. While he never had the opportunity to become a hero in the major leagues, in the words of Bob Feller, he became a "real hero," nonetheless. Jimmy Trimble put his country ahead of himself and everything he held dear: his fiancé, his family and friends, and baseball. He volunteered to serve on the front lines and he died as the man he wanted to be: "Private Jim."

Jimmy Trimble was remembered at a Veterans Day 2000 tribute to the baseball heroes of World War II. Christine White quoted General Erskine's words about Trimble's character—his courage, loyalty, and high ideals. "These are qualities that are desperately needed today," she said, closing with, "If we remember Jimmy Trimble and his example, then his death was not in vain."

An evensong service in honor of World War II veterans followed at Washington's Church of the Epiphany. Taps was sounded in memory of the dead, and the choir sang:

The souls of the righteous are in the hand of God, and the pain of death shall not touch them. To the eyes of the foolish they seemed to perish. But they are in peace.

INDEX

INDEX

INDEX